Morris
&
Lois Watki...
attended the
Feb. 1989 TM con...
Ambassador Hawaii...
in Lake Havasu...
City, AZ

Seven Worlds to Win

By Morris Watkins
Doctor of Missiology

Published
by
R.C. Law & Company, Inc.
579 S. State College Blvd.
Fullerton, CA 92631

©Copyright 1987 by Dr. Morris Watkins

ISBN 0-939925-00-1

Printed in the United States of America

Publication of
THE GREAT COMMISSION RESOURCE LIBRARY
Fort Wayne, Indiana

Introduction

For years I have felt compelled to write a book like this one for two major reasons.

First, it is my fervent prayer that this book will be used in Christian schools across this great land, as supplementary material for geography classes, that young people may learn to see God's world as God sees it, that they may pray more intensely and intelligently for the people of the world for whom Christ died, for God's servants around the world, and that they might begin at an early age to seek God's perfect will for their lives regarding the Seven Worlds to Win.

At present most young people as well as their parents have little or no understanding of the great unfinished task of making disciples of all nations. Many believe that there is no more need to send missionaries to other lands. Others believe that one has to be an ordained minister in order to serve Christ overseas.

It is quite possible for a young person to go to church every Sunday and to a Christian school every school day for twelve years and hear little or nothing about the Seven Worlds to Win, except perhaps the so-called Christian world. Our children grow up thinking that if they want to serve Christ, the only way they can do it is by becoming a pastor of a church in the U. S. or Canada, or by becoming a parochial school teacher. But that shouldn't surprise us. How can they possibly know how God would have them serve and glorify Him when they have no idea of what the needs are and what opportunities of service exist in other lands? How can anyone make the right decision on the basis of facts he does not know?

It is also my fervent prayer that every pastor, every Bible class teacher, every prayer group leader and every missions committee chairman will study this book and use it as a handbook for world intercession. We cannot begin to demolish Satan's strongholds and win the Seven Worlds to Christ without an ongoing intensive and intelligent prayer effort on the part of children and adults alike.

It is my fervent prayer that this book will be a blessing to everyone who reads it and that the readers in turn will be a greater blessing to peoples of other lands as a result of reading these pages about the Seven Worlds to Win.

Morris G. Watkins, President
All Nations Missions

FOREWORD

Dr. Morris Watkins is a man with a vision for lost people. Morrie and his devoted wife Lois see the Great Commission of our lord Jesus Christ in flashing neon lights. For them, "God would have everyone to be saved and come to the knowledge of the truth" are not just words in I Timothy 2:4 but marching orders for every Christian who has received forgiveness and eternal life by God's grace through faith in the Savior Jesus Christ.

This world view led the witnessing Watkins family onto the road. They personally shared the Good News of Jesus Christ and the challenge of world evangelism with others in teacher training college and Seminary, from west to east in the United States and into the continents beyond. When sickness and death forced the Watkins family back from Nigeria to the United States in 1964, they understood it not as defeat but as an open door for a new direction in work and witness.

The new challenge was recruiting and sending workers to the world's white harvest fields particularly in the areas of translation and literacy evangelism. Messengers of Christ (later called Lutheran Bible Translators) and All Nations Literacy Movement (later called All Nations Missions) were organized. During the past twenty plus years over 500 translation and literacy missionaries have been sent out by these two organizations to over forty different people groups in five different continents.

Now Dr. Watkins is on the move again. He says, *"We can't wait. The young Christians of our generation must learn to see God's world as God sees it before they choose a career."* His resolve has caused his pen to flow and out of years of mission experience gives us **7 Worlds to Win.**

Within the challenging, overall framework of over 3,000 Bibleless languages, nearly 17,000 unreached people groups, containing over one half of the world's population and the need for 200,000 additional cross-cultural missionaries by the year 2000, Watkins, in **7 Worlds to Win,** will systematically open your eyes to the world wide mission challenge of today. He does it insightfully, incisively and interestingly. With each new page you will find compelling reasons for personal world witness and outreach and invaluable insights and assistance as you work with others to become witnessing, world Christians.

7 Worlds to Win is chuck full of historical insights about the success and failure of Christian witness. It is also full of challenges for the future. In order to get the most out of this book, think of each chapter as a case study of another world or culture or society into which God wants the Good News of His love, forgiveness, salvation and life-changing power to come. Do not try to read the whole book in one sitting. Read it slowly, and meditate on what you have read. As you read, keep the following questions in mind:

1. Historically, what blocked the communication of God's message in this particular culture or world?
2. Historically, what opened or facilitated the communication of God's message in this culture or world?
3. What, at the present time. are the road blocks to a full communication of the gospel in this culture or world?
4. Do I feel personally challenged to be God's witness in this culture or world?
5. If so, what must I do to accept that personal challenge?

Good reading, and may God make it a life-changing experience for you and for others through you.

Professor Eugene W. Bunkowske, Ph.D.
April 1986, Fort Wayne, Indiana

ABOUT THE AUTHOR

Dr. Morris Watkins is well qualified to write on this subject. He is a graduate of Concordia Teachers College in Seward, Nebraska (1949), of Concordia Theological Seminary in Springfield, Illinois (1959) and has his Doctor of Missiology degree from the Fuller Theological Seminary School of World Mission in Pasadena, California (1978). He also attended the Kennedy School of Missions in Hartford, Connecticut from 1962 to 1963 and the Summer Institute of Linguistics at the University of North Dakota and the University of Oklahoma.

He has had teaching experience on virtually every level from the fourth grade through high school as well as in a teacher training center and a Bible Institute in Nigeria, West Africa, where he also planted a number of churches in many villages in two different provinces. He also helped establish a School of World Mission at Faith Seminary in Tacoma, Washington and has served as adjunct professor at Fuller Seminary and at the William Carey International University in Pasadena.

After six years in Nigeria, Dr. and Mrs. Watkins were forced to return to the States following the death of their two year old daughter and the near death of two other children. Within a few months after their return to the States, the Lord led Morrie and Lois Watkins to start Lutheran Bible Translators to help get Lutherans involved in the monumental task of bringing Christ to the 3000 Bibleless tribes. Morrie was the Executive Director of LBT for eight years, until he felt God calling him to an even more staggering task—that of training literacy workers to prepare materials and train teachers for the 1.4 billion adults and teenagers throughout the world who have Scripture in their own language but can't read a word of it. That was in 1972 when a small group banded together to form the All Nations Literacy Movement, known better today as All Nations Missions.

Over these past 23 years, God has used Dr. Watkins to help recruit and train hundreds of God's people for Bible translation, literacy work, evangelism and church planting and for many supporting roles. They are serving Christ on five continents and on many islands of the South Pacific in more than 40 different languages. For the most part these have been people groups who were beyond the reach of any national church or any other existing missionary efforts.

While Dr. Watkins is grateful to God for having a part in the training and sending of some 500 missionaries, he is fully aware that at least *30,000 missionaries must be recruited within the next ten years* just to replace the missionaries who will be retiring or returning from the field for one reason or another.

"We can't wait," says Watkins, "until young people graduate from high school before we talk to them about missions. Most of them have already decided upon a career by then. We need to begin talking to children about missions in the early elementary grades and keep the challenge of the unfinished task before their eyes throughout the school year. They need to know something of the history of Christian missions in each country, the status of Christianity in that country today, the spiritual, social and economic needs, the problems of bringing the Gospel to these neglected (often resistant) people, the training required to break down cultural, social and linguistic barriers, and where to obtain this training, and they need to be aware of the many kinds of opportunities for Christian service. They need to begin at an early age to seek God's perfect will for their lives—how and where He would have them serve and glorify Him."

SEVEN WORLDS TO WIN
CONTENTS

SEVEN WORLDS TO WIN

PUBLISHER'S INTRODUCTION
To the Purpose and Plan of the Book

Seven Worlds to Win has been prepared for Christians. It has been written in order that they might better understand the world about them and see it through the eyes of their Savior and God. It is a book about people, people nearby and people far away, but all people loved by God. For that is part of the wonderful miracle, that He gave His Son for all people.

Before His ascension Jesus left His disciples with a supreme commandment. We call it "the Great Commission." It is well known to most of us as Christians, but often overlooked. We need to review it briefly in order to put this book in context.

"Then the eleven disciples went to Galilee, to the mountain where Jesus had told them to go. When they saw Him, they worshipped Him; but some doubted. Then Jesus came to them and said, 'All authority in heaven and on earth has been given to me. Therefore go and make disciples of all nations, baptizing them in the name of the Father and of the Son and of the Holy Spirit, and teaching them to obey everything I have commanded you. And surely I will be with you always, to the very end of the age.'" Matthew 28:16-20 (NIV)

It is interesting to observe that even as they saw and worshipped Him, some doubted! It is to this doubt that Jesus responds, reaffirming His divinity and authority, and issues this compound order, "go . . . make disciples . . . baptize . . . and teach . . ."

Jesus' response to doubt in the Christian life is the simple declaration of His authority and a command to proceed. Perhaps He is directing us to say to our doubts, "Satan, get thee behind me" and get on with the business He has called us to. This 'business' is the go-make-baptize-teach task which we, today, loosely define as "missions."

Jesus says, "Go!" Where? "To all nations." "But Lord," I reply, "I can't." Too often we excuse ourselves from responsibility with the "I can'ts" of our life. And, too often, the "I can't" is really an "I won't."

Theology is complex, and easily made more so! But Jesus' teachings are remarkably simple and equally direct. He does not call upon us to do that which we cannot! His every command includes the implicit "And surely I will be with you always" and "I have all authority." We do not have to be theologians to understand or obey His will!

No, no one of us can physically go "to all nations" and fulfill the Master's orders. In fact, there are countless disciples who will be unable to go beyond their community or, perhaps, even beyond their home. This command of His disciples is to the body of believers who, over the centuries, has carried and will carry the gospel around the world, some by going, but far more by praying, preparing, sending, and supporting. Paul refers to this as "service of the saints" (I Cor. 16:14 NIV). In discipleship we each go as we participate in the collective going of those who are physically enabled to do so. After all, we do none of this of ourselves, ". . . I no longer live, but Christ lives in me." (Gal. 2:20)

Jesus says, "Make!" What? "Disciples." Not just converts, not just intellectual believers, not congregations, but disciples! Reproduce and multiply yourselves by making disciples of all nations. What is the role of a disciple? Well, for one thing, it is to carry on this same task! We have come full circle. This is "mission" as God intended it.

Cross-Reference
Great Commission, *196*

Jesus says, "Baptize . . ." Why? Our role is not social, it is spiritual. Our call is not the saving of lives, it is the saving of souls. The importance of welfare and caring for others is clearly scriptural and vital to being wholly Christian, but the ultimate objective is the heart and soul of believers. Only those so won can be disciples.

Jesus says, "Teach them . . ." What? " . . . to obey everything I have commanded you." Our work is not completed with saving souls. We do not bring the gospel for the purpose of enlisting an army of "babes in Christ." We must bring the solid food of Christian maturity as well.

This is the Great Commission. It is for us then to seek God's will as to how these gifts and talents may be used and in what fashion our personal "going" will take place. To do this we are compelled to consider the world about us and study the nature, needs, and spiritual state of its nations.

The world of today is very complex. It is dominated by a number of profoundly different religions. There are many contrasting political systems. Ethnic, racial, cultural, social, and other disparities divide us. Tension between factions inhibits communication. Barriers are imposed, wars fought, revenge pursued, and power seized and sought. Preoccupied by the forces and effects of these divisions, mankind has no time for the still, small voice of God.

Yet we are commanded to make disciples of all these nations. But where do we begin when the world turns deaf ears to hope and sanity? How do we communicate the love of God to those who do not even know human love?

We begin in humility. We must humble ourselves before God, that we may be yielded to Him. We must humble ourselves before others, that we be not judgmental or self-righteous. We must humble ourselves of self, casting off pride, envy, boasting, and self-gain. Then, in submission to God's will, we seek through His word, through prayer, and through study to learn how we may participate in winning the world to Christ.

This text is presented to help us better understand and communicate with the people of the world we live in. If we are to communicate, we must get ourselves onto a plain of communication. We must be able to talk at the same level. This requires that we must be comfortable with those we would reach in order that they may be comfortable with us. We cannot accomplish this unless we recognize their special qualities and character.

With hundreds of nations on earth most of us could not hope to learn much about each of them. However, many nations have much in common with other nations and can be studied together. This objective has led Dr. Watkins to classify nations by various common characteristics and to define the "seven worlds" of this text. He has chosen seven blocs of peoples or nations having sufficient in common to study together.

What they have in common differs. For three it is a specific prevailing or historic religion. He has designated these as the Buddhist, Hindu, and Muslim Worlds. A quick observation of the state of our world and its history reveals that more wars are fought and alliances formed on religious grounds than any other. Ethnic, racial, linguistic, and political differences have less impact on international relations than religion!

Another we may think of in the same context is animism or natural religion. These are bodies of belief not generally the product of a prophet or seer like Buddha or Mohammed. They reflect man's awe of nature and his inborn desire to know God manifest in worship of spirits in nature and in the objects about him. In *Eternity in their Hearts,* Don Richardson has shown how God has prepared mankind through special "redemptive analogies" placed within his own culture and beliefs. Today we find animism and spiritism prevalent in areas which remained separated from

Christian influence until only very recent times. These are lands where the Bible has not until recently, if ever, appeared in the mother tongue or where no written language form exists even today. We call this the Bibleless World.

Almost a religion in itself is opposition to religion! Man's obstinate rejection of a loving God can assume all the elements of worship except a worthy objective. The Communist World we think of as political in nature but the most profound claim of communism is the substitution of state for God. The state is the object of worship and the state defines moral, ethical, and social values. The documents of marxism are its bible and Lenin, its Moses.

At the opposite political pole, the Western World represents all the plusses of Christian heritage, yet we look about it (for we live in it) and wonder, "what has gone wrong?" This so-called "Christian World" of ours is ravaged by humanism, atheism, gnosticism, and general moral decay.

Distinctive from the other worlds, yet having elements in common with several, is the Chinese World. This most populous nation of all, with its unique history, religious variety, and political adventures, has a place all to itself in our study.

In *Seven Worlds to Win* we will study the world's peoples in these seven blocs. In each bloc we examine the characteristics which make it unique and the factors we must consider if we are to win it to Christ. You will find listed the nations most readily ascribed to it and maps, statistics, and helpful insights into it. You will also be given much to aid in praying for the people in it. As you study you will become a "world Christian" better prepared to go-disciple-baptize-teach whether in person or as a servant of discipleship.

To further assist your study and use of this text as a reference, a detailed index is supplied together with an exhaustive marginal cross-reference. Each "World" chapter concludes with a suggested reading list and resource list. Three chapters at the conclusion focus on praying for missions, the world at a glance, and other missionary resources.

A GUIDE TO STUDY

The individual reader's approach to the use of this book will differ according to need and circumstance. *Seven Worlds to Win* has been prepared so that it can be used equally well in a variety of ways.

It may be read cover to cover. As you do so you will become progressively more conscious of the spiritual needs of the whole world and of the opportunities for your personal ministry. It is not a difficult reading task and will serve you well.

Topical study is also possible. You may choose to study one subject whether a world or a nation or an area of ministry. Consult the index for the topic(s) of interest and use the marginal cross references to expand your study.

Group study is excellent, whether in an organized class, formal Bible study, missions conference or committee, or informal home or family study. Interaction is particularly helpful in group study. You may wish to obtain a copy of "The Great Commission Study Guide" to help you further. (See the resource list at the end of the text for study helps.)

Whatever the method of study consider these helpful hints:

1. Proceed logically. Have a plan of study, don't read at random.
2. Refer to the maps, visualize the location, size, and people of the lands you study.
3. Obtain suggested reading material on topics of special interest. This text is an overview. Expand upon it freely from outside sources.
4. Seek other sources such as "National Geographic Magazine" references and other publications. Consult your librarian.

5. Discuss your study with others, your pastor, missionary friend, other Christians.
6. Pray for your study, sensitivity to the unreached world, and missionary endeavor.

THE SEVEN WORLDS

The maps on the following pages illustrate the seven worlds of this text. Under each map is a list of the nations most identified with that "world." Listed in the margin are the pages to which the reader should refer for information, charts, diagrams, maps, and other special references which pertain.

A few nations appear more than once because of dual identity. For example, China is (of course) in the Chinese World. However it is also in the Communist World. Refer to the *Chinese World* to study China from an ethnic and cultural perspective and the *Communist World* to see it in the political sense. In each world study you will be able to relate it to other nations of the same "world" according to that aspect.

If you do not find a nation listed under any map, locate it as a shaded area of one of the maps and refer to that area of study. Remember, many nations are known by more than one name, example: *England, Great Britain, United Kingdom.* Others have new names gained through independence, example: *Belgian Congo, Zaire.*

Bob Law

LOCATING THE SEVEN WORLDS

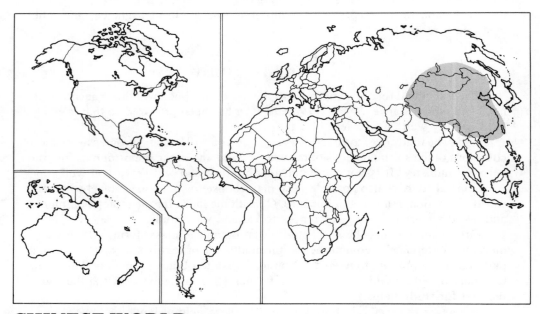

CHINESE WORLD

China   Hong Kong   Macau   Taiwan

Predominately ethnic Chinese.

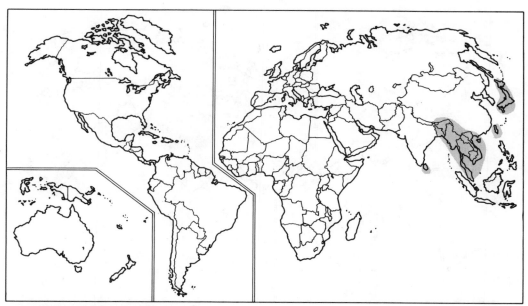

BUDDHIST WORLD

Bhutan	Cambodia	Korea*	Sri Lanka	Thailand
Burma	Japan	Laos	Taiwan	Vietnam

30% or greater Buddhist population.
*Dramatic growth of Christianity in recent decades has greatly diminished Buddhism in Korea.

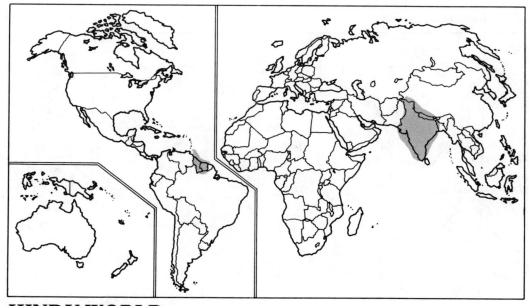

HINDU WORLD

Guyana	India	Mauritius	Nepal	Surinam
Trinidad				

30% or greater Hindu population.

TOPICAL INDEX

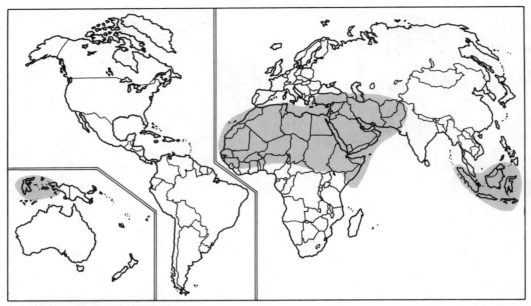

MUSLIM WORLD

Afghanistan	Ethiopia	Kuwait	Nigeria	Sudan
Algeria	Gambia	Libya	Oman	Syria
Bahrain	Guinea	Malaysia	Pakistan	Tunisia
Bangladesh	Guinea Bissau	Maldives	Qatar	Turkey
Chad	Indonesia	Mali	Saudi Arabia	United Arab
Comoros	Iran	Mauritania	Senegal	Emirates
Djibouti	Iraq	Morocco	Sierra Leone	Yemen
Egypt	Jordan	Niger	Somalia	

40% or greater Muslim population.

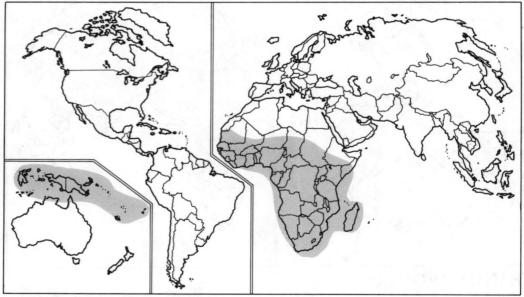

BIBLELESS WORLD

Botswana	Ghana	Maldives	Rwanda	Tanzania
Burundi	Indonesia	Mauritius	Senegal	Togo
Cameroon	Ivory Coast	Mozambique	Sierra Leone	Uganda
Chad	Kenya	Niger	South Africa	Zaire
Congo	Liberia	Nigeria	Sudan	Zambia
Gambia	Malawi	Papua New Guinea	Swaziland	Zimbabwe

Many bibleless tribes are found in India, other Asian countries, and the Americas.

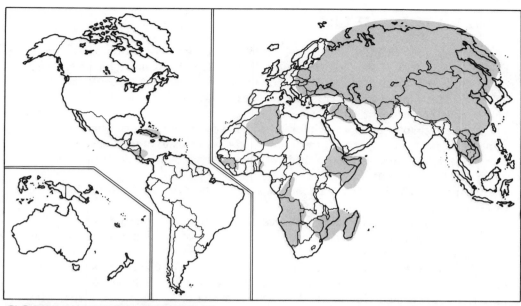

COMMUNIST WORLD

Afghanistan	China	Ethiopia	Mongolia	Romania
Albania	Congo	East Germany	Mozambique	South Yemen
Angola	Cuba	Hungary	Nicaragua	U.S.S.R.
Bulgaria	Czechoslovakia	Kampuchea	North Korea	Vietnam
Burma	Equatorial Guinea	Laos	Poland	Yugoslavia

Communist or communist inclined governments.

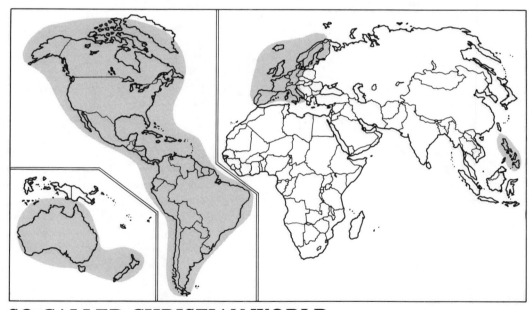

SO-CALLED CHRISTIAN WORLD

America (U.S.A.)	Canada	Finland	Jamaica	Spain
Argentina	Chile	France	Mexico	Sweden
Australia	Colombia	Guatemala	New Zealand	Switzerland
Austria	Costa Rica	Haiti	Norway	United Kingdom
Belgium	Denmark	Holland	Panama	Uruguay
Belize	Dominican Republic	Honduras	Paraguay	Venezuela
Bolivia	Ecuador	Iceland	Philippines	West Germany
Brazil	El Salvador	Italy	Portugal	

The So-called Christian World includes many bibleless peoples as well.

OTHER STUDY HELPS

Cross-Reference
Study Helps, *3*

The final four chapters of this text contain important information pertaining to missions. The first is devoted to prayer. This study is excellent for missionary fellowships and committees and for individuals who earnestly seek to be more effectual in their missions prayer life. It includes a "Lord's Prayer for Missions," and help in praying for missionaries, cultures, and the lost.

The next chapter provides helpful information pertaining to missionary support. Support begins with prayer but prayer almost always leads to other areas of mission involvement. This includes stewardship of finance, time, and talent. It may include going, full time or short term.

Chapter X, *The World at a Glance,* is a general overview of the world, its needs, its peoples, and religions.

The last chapter, *Missionary Resources,* lists general mission study sources such as books and periodicals and names and addresses of mission agencies offering information or opportunities to serve.

All of the seven worlds have one need in common, Jesus Christ, the one hope for eternity. As Christians, we have been directed by Him to reach out to those who have not yet accepted Him as Lord and Saviour and bring this Good News. May God richly bless you as you seek to fulfill this command.

CHINA

As far as we know, it was not until the seventh century that Christianity came to China. In the first third of the seventh century a bishop and a young monk started eastward from their home in Persia. They were received in the palace of T'ai Tsung, the emperor of China, in the year 635. The Chinese gave the bishop the name, Alopen, which means, "The man who was sent by God". The emperor commanded that a monastery be built for these men and for twenty-one monks at his own expense, and that they be permitted to preach anywhere in China. [1]

Alopen never returned to Persia, and we would know nothing about him if it had not been for the discovery of the "Nestorian Monument" in 1625, on which this story is recorded. Engraved in the year 781 in Chinese characters, the tablet informs us that Christian monasteries were built in different parts of China and that Christian literature had been produced. [2]

The list of translations of Christian books in Chinese suggests that the monks learned the language and made themselves at home in China. But we cannot help but wonder to what extent they made their presence felt. Were their translations printed and circulated? If so, to what extent were they read? It is doubtful that more than five percent of these Chinese people could read and write. It is known that as late as 1950, only twenty percent of China could read and write. According to one authority, only one or two percent of the people throughout most of Chinese history have been able to read the ideographic script. [3]

In 845 the Emperor Wu Tsung, an ardent Taoist who opposed monasticism in all its forms, issued a decree prohibiting Buddhism, dissolving monasteries, and ordering the monks to return to private life. Since the Nestorians were monks, the decree applied to them also.

It is unlikely that the Christian Church was exterminated, but its power was apparently broken. In 987, a monk and five other men were sent to inquire into the state of the Church in China. They returned to report that they could find *no trace of Christianity in the Empire*. [4]

There may have been some Nestorians somewhere in China, however, since we hear about them again near the end of the 13th century. In the latter third of the 13th century, the father and uncle of Marco Polo arrived at the Imperial Palace in Cambaluc (now Beijing). They were received with high honor by Kublai Khan, the most powerful ruler at the time. His attitude toward Christianity was favorable. He even dictated a letter to the Pope requesting a hundred missionaries. The Polos traveled back to Italy, and in 1269 delivered the letter to the Pope.

But the Pope didn't respond. After several years, the Pope appointed two friars to go with the Polos to China. But they had not gone far when the friars took fright and returned to Rome. Later the Pope sent five more friars, but none of them ever reached China. Twenty-five years after the Pope had received the letter, Kublai Khan died without having seen a single missionary in response to his invitation. How tragic! If the Pope had responded to this request in full obedience to our Lord's command, it might have changed the history, not only of China, but of the entire world.[5]

Shortly after the death of Kublai Khan, however, in 1294, an Italian Fransiscan monk known as John of Montecorvino, arrived in Cambaluc with a letter from the Pope. After a five year imprisonment because of false accusations against him by Nestorian Priests, John began his missionary work in China, which was to continue for thirty years. He claims to have translated the New Testament and the Psalms into "the language and character which is in general use among the Mongols"[6] Although a letter of Pope Benedict XIII (A.D 1335) mentions the finding of a Mongolian Bible in China, no trace of these early versions has been found.[7] John also claimed to have baptized some six thousand people in a period of six years. We cannot help but wonder how well they were instructed, for the work completely disappeared.[8]

Three more bishops joined John in 1308. Others arrived in 1342, twelve years after John's death. But with the collapse of the Mongol dynasty in 1368, Nestorian and Catholic Christians totally disappeared from Chinese history for nearly two hundred years.[8]

Apparently neither the Franciscans nor the Nestorians made any great effort to train the nationals for the ministry, and if the New Testament or any part of God's Word was translated into the Chinese language, there is no trace of it today.

In 1552 Francis Xavier, the first Jesuit missionary, tried to enter China, but without success. The door of China had been slammed tight against missionaries of the Gospel due to the cruelty of Portuguese traders. Xavier died on an islet near Hong Kong while waiting for an opportunity to get into the country.[9]

Xavier was succeeded by Valignano as superintendent of missions in Asia. At Macao (on the mainland not far from Hong Kong) Valignano was training something like a Christian "commando" group of young men to break through into China. Matteo Ricci joined the group. After mastering the Chinese language, Matteo gained entrance to the country. Eventually, he made his way to Cambaluc (Beijing), and, being a brilliant scholar, was invited into the Emperor's palace. Within a few years members of the Imperial family had joined a church whose two hundred members included many others of the highest of the land.[9]

Ricci mastered the Chinese classics, especially the teachings of Confucius. In these classics the names for the Supreme Spirit, Shang Ti and T'ien, meant something very impersonal. Ricci used these words for God in Christian worship and in teaching about Christianity. He also allowed converts to continue the ceremonies in honor of ancestors and of Confucius. When he died in 1610, he had called thousands into the Church. Forty years later, the Catholic Church in China numbered over two hundred fifty thousand, and by 1708 the number of Chinese Christians had risen to a third of a million.[9]

But then the decline set in, due to a fierce controversy over Ricci's policy. In 1704 the Pope forbade the use of the Chinese terms for God that Ricci had used, and he ordered the Christians to stop participating in the sacrifices to ancestors and to Confucius. The Emperor was furious that a foreign "barbarian" like the Pope should disagree with him about the use of Chinese words. The missionaries found themselves in quite a dilemma. They had to obey the Pope and anger the

Emperor or please the Emperor and be excommunicated by the Pope. The debate continued until 1742 when the Pope ordered disobedient missionaries to return to Rome for punishment.

But there were at least four other causes for the decline of Catholic missions in China in the latter half of the eighteenth century:
1. The Spanish and the Portuguese empires were in decay;
2. The Jesuits were suppressed by the Pope in 1773, after having been expelled a few years earlier from French, Spanish and Portuguese territories;
3. Persecution increased with the growth of the Church;
4. The French Revolution, followed by the Napoleonic wars, cut off the support of missionaries from Europe.

Although there are many reasons for the failure of the Church to grow in China, one of the greatest reasons may be the fact that they were not given the written word of God in their own language until the nineteenth century, and even then, as we shall see, it was a long, long time before many people had access to it and could read it for themselves.[10]

At the beginning of the nineteenth century there were probably between two hundred thousand and two hundred fifty thousand Christians in China, mostly Roman Catholic, but also a small number of Russian Orthodox. The Roman Catholic Church, however, was on the decline, and there were only a few European priests and bishops scattered throughout the empire.[11]

There was no Protestant mission work in China at all until Robert Morrison arrived in Canton in 1807 and began translating the Scriptures under extremely dangerous and difficult circumstances. To discourage translation of the Scriptures, the Chinese government forbade, under pain of death, the teaching of Chinese to a foreigner. Morrison's teacher always carried poison, and was ready to commit suicide if he should be detected. In spite of the danger, Morrison worked steadily at the task and completed the New Testament by 1814 and the entire Bible by 1823. For nearly thirty years, Morrison's translation served as the basis for other and better versions.

As printed Scriptures became more abundant throughout China, the government decreed the death penalty for any European preparing or disseminating Christian literature and exile to northern Manchuria for any Chinese who were deluded by them. The Imperial edict was posted on every gate in the walls of the ancient city of Canton.[12]

In spite of these difficulties, attempts were made to circulate the books through Cantonese booksellers. These efforts were largely unsuccessful, so when Morrison's New Testament was issued in 1814 it was arranged that his young colleague, the Reverend W. Milne, should visit Java, Malacca, and Penang to circulate the Sacred Word among the many Chinese settlers in those places! For the next twenty-five years, Malacca and Singapore were the chief distribution centers for the Chinese Scriptures.[13]

In the 1830s Gutzlaff, Medhurst, and others sailed in Chinese junks up the coast of China distributing thousands of New Testaments and Bible portions as far north as Korea. But getting beyond the coast was virtually impossible. All foreign nations were suspect and must be kept out at all costs.

Protestant mission work did not really begin in China proper until 1842 with the Treaty of Nanking following the Opium War. This brought an end to the restrictions on the distribution of God's Word. Also as a result of the war, the island of Hong Kong was ceded to Great Britain, and five ports, later known as Treaty Ports, were opened to foreign trade. These were Canton, Shanghai, Amoy, Foochow, and Ningpo. Shanghai, at that time a small village, became the headquarters of missionary societies from all over the world.[14]

Cross-References

Canton, *17*

Jesuits, *48*

Korea, *4, 17, 29, 37, 38, 100, 123*

Persecution, *14, 38, 77, 80, 109, 116, 123, 129, 143*

Shanghai, *17*

Singapore, *23, 29, 59, 101*

Translation, *9, 45, 48, 52, 66, 89, 91, 96, 106, 108, 214*

Cross-Reference
Mandarin Language,
202

Missionaries immediately settled in all of these ports, and efforts to print and circulate Scripture were intensified. But the work of distribution was still on a very small scale.[15]

A second war broke out with Great Britain in 1856 and the work of distribution almost came to a complete standstill. The war continued until 1860. But with the coming of peace, ten more Treaty Ports were opened, the Christian religion was to be tolerated, and missionaries were granted the right to buy land, erect buildings, and travel and reside in the interior. The Treaty of Tientsin, which granted these privileges, was the *turning point* in the whole missionary enterprise in China. The ten new treaty ports were immediately occupied, and exploratory trips, involving months of arduous travel, were undertaken in many parts of the empire never before seen by the white man.[16]

Up until the middle of the nineteenth century all versions of the Bible were in what is known as the Literary or Wen-li style, a classical form of expression understood only by well-educated people. To the average person, the Wen-li language was comparable with what Latin is to English, so that the Wen-li Bible reached only a very small fraction of the people. To remedy this in the 1850s several missionaries began translating the Scriptures into the vernacular, Mandarin, which extended over about 80 percent of the country. Between 1857 and 1889 several new translations appeared. Each of these translations had its respective value, and within a few years the Wen-li Bible was largely replaced. In the family, in the classroom, in the chapel and church services, the Mandarin versions were read with interest and excitement. As Christianity spread and the number of missionaries increased,there developed a widespread desire and an ever-increasing demand to have one unified translation for the whole Protestant Church. But it was not until 1919 that this unified translation, the Union Mandarin Version, was published. This is the version now used by ninety-nine percent of the Protestant Chinese Christians.

In 1860 there were only twenty-five hundred Protestants in all of China and not quite a hundred Protestant missionaries. But as we mentioned earlier, 1860 was the turning point for Protestant missions in China. The period from 1860 to 1900 was a time of rapid expansion. Wherever missionaries went, churches, schools, and hospitals were established. By 1907, Protestant forces comprised a total of ninety-four societies with a total membership of 3,445 missionaries, living in 632 stations, and there were 389 schools of higher learning.[16]

The China Inland Mission, founded by Hudson Taylor in 1865, became by far the largest of all the missions in China, with nine hundred members and four hundred associates, working in fifteen of the eighteen provinces.[16]

During this period there were also three Bible Societies at work and eleven tract societies. Eleven mission presses turned out a steady stream of Christian literature. In 1860, some thirty thousand Scripture portions were circulated. Within ten years, circulation had reached a hundred thousand copies per year throughout seventeen of the eighteen provinces of China. By 1876, a million Testaments had been distributed. This seems like a lot of Scripture, but it was still only one New Testament for every four hundred people in that vast land of four hundred million people.[17]

In 1900 there was another fanatical outburst of anti-foreignism known as the Boxer Rebellion. One hundred and eighty-nine Protestant missionaries and their children were killed, and scores of other missionaries barely escaped to the coast, suffering severe hardship along the way. This was the largest massacre of missionaries in modern times. It is not known how many Chinese Christians were put to death at this time but it would be safe to say that they numbered in the thousands.[16]

When peace was restored, a large number of reforms were made. An ancient scholastic method was changed into an ever-expanding modern system, railways began to replace the cart and mule, a government postal and telegraph system was introduced, and newspapers began to appear.

During the decade 1900 to 1910 the church grew faster than ever before. In fact, if statistics are any criterion, more progress was made in that decade than in any previous fifty years.

By 1914 there were 543 high schools with an enrollment of thirty-three thousand. There were probably about 1,750,000 Christians in China by that time. About one-third to one-fourth of these were Protestants. These church members were from all ranks of society. Many Christians, especially Protestants, were well-educated, bringing into being a leadership which was influential out of all proportion to the size of the Christian community. Even so, the fact remains that after nineteen centuries, China was less than one-half of one percent Christian, in spite of the intensive efforts made during the 19th century, especially during the last half of it.[18]

During the early part of the 20th century there was a steady growth in anti-foreign feelings. The murder of missionaries was not an uncommon event.

Being a missionary in many parts of China was an extra hazardous occupation, and being a Christian did not carry as much immunity from attack as in the first years after the Boxer uprising.

Nevertheless, the missionary forces grew in China, reaching a peak of 8,158 missionaries in 1925 throughout the country. But by 1927, 62 percent of the missionaries had been withdrawn from the interior.[19]

The emergence of Chaing Kai Shek as a ruler of increasingly large areas in the country gave a period of relief from persecution. In 1930, Chiang declared himself a Christian and was baptised though some have questioned the depth of his conversion.

In spite of the uncertainties of life, the Christian cause continued to make progress, although the Marxists were already at work in the 1920s, attempting to obtain a stranglehold on the life and thought of China. In two successive years, the Protestant missions reported an increase in membership — among them men and women of stature who were to enter into positions of leadership and power. At the time of the final collapse of Free China, several cabinet ministers in the government of Chiang Kai Shek were Christian men of the highest integrity and capacity.

The time of respite came to an end with the Japanese invasion of 1937. The sufferings of the country were intense. The ruthlessness of Japanese methods brought grave losses to Christians and others.

But even this time gave new opportunities of Christian service. Mission compounds were opened to the thousands of refugees and wounded who were able to receive at least minimal treatment and sustenance. Missionaries, along with their Chinese Christian friends, retreated before the advancing Japanese armies. Many schools and colleges started a new existence in western China, beyond the farthest reaches of the Japanese. Here the work went forward, and students continued to be baptized.

In 1945 the Japanese were at last thrown out. Christian forces emerged from exile, and set to work everywhere to reconstruct, to restore, and to renew. But no sooner had one enemy been overcome than another appeared. The *Communists* had only been waiting for the chance which now presented itself. The Communists armed themselves with the munitions sent by the Americans (to defend themselves against the Japanese) and all too easily won victory after victory against the nationalist forces of Chiang Kai Shek. The end came suddenly and unexpectedly. On October 1, 1949, the Peoples Democratic Republic of China was proclaimed in Peking; Chiang Kai Shek and his friends fled to Taiwan.

Missionaries prepared to make the most of the situation and to stay in China. Their numbers had been steadily decreasing since 1925 but there were still 4,062 Protestant missionaries in China in 1949 and probably an equal number of Roman Catholics. Missionaries knew that they would live under constant suspicion. All this they were prepared to accept, if only they might continue to serve the people.

It soon became clear not only that the missionaries would be permitted to do nothing, but their continued presence in China would bring danger to their Chinese friends. By 1951 a policy of withdrawal was agreed upon, and by 1953 it was almost complete. A few westerners were killed; and a larger number suffered imprisonment, including solitary confinement and "brain-washing".

Since the Communist takeover in 1949, all educational, medical, and social work has been taken out of the hands of the Church. Church buildings, however, were not at first confiscated; services could be maintained, and the regular work of the Church carried on. [20]

Before World War II, liberal theology had permeated most of the large Christian colleges. The majority of the graduates of these schools soon gave up any profession of the Christian faith. Some still professed to be Christian, but tried to please the Communists. [21]

In 1950, Communist leaders gave to Wu Yao-tsong (a prominent YMCA leader) the task of forming a new church that would be free from the influences of imperialism. Before long, Wu Yao-tsong launched a movement commonly known as the Three-Self Movement — later known as the "Chinese Christian Three-Self Patriotic Movement".

The stated aims of the movement were very good. The Three-Self Principles — self-governing, self-supporting, self-propagating — have been the goals of every good missionary society for centuries. Now these principles were absolutely necessary in China. But under Communism, these principles were, of course, given a new interpretation, and the entire emphasis was to destroy imperialistic and anti-socialist influence within the church.

In conferences organized by the Three-Self Movement and in the official church publications, the teaching of God's Word, evangelism, spiritual life were almost completely ignored. Instead, there was a constant indoctrination regarding the church's attitude to the Communist way of life.

Churches became centers of intense political discussion. Instead of Bible study there were discussions of Communist principles and denunciation of people who were not "progressive" enough in their thinking.

Some churches were not allowed to continue services. In small towns and villages church buildings and furnishings were appropriated by various government agencies and the religious life of Christians was interfered with. Some churches were used as stables. Churches that remained open were not allowed to make repairs or take in new members.

Many pastors tried to compromise their faith. Others, like Wang Ming-tao, boldly confessed their faith in Jesus and continued to preach the whole counsel of God, even though they knew it would cost them their lives. Mr. Wang was arrested in 1955 and this heralded the beginning of a great campaign against evangelicals throughout the country. Many were sent to prison and labor camps. Christian workers throughout China were required to express their personal condemnation of uncompromising Christian leaders like Wang Ming-tao.

It wasn't long before most of the evangelical leaders were either in prison or disgraced, and the Communist control over the church tightened. A decree was issued making illegal all Christian activities outside the jurisdiction of the Three-Self Movement. Sunday Schools were abolished.

In Shanghai many students belonged to the "Little Flock", an indigeneous movement containing a very great number of Christians scattered throughout China. Terrible charges had been brought against their leader, Watchman Nee (Nee-To-sheng), and he was sentenced to a 15-year prison term in 1952. He was still in prison twenty years later, and died there June 1, 1972.

A few months after Wang Ming-Tao's arrest, the leaders in Shanghai were also arrested, and twenty-five hundred Christians were summoned to a mass denunciation meeting. All the members of the "Little Flock" had to go through a special indoctrination course and a reformed "Little Flock" was taken into the Three-Self Movement.

Outward opposition to the government-sponsored church had now been overcome and leadership was completely in the hands of men and women who had been well indoctrinated and had fully accepted the government's religious policy. Those who remained in the official church enjoyed a measure of freedom for a time, while others who met secretly outside were in constant danger of arrest. But peace within the official church was to be shortlived.

In 1967, the Cultural Revolution accompanied by the rampage of the Red Guards completely changed the situation. The church was now regarded as a part of the old tradition which must be completely crushed. Church buildings were closed and desecrated. Christians were humiliated. Bibles and other Christian books were burned. Christian homes were ransacked by zealous Red Guards eager to seek out and destroy everything connected with religious observances. The Christian population within prisons and labor camps increased. Those who had sought to survive through holding membership in the Three-Self Movement now found themselves obliged either to deny the faith or join with secret disciples in hidden cell groups.

For some real Christians who had bought physical safety at the cost of the loss of peace of mind the moment of truth had come. They realized they had betrayed their Lord and their fellow Christians. The so-called "freedom of religion" was only temporary, and they too had to face persecution, if they were to continue in the faith. At least the issue was now clear. Christian faith must be maintained in secret. Only those who were prepared to suffer could remain true to their Lord. [22]

Despite the many years of intensive persecution, the Church in China has grown beyond anyone's wildest expectations. When the bamboo curtain began to lift in the late seventies, it soon became evident that the million Christians were still there. Then the estimates grew to 3 million, then 5 million, then 10. Now even conservative estimates range between 30 million and 50 million.[23]

One of the reasons for this church growth, no doubt, is the fact that the broadcasting of the Gospel via short wave and medium wave transmissions has never ceased, but has continuously increased. By 1975, total broadcast hours per week in Chinese were about 150. The Far East Broadcasting Company alone was broadcasting the Gospel into China 103 hours each week. Between 1970 and 1978, FEBC received an average of just 18 letters per year from listeners in China, but in the first four months of 1979, they received 5,644 letters, 90% of them from non-Christians.

In a major development, in 1975, FEBC began broadcasting into China not only shortwave (potentially reaching China's 12 million sets), but also with AM transmissions, audible over China's 100 million local radio receivers and hence potentially reaching 90% of China's total population for (in 1978) 19 hours of broadcasting each day.[24]

Cross-References
Cultural Revolution, *121*
Far East Broadcasting Co. *123*
Radio Broadcasting, *67, 72, 106, 111, 118, 123, 151, 163, 191*

Great efforts have also been made to provide the Christians in China with the written word of God. Copies of the Bible were brought in first through smuggling, then through visitors who are now allowed to bring in almost any reasonable quantity of Bibles. In cooperation with other agencies, the Hong Kong-based Asian Outreach has produced the Living New Testament and the Living Bible in simplified Chinese script, along with the popular daily devotional Streams in the Desert. These are now available to all Christians who want to bring or mail them into China.[25]

Since 1979, Christian teachers have been allowed into China to teach English as a second language in the universities. Now the government is asking for teams of four teachers each to teach English in the high schools. The leader of each team must have a Master's degree in teaching English as a second language, but the other three teachers need only a bachelor's degree, and that degree can be in almost anything. Further information can be obtained from the William Carey International University, 1539 E. Howard St., Pasadena, CA 91104 or from the Overseas Counseling Service, P.O. Box 33836, Seattle, WA 98133, or Global Opportunities, 1600 E. Elizabeth St., Pasadena, CA 91104. You can also write to English Language Institute/China, 448 E. Foothill Blvd., San Dimas, CA 91773. ELIC sends teams of 10 teachers to 10 or 12 universities each summer and teams of 2-4 to more than 40 schools during the regular school year. China is also looking for teachers of many different disciplines on the university level. Write to the Overseas Counseling Service for details.

We praise God for what He is doing in China, and we expect to see even greater things in the years ahead.

China

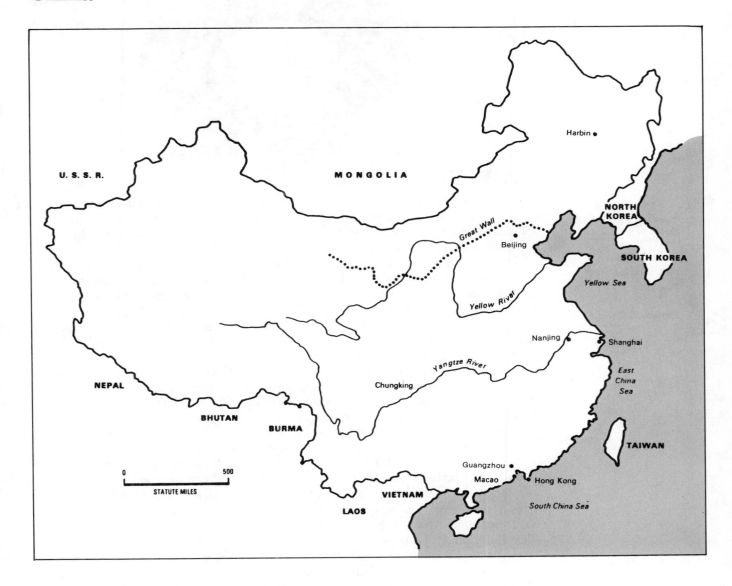

TAIWAN

Forty percent of all the Chinese people outside of mainland China live on the island of Taiwan, 100 miles east of the China coast. Only two percent of these Chinese people are evangelical Christians, making Taiwan *the largest field* for Chinese evangelization in the Free World.

Who are these people and why has it been so difficult to win them to Christ?

About two percent of the inhabitants of Taiwan are descendants of early settlers who may have come from the Malay Peninsula, although some may have come from tribal areas of China. They are known as Mountain People although many of them have migrated to the plains and to the major cities. They have been more responsive to the Gospel than the Chinese. About twenty percent of them are Christians.[26]

By far the largest ethnic group on the island is the Minnan people. They constitute seventy-five percent of the total population. Their language is also referred to as Taiwanese. Most of their ancestors came from South China less than four hundred years ago. The largest migration took place in 1661 when Koxinga brought thousands of them with him to recover the island from the Dutch who had est˙blished a trading and military post there in 1634.

Ten percent of the inhabitants of Taiwan are the Hakkas. Their ancestors came from Northern China. They speak a distinctly different language known to few others on Taiwan. They came to the island in large numbers somewhat later than the Minnan Taiwanese, but long enough ago to allow them to have established many distinct Hakka communities.

The Religion of Taiwan

Most of those who practice religion in Taiwan today can be classified as "folk religionists". Although government classifications prefer to distinguish between Buddhism and Taoism, these two main schools of thought are merged together in Taiwan, held together and undergirded by an animistic world which views all of nature as filled with spirits, gods and ghosts — objects to be divinely manipulated in order to produce the ideal Chinese goal of wholeness, unity, and harmony.

Dutch missionaries came to Taiwan in 1627, 165 years before William Carey launched the modern missionary movement. Between 1627 and 1664 the Dutch Reformed Church sent 37 missionaries to Taiwan to minister to Dutch traders. They also made a major missionary outreach into the aboriginal communities. The local Chinese, for unknown reasons, received little missionary attention.[27]

With the establishment of Manchu control over Taiwan in 1683 the last missionaries were driven out. The door didn't open again to the gospel for 175 years.

In 1859, several Dominican Catholic missionaries arrived in Taiwan and the modern movement on that island began.

The Protestant banner was carried back to Taiwan by the English Presbyterian, Dr. James Maxwell, who arrived in south Taiwan in 1865, but the Chinese hatred of foreigners, so prevalent at that time, made his pioneer work difficult and dangerous. In 1872, the Canadian Presbyterian entered northern Taiwan. The founder, Dr. George Leslie Mackay, was one of the 19th century missionary giants. His gifts of preaching, teaching, and healing, together with an endless supply of energy, faith, and courage enabled Mackay to make a profound impact in northern Taiwan.

Progress was slow in the early church. In 1895, Taiwan was ceded to Japan. The Japanese gave the missionaries considerable freedom until the threat of World War II led to their expulsion in 1940. The young Taiwanese Church was now on its own, a small but vital Christian witness in an increasingly hostile environment. They did not falter. When freedom came in 1945, a faithful church emerged.

Several other churches also labored in Taiwan beginning in 1926.

Four major churches with approximately 51,000 members were on hand to greet the flood of refugees and missionaries that poured into Taiwan during the first decade after the war. Broken hearts and homes helped prepare the people for a new message.

A few Christians were among these refugees. Christianity on the mainland had found its greatest acceptance among government workers, students, and the military, the same groups that fled to Taiwan in the greatest numbers. These Christians provided a base for new outreach to tens of thousands who were filled with fear and frustration, and searching for a new faith that could renew their crumbling social and family structures.

An unprecedented opportunity for evangelism had opened for the Christians in Taiwan. Almost overnight the formerly little-known island became a major new mission field. Unfortunately, these were also days of indecision for many missions. Would Taiwan fall to the Communists? Would the Mandarins return home again in a short time? Was the upheaval just a temporary phenomenon as some claimed?

By 1952 the picture was coming into sharper focus,"Settle down and seek the welfare of the place where I have sent you", (Jer 29:7) became wise counsel. The time for sowing seed into receptive hearts was at hand. Cooperative efforts were common as many missions joined hands in the harvest field. By 1955 the original four denominations in Taiwan had grown to 36. By 1980, there were 57.

By the latter part of the decade, the seed sown in the early 50s was bringing a harvest unprecedented in the history of China missions. Roman Catholics soared from 13,000 in 1945 to 180,000 by 1960. The Protestant community shot up from 37,000 after World War II to more than 200,000 in the same period.

Most of the receptivity was found among the Mandarins and the mountain aborigines. One reason for the good response among the Mandarin was that most of the missionaries were transfers from the China Mainland. It is only natural that they would work with the people whose language they had spent years to learn. With the fate of the mainland sealed, Bible schools and seminaries began rapidly opening all over Taiwan, especially where the Mandarin refugees tended to congregate.[28]

A community of 51,000 Christians in 1948 had expanded to almost 380,000 by 1960. But the era of rapid growth was over. Many of the Mandarin Churches in Taiwan today are hardly any larger than they were in 1960. Some have lost ground. Why this stagnation?

1. Some had come to the church for material gain and left when the material goods were no longer available. As receptivity decreased so did evangelistic zeal of the laity.

2. The increased number of "trained" pastors, subsidized by the parent mission had an adverse effect on small struggling congregations. These people saw little reason to continue their voluntary labors. Now the pastors were only too willing to assume all of the responsibilities that formerly were shared by the laity.

3. The laity lacked Bible training.

4. Because the Chinese place such a high value on family unity, members won out of such a matrix often leave the impression that Christianity contributes to the disintegration of the Chinese family system.

5. Many churches entered the 1970s strapped by major financial burdens and church structures created by missions that had built beyond the ability of the local churches to support. While missionaries and national church workers are striving to overcome these obstacles, church growth in recent years continues to be slow.

Today about thirty-three percent of the Christians in Taiwan are Mandarin, forty percent are Minnan (Taiwanese), twenty-three percent are Mountain People (whose population is only two percent of the total Taiwan population), and three percent are Hakka. Fewer than one percent of all Minnan and Hakka people are Christians. The two million Hakka people still have no Bible in their mother tongue and only about six missionaries are ministering in this language.[29]

There are still about 500 towns and villages without a single gospel witness.[30]

Pray that this land may be evangelized while there still is time. The growing power of mainland China may be used to occupy Taiwan. It could happen almost any time.

HONG KONG

Hong Kong is one of the most strategic centers for the Gospel in Asia because of its close links with mainland China, the 42 million Chinese outside mainland China, and all Asia.

Hong Kong's population at the end of World War II was 600,000 but refugees flooding into the city from Red China and Southeast Asia have swollen the population to five and a half million. With all these people crowded into 398 square miles, Hong Kong is one of the most densely populated areas in the world—nearly 14,000 per square mile.

Hong Kong is most strategic because of the threat of a takeover by mainland China at any time. Then, too, the lease of the New Territories expires in 1997. The New Territories constitute nine-tenths of the total area of Hong Kong. It is therefore imperative that Christians plant all the house churches they can plant before the reintegration into mainland China in 1997.

One way to plant house churches is by teaching English in the teacher's own home or one of his students' homes. Since English is the official language, along with Cantonese, most people want to learn English. Teaching English gives the teacher a golden opportunity day after day to share his Christian faith with his students. Missionaries are enjoying much success in leading people to Christ in this way and making them responsible members of His Church.

Only about 5% of Hong Kong's population are evangelical Christians, but churches are growing in number and maturity wth outstanding Christian leaders, theological training, literature and mass media. The expensive land and overcrowded conditions have compelled many groups to meet in homes, roof-top churches, or build high-rise multipurpose, church-school-hostels.

There are over 20 seminaries or Bible Schools. A new interdenominational Graduate School of Theology was opened in 1975 and promises to be a great boon to the Church of South East Asia as well as to the churches and pastors of Hong Kong.

Refugees continue to arrive illegally (and often with great danger) at the rate of about 30,000 a year. Some are repatriated by the government to mainland China and an unknown future. At least two out of every three in Hong Kong are refugees. These needy and despairing refugees often become embittered and disillusioned in the overcrowded and difficult conditions of Hong Kong. Many missionaries are making efforts to reach these people, and with much success, but much more needs to be done.

Cross-References
Printing & Publishing (General), *90, 105*

Christian communications are very well developed. There are many publishing groups producing new translations of the Bible in the new simplified Chinese script. Other Christian literature is also being produced for Mainland China and other countries of Asia as well as for Hong Kong.

Missionary vision is increasing. There are now more than ten Chinese sending agencies or churches with over fifty missionaries serving in other lands. But with more than a billion people in mainland China and another 42 million Chinese in other lands, the amount of work to be done cannot possibly be exaggerated. Just in Hong Kong alone the need is staggering. Here is abject poverty, starvation, lust, intrigue, avarice, fabulous wealth, love, hate, and mercy all jammed together. Man gluts on the sins of others, feeds on the misery of the starving. There is indescribable callousness to suffering. Here the marvelous compassion of Christ is poured out upon some of the most needy people in the world, and hope springs anew from the ashes of despair.

Chinese Around the World
From the Chinese World Handbook

People's Republic of China—1,042,000,000 with about 60 million Christians! (1985)

COUNTRY	TOTAL POPULATION	TOTAL CHINESE POPULATION	CHINESE PROTESTANT POPULATION	CHINESE PROTESTANT CHURCHES
Predominantly Chinese Countries				
TAIWAN	19,600,000	18,880,000	203,500	2,300
HONG KONG	5,700,000	5,050,000	215,000	634
MACAU	400,000	300,000	1,300	20
SINGAPORE	2,600,000	1,700,000	44,000	229
Islamic Countries				
INDONESIA	168,400,000	5,500,000	40,000	350
***a) W. MALAYSIA	10,000,000	3,557,000	39,000	269
b) SARAWAK	1,300,000	350,000	10,000	70
c) SABAH	800,000	230,000	21,000	52
BRUNEI	200.000	50,300	1,500	7
Buddhist Countries				
THAILAND	52,700,000	4,000,000	6,000	71
BURMA	36,900,000	520,000	7.400	65
JAPAN	120,800,000	49,000	750	10
KOREA	42,700,000	28,000	400	9
Western Countries				
CANADA	25,100,000	130,000	6,000	70
U.S.A.	236,300,000	1,350,000	60,700	600
EUROPE	491,000,000	300,000	2,600	64
AUSTRALIA	15,800,000	140,000	1,200	16
NEW ZEALAND	3,300,000	15,000	300	7
Third World Roman Catholic Countries				
PHILIPPINES	56,800,000	600,000	16,000	53
LATIN AMER.	397,000,000	156,500	1,080	15
CENTRAL AMER.	252,000,000	105,000	200	?
Other Lands				
** AFRICA	531,000,000	73,000	1,700	6
INDIA	762,200,000	60,000	400	3
PACIFIC ISLANDS	4,900,000	10,300	800	2

Notes:

* Statistics only include U.K., France, and the Netherlands.

** Statistics only include Nigeria, Mauritius, Madagascar and Reunion.

***All three of these are part of the country of Malaysia.

Population statistics from 1986 World Population Data Sheet.
All other statistics are from the 1982 Chinese Churches Handbook.

SUGGESTED READING

CHINA YESTERDAY, CONFUCIUS, MAO & CHRIST: *By Paul E. Kauffman (Founder/President of Asian Outreach) Hong Kong: Asian Outreach Ltd.. 1975.*

This book is part of Paul Kauffman's China trilogy which includes CHINA TODAY—Through China's Open Door, and CHINA TOMORROW—China's Coming Revolution. Paul Kauffman writes as one who has spent half his life in China. His love for the Chinese people is apparent, having lived in Hong Kong for a long time. He has been in a privileged position to study the changing scene on China's mainland. His books clearly and authoritatively show that God is still at work in China.

HUDSON TAYLOR'S SPIRITUAL SECRET: *By Dr. and Mrs. Howard Taylor. Chicago: Moody Press, 1935*

"The story of the founder of the China Inland Mission, a man full of the Holy Ghost and of faith, entirely surrendered to God and to His call—a man of great self-denial, heartfelt compassion, rare power in prayer, marvelous organizing ability, energetic initiative, indefatigable perseverance, and an astonishing influence with men, and with a childlike humility."

HUDSON TAYLOR AND MARIA: *By John Pollock. Kingsway Publications Ltd. in Eastbourne, E. Sussex, 1983; 1st published in 1962 by Hodder & Stoughton Ltd.*

Hudson Taylor was a remarkable missionary and statesman who, with the help of his gifted wife Maria, founded the China Inland Mission. This is the story of their youth, romance, and early years as missionaries to China.

NEVER SAY DIE: *By Cyril Davey. Fort Washington, PA: Christian Literature Crusade, 1964*

The story of Gladys Aylward (missionary to China).

ON THE CLOUDS TO CHINA: *By Cyril Davey. Ft. Washington, PA: Christian Literature Crusade*

This is the great story of the most famous man who ever carried the good news of Christ to China. Hudson Taylor was founder of the China Inland Mission and as a dauntless pioneer his story is a classic of Christian Adventure.

COME WIND, COME WEATHER: *By Leslie T. Lyall. Chicago: Moody Press, 1960*

The aim of this book is to show in an unbiased manner the way in which the Communist government has handled the Protestant Church in China. The picture is sharp and clear as told by a missionary forced to leave China by godless Communism. A warning glimpse of what we may expect if Communism is victorious.

PROVING GOD: *By Phyllis Thompson. Chicago: Moody Press*

This is the testimony of S. Oswald Sanders, General Director of Overseas Missionary Fellowship (formerly China Inland Mission). Proving God records God's provisions for His children during the tumultuous quarter century when missionaries of CIM were persecuted, tortured, and martyred by Chinese Communists.

HAVE WE NO RIGHT: *By Mabel Williamson. Chicago : Moody Press*

While serving the Lord in China for many years, Miss Williamson learned that she was not her own—she was bought with a price. She could not stand up for her rights. She had no rights. Her sincere and frank remarks about her problems of adjusting on the mission field provide fascinating, instructive, and extremely valuable material for missions, students and all Christians.

CHINA—CHRISTIAN STUDENTS FACE THE REVOLUTION: *By David H. Adeney. Madison, WI: Varsity Press, 1973*

When Communism came to China in 1949, David Adeney was there, helping Christians establish and maintain a witness. Now he tells a powerful story of Chinese Christians under Communist pressure—their sorrows and joys, their triumphs and failures. He also outlines the prospects for continued Christian witness.

THE GLORIOUS AGE OF EXPLORATION: *By Felix Barker. New York: Doubleday, 1973*

Chapters of the Silk Road, Genghis Kahn, Kubla Kahn, and the Polos are accompanied by numerous reproductions of contemporary representations. (488 pp.)

THE SINKIANG STORY: *By Jack Chen. New York: Macmillian, 1977*

The story of China's westernmost province and the locus of the ancient Silk Road is told from an official People's Republic perspective. It includes a glossary, a gazetteer, and a superior chronological table of Chinese history. (386 pp)

THE MAN WHO CHANGED CHINA: THE STORY OF SUN YAT-SEN: *By Pearl S. Buck. New York: Random, 1953*

A sympathetic presentation by the compassionate American woman who grew up in China and was a prolific author of books about China for both children and adults. Dr. Sun (1855-1925) devoted his life to the overthrow of the Manchu dynasty and the achievement of national unity under a republican government. (185 pp., illus.)

TAIWAN, ISLAND CHINA: *By David C. Cooke. New York: Dodd, 1975*

This author of numerous nonfiction books for young people writes clearly and understandably about the land and people, the philosophy and religion, food, language, family, festivals and celebrations. (158 pp. for grades five through nine)

THE GOOD EARTH: *By Pearl S. Buck. New York: Crowell, 1931*

The first realistic novel about China and a Pulitzer Prize Winner. The author had grown up in China, and went on to write many more books on Asian themes for young people as well as for adults. (323 pp. for grades nine and up)

THE DRAGON'S VILLAGE: AN AUTOBIOGRAPHICAL NOVEL OF REVOLUTIONARY CHINA: *By Yuan-tsung Chen. New York: Pantheon, 1980*

The heroine, who was a graduate from a missionary high school, idealistically works to bring land reform to a remote village in northwest China. She finds living conditions that her middle class up-bringing never prepared her for and peasants distrustful of change. (285 pp. $10.00, for grades nine and up)

THE FAR EAST AND THE SOUTH PACIFIC: *By Harold C. Hinton, ed.. Washington, D.C.:Stryker-Post, illustrated, maps, tables.*

This annually revised overview includes chapters on China (including Taiwan) and Hong Kong, each full of current data on area population, economy, and politics, as well as geographical and historical summaries. (99 pp. Annual $2.95 for 9th grade and up)

MARCO POLO'S ADVENTURES IN CHINA: *By Milton Rugoff. Horizon Caravell Book. New York: American Heritage, 1964, illus.*

Superb with varied illustrations. (152 pp. for grade six and up)

GOFORTH OF CHINA: *By Rosalind Goforth. Minneapolis: Bethany*
One of the truly all-time missionary classics in the English language.

TO CHINA WITH LOVE: *By J. Hudson Taylor. Minneapolis, MN: Bethany Publishers*

The remarkable story of one man's love for China and his unflinching determination to bring the message of Christ to that nation. Especially relevant in our day. ($3.50)

NEW SPRING IN CHINA: *By Leslie T. Lyall. Grand Rapids, MI: Zondervan, 1979/80*

Leslie T. Lyall, a resident of China before the Communist regime came to power, recently returned to see firsthand China's new way of life, her efforts at modernization, and the state of the Christian church.

This is his appraisal. In this book Lyall seeks to answer the questions that confront us after China's reawakening to the West during the seventies: What changes have taken place in China's way of life? How has the church fared during thirty years of Communism? What are the prospects for genuine religious freedom? What can we expect of China's government and her people in the decade to come?

REFERENCES

1. Mathews, Basil.
1952 **Disciples of All Nations,** London: Oxford Press, page 68.

2. Broomhall, Marshall
1934 **The Bible in China.** London: British & Foreign Bible Society, page 17.

3. Francis, J. de
1950 **Nationalism and Language Reform in China.** Princeton: Princeton University Press, page 222.

4. Neill, Stephen
1964 **A History of Christian Missions.** Baltimore: Penguin Books, Inc., page 97.

5. Mathews, Basil.
1952 **Disciples of All Nations,** London: Oxford Press, page 72.

6. Moule, A. C.
1930 **Christians in China Before the Year 1550.** London: SPG, page 176.

7. Nida, Eugene
1972 **The Book of a Thousand Toungues.** New York: United Bible Societies, p. 303.

8. Hudspeth, W.H.
1952 **The Bible in China.** London: British and Foreign Bible Society, page 10.

9. Mathews, Basil.
1952 **Disciples of All Nations,** London: Oxford Press, page 107.

10. Watkins, Morris G.
1978 **Literacy, Bible Reading and Church Growth.** Pasadena: Wm Carey Library, page 78.

11. Latourette, Kenneth Scott
1970 **A History of the Expansion of Christianity.** Grand Rapids: Zondervan Publishing House, Volume 6, page 257.

12. Mathews, Basil.
1952 **Disciples of All Nations,** London: Oxford Press, page 173-174.

13. Hudspeth, W.H.
1952 **The Bible in China.** London: British and Foreign Bible Society, page 16-17

14. Kane, J. Herbert
1971 **A Global View of Christian Missions.** Grand Rapids: Baker Book House, page 214.

15. Hudspeth, W.H.
1952 **The Bible in China.** London: British and Foreign Bible Society, page 18

16. Latourette, Kenneth Scott
1970 **A History of the Expansion of Christianity.** Grand Rapids: Zondervan Publishing House, Volume 6, page 253.

17. Kane, J. Herbert
1971 **A Global View of Christian Missions.** Grand Rapids: Baker Book House, page 253.

18. Latourette, Kenneth Scott
1970 **A History of the Expansion of Christianity.** Grand Rapids: Zondervan Publishing House, Volume 6, page 256.

19. Neill, Stephen
1964 **A History of Christian Missions.** Baltimore: Penguin Books, Inc., page 467.

20. Neill, Stephen
1964 **A History of Christian Missions.** Baltimore: Penguin Books, Inc., page 465-469.

21. Adeney, David H.
1973 **China: Christian Students Face the Revolution.** Downers Grove, IL: InterVarsity Press, page 88.

22. Adeney, David H.
1973 **China: Christian Students Face the Revolution.** Downers Grove, IL: InterVarsity Press, page 104-107.

23. Wagner, C. Peter
1983 **On the Crest of the Wave.** Ventura: Regal Books, page 30.

24. Barrett, David (ed.)
1982 **World Christian Encyclopedia.** New York: Oxford University Press, page 234.

25. Liao, David C. E. (ed.)
1979 **World Christianity: East Asia.** Monrovia, CA: MARC, page 39.

26. Law, Gail (ed.)
1982 **Chinese Churches Handbook.** Hong Kong: Chinese Coordination Center of World Evangelism, page 26.

27. Law, Gail (ed.)
1982 **Chinese Churches Handbook.** Hong Kong: Chinese Coordination Center of World Evangelism, page 29.

28. Law, Gail (ed.)
1982 *Chinese Churches Handbook.* Hong Kong: Chinese Coordination Center of World Evangelism, page 30.

29. Law, Gail (ed.)
1982 *Chinese Churches Handbook.* Hong Kong: Chinese Coordination Center of World Evangelism, page 31.

30. Johnstone, Patrick
1979 *Operation World.* Bromeley, Kent England: Send the Light Publications, page 129.

BUDDHISM

For centuries, Buddhism was the chief religion of China, Korea, and all of Southeast Asia. It still is the predominant religion of Burma, Thailand, Sri Lanka, Taiwan, Hong Kong, Japan, Singapore, and Bhutan.

A few decades ago, it was estimated that one fifth of the people in the world were Buddhists. But since World War II, godless Communism has conquered China, North Korea, and much of Southeast Asia and murdered millions of Buddhists, as well as thousands of Christians.

A whole generation has grown up in China and North Korea where the teaching of the "Buddha" or "Enlightened one" has been forbidden. So it is difficult to know exactly how many Buddhists there are in the world. Estimates vary from 250 to 300 million.

Even before the Communist take-over of the above lands, it was difficult to know how many Buddhists there actually were because many Buddhists also practice Confucianism and/or Taoism.

Buddhism consists of a number of different sects with varying practices and beliefs. Some sects are so different from the others that they appear to be separate religions. But all sects have in common the belief that they are following the principles laid down by Siddhartha Guatama who lived in India about 500 B.C. Today there are two main branches of Buddhism. Hinayana Buddhism is practiced in Southern Asia, Mahayana in Northern Asia.

Although Buddhism was originally a reform movement that rejected certain beliefs and practices of Hinduism, the two religions have several important beliefs in common. Among them are (1) *reincarnation* the idea that a living thing can be reborn in a new body, (2) the law of *Karma*, the belief that events in this present life are the result of things (sins or outstanding achievements, for example) that happened in a previous life, and (3) *liberation*, or salvation, which is the state of being free of the law of Karma and rebirth.

According to Buddhism, liberation is attained through understanding and practice of the Four Noble Truths, which are as follows:

1. There is suffering in life.
2. Suffering is caused by desire for pleasure, existence, and prosperity.

3. Suffering and rebirth cease when one ceases such desires, leading to enlightenment or Nirvana, a blessed state in which peace, harmony, and joy are attained.
4. The way, or path, to Nirvana is the Eightfold Path, summarized as:
    (1) Right understanding
    (2) Right thoughts
    (3) Right speech
    (4) Right conduct
    (5) Right occupation
    (6) Right effort
    (7) Right mindfulness
    (8) Right meditation

The Eightfold Path is also called the Middle Way because of its emphasis on avoiding such extremes as following sensuous pleasures on the one hand, and self-punishment on the other. The Buddhist must always observe the high moral principles described in the Eightfold Path, which emphasizes non-violence and brotherhood of all.

The name Hinayana means "small vehicle", a system of religion that is practiced by a limited number of persons. Hinayana is an austere religion that requires solitude, meditation, and self-mastery through which each member hopes to achieve Nirvana for himself. For this reason, many of its followers are monks or nuns. They spend most of their time in meditation and teaching.

Mahayana means "large vehicle", a less demanding system of religion that is practiced by a larger number of persons. Many Mahayana Buddhists believe in liberation through faith and good works.

Their object is not only to obtain a personal Nirvana, but to help others to that goal.

Mahayana Buddhists have temples presided over by priests. They have colorful festivals and solemn rituals. Mahayana Buddhism is divided into many sects including Zen, Jodo, Shin, Tendai, and Soka Gakkai.

HISTORY

Guatama "the Bhudda" himself did not leave any writings and his teachings were not written down until many centuries after his death.

Like Christianity and Islam, Buddhism is a missionary religion. Within 300 years after Buddha's death, it had spread throughout India and reached Sri Lanka (Ceylon). Monks and travelers carried it to other parts of Asia. It first came to China about 65 A.D. (about the same time that St. Paul was beheaded in Rome). Buddhism first came to Japan in the sixth century—about the same time it came to Tibet. Here it was combined with native religions and developed into Lamaism.

In India, the religion turned more and more to the ideas of Hinduism, until by the year 1000 A.D. Buddhism had all but disappeared from the country of its origin.

One cannot help but wonder what would have happened if Christians had been more obedient to the Lord's command to "make disciples of all nations." If Christian missionaries had brought the Gospel of Jesus Christ to China in the first century, no doubt millions could have been won to Christ. Perhaps Buddhism would never have gained a foothold. But there is no record of any Christian missionaries arriving in China before 635 A.D.

If missionaries had come to Japan in the first century, or even in the sixth century, that country may have been predominantly Christian today rather than Buddhist. But, as far as we know, there was no Christian work before the 16th century and no Protestant work before 1859.

The Buddhist World

The Spread of Buddhism and its First Encounter with Christianity

COUNTRY	BUDDHISM INTRO.	% BUDD. TODAY	1st CHR. MISSION	1st RC MISSION	1stPROT. MISSION	% CHRISTIAN TODAY
* INDIA	500 BC	0.8%	55 AD	1293	1706	3.9%
CEYLON (SRI LANKA)	246 BC	67.0%	55	1505	1665	8.3%
CHINA (P.R.C.)	65 AD	3.0%	635	1294	1807	5.0%(?)
ANNAM (VIETNAM)	220 AD	55.3%	1580	1580	1911	7.4%
KOREA, S.	372 AD	1.7%(?)	1592	1592	1884	30.0%
BURMA	438 AD	87.0%	1544	1544	1813	5.6%
JAPAN	552 AD	59.0%	1549	1549	1859	3.0%(?)
SUMATRA/JAVA	600 AD	1.0%	1323	1323	1605	11.0%
#TIBET	642 AD	?	1857(?)	—	1857(?)	.0%
SIAM (THAILAND)	720 AD	92.0%	1554	1554	1828	1.1%
CAMBODIA (KAMPUCHEA)	800 AD	88.4%	1555	1555	1922	0.6%
LAOS	1340 AD	58.0%	1630	1630	1902	1.9%
MONGOLIA	1577 AD	1.9%	700(?)	1298	1817	.0%
BHUTAN	?	69.0%	1892(?)	—	1892	.1%
TAIWAN	?	43/0%	1621	1621	1624	7.4%
HONG KONG	?	17.2%	1847	1847	1842	17.7%

* Buddhism flourished in India, the land of its birth, for several centuries, but then gradually died out until there were hardly any Buddhists left by the year 1000.

For centuries Tibet was 100% Buddhist (Lamaist), but since 1949 they have been ruthlessly secularized by the Communists. By 1976 less than a dozen of Tibet's former 5,000 monasteries were functioning, no new monks were being recruited, and the practice of Buddhism had virtually disappeared. In 1978 there were only 300 practicing monks in Tibet compared to over 100,000 in 1950.

There are also 2.7 million Vietnamese in the United States, 120,000 Laotians, 120,000 Thais, 700,000 Japanese, and 1.3 million Chinese. Not all of these are Buddhists, however. In fact, it is estimated that only about 180,000 of them are practicing Buddhists. On the other hand, very few of them are Christians. There are about 600 Chinese Protestant churches in the U.S., with a total membership of about 60,700. One-third of the Japanese in the U.S. live in Hawaii. There are 100 Buddhist temples in Honolulu and practically no evangelical mission work among these people.

THAILAND

After more than a century and a half of Christian mission work in Thailand, only about one-tenth of one percent of the country's 52 million people are Christians. Ninety-four percent are Buddhists, four percent are Muslims, and two percent practice their traditional animistic religion.

Why hasn't Christianity made more of an impact on Thailand? Maybe its because being a Thai and being a Buddhist are thought to be one and the same thing. It's almost regarded as unpatriotic for a Thai to leave Buddhism and become a Christian or Muslim or anything else. Maybe there are so few Christians because there have never been very many missionaries. Even today there is only one missionary for every 86,000 people and many of them are involved in medical and other institutional work; not many are even trying to win Buddhists to Christ. Another reason for the small number of Christians in Thailand may be that there is not a single Christian college or university in the country. So it has been difficult to establish rapport with the intellectuals, But a more important reason for so few Christians, perhaps, is the fact that there are so few who can read the Scriptures. Before World War II half the adult population was illiterate. Even today, in the rural areas, there is a high percentage of illiteracy. Most of the Christians in rural areas are only semi-literate or totally illiterate, and many of them are converts from among "outcast" leprosy patients.

The country really needs a lot of prayer. The Message of salvation through faith in Jesus Christ has made little impact on these Buddhist people, even though there is freedom of religion. This freedom could be lost almost overnight. The Communists who have taken over Vietnam and neighboring Cambodia and Laos, slaughtering two to three million people in the process, have been increasing their terrorist activities. The Communist goal, of course, is world conquest, and Thailand seems to be one of the next countries on their list. Thailand may have already fallen to the Communists if it had not been for a military coup in 1976 which restored morale and put an end to defeatist talk of an imminent fall to the god-denying Communists.

The Communist threat, however, has had a good effect. It has contributed to a growing interest in the Gospel of Jesus Christ. There seems to be more interest now than ever before.

Another reason for the increased interest in Christianity is no doubt the excellent witness of Christian medical work. At present there are 30 Christian hospitals plus several leprosy hospitals and scores of leprosy clinics. Leprosy control treatment among the 400,000 sufferers of leprosy has resulted in the planting of many small churches.

But even with the increased interest in the Gospel, 99.9% of the population is still held in the grip of demonic powers. Pray that God would bind these demonic powers, that souls now in bondage may be delivered from the chains that bind them, that they may find new life in Jesus Christ our Lord.

Pray for the 3,500 believers among the 3 million Chinese people in Bangkok and other cities. Pray that the tiny minority might not only remain faithful but that they might witness boldly and effectively to the other Chinese and to all the Buddhists in this land.

Pray also for other minority groups such as the one million Malays who live in provinces that border Malaysia. This is the only Malay community open to evangelism in Asia. After many years of missionary work, there are only 30-50 believers. Pray that these few believers may receive power from on high to witness effectively to other Malays and to the Thai people as well.

Two percent of the population of Thailand are animistic tribal people who are very poor, illiterate, and under terrible domination of evil spirits. Bible translation, literacy work, and the encouraging of potential leaders are some of the urgent needs. Pray for these people who are without Christ, and thus without God and without hope, for no one comes to the Father but through Jesus Christ our Lord.[1]

Cross-References

Malaysia, *6, 23, 34, 59, 69, 91, 100, 171*

Medical Missions, *32, 68, 109, 191*

Southeast Asia
Bangladesh, Burma, Thailand, Laos, Kampuchea, Vietnam, and Nicobar Islands

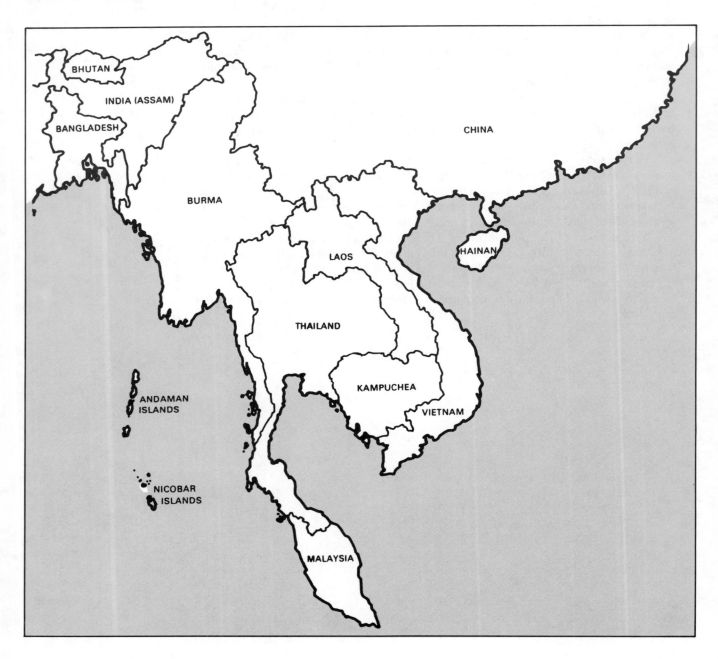

JAPAN

Japan is a 1300 mile arc of four large islands and 3400 smaller ones, extending from Hokkaido in the north to Okinawa in the south through latitudes and temperature ranges similar to the east coast of the United States from Maine to Florida. It is one of the most homogenous nations in the world with 98% Japanese and 2% foreigners including almost one million Koreans, many of whom were forceably brought to Japan during their earlier occupation of Korea before World War II. These figures, however, cover up the fact that there are different people groups in both the southern and northern islands, namely at least twenty thousand Ainu in Hokkaido and over one million Ryukyuan peoples of various island dialects, and thousands of "love-children", a term politely given to describe children of interracial marriages, especially between American GIs and Japanese women.

The largest cities of Japan are Tokyo, Osaka and Yokohama with populations of 12, 3 and 2.5 million respectively. With only about 15% arable land, Japan is very highly industrialized and urbanized (about 75%). Known for its dramatic and rapid post war economic development (thanks, in large part, to the United States), Japan is now the leading nation of Asia in both per capita income and output. Japan remarkably has one of the world's most powerful economies, despite a lack of raw materials and limited farm land.

To date there is still complete freedom of religion and entry of missionaries is allowed. There are about half as many Mormon missionaries as there are true evangelicals, however. The government is a constitutional monarchy (since the U.S. allowed Emperor Hirohito to survive World War II). Japan's democratic government is under pressure from both leftist and radical Buddhist elements, which control over 15% of parliament already.

Both Buddhism and Shintoism are intertwined in Japanese society, together with Shamanistic animism and Confucian ancestor worship. Probably the most dangerous movement in Japan is called 'Sokka Gakai', a militantly nationalistic offshoot of Buddhism that is very anti-Christian and seeks political power, already having won 15% of both the populace and parliament. Cults such as the Moonies, Mormons, and Jehovah Witnesses are also very active, but still small. The total number of Christians in Japan is only about 2%, counting both Protestants (1.2%) and Roman Catholics (.5%). There are over 100 denominations in Japan. This may be one cause for the small number of churches in Japan. Among the evangelicals, .6% of the churches have a good annual growth rate of 10%.[2]

Cross-References

Buddhism, *2, 18, 29, 32, 39, 122, 171, 199*

Confucianism, *29, 39, 122, 154, 171*

Japan, *5, 23, 29, 31, 37, 100*

Jehovah's Witness, *158*

Okinawa, *37*

Shamanism, *39*

Soka Gakkai Buddhism, *30*

Tokyo, *37*

The Japanese are a very talented people, many of whom today, unfortunately, seem too materialistic, unresponsive and hidden in a centuries old cocoon of cultural traditions and bondage to ancestor worship and a mixture of Buddhism-Shintoism. Relatively few have been willing to make the decisive break with the past, despite many being outwardly friendly to Christianity.

Please pray for a mighty work of the Holy Spirit to break down these barriers and liberate these people into the glorious liberty of the children of God, even as a beautiful butterfly is released from its cocoon. Pray for churches that do exist to maintain a biblical theology, and to grow in both evangelistic zeal and missionary vision. Japan has great resources to aid in reaching the rest of Asia. Please pray for a vast harvest of souls to be won by various methods of outreach and to be discipled and incorporated into strong growing churches. Also ask the Lord to help those who become Christians not to backslide due to social pressures but to go on with the Lord, becoming full of evangelistic zeal and love for the Savior.

OPPORTUNITIES FOR OUTREACH

With almost one thousand colleges and two million college students, there is a large field for student ministry in Japan, A majority of urban dwellers have never had a clear presentation of the Gospel. Sixty-five percent of the towns and eighty-five percent of the villages in Japan have no Gospel witness. Unfortunately, the church in Japan is still quite small and her evangelistic efforts rather uncoordinated and weak.

Pray that churches in Japan will begin to do more cooperative evangelism and fellowship, taking full advantage of the good development of media for better outreach and follow up of the unreached masses. Literature, hospital and radio ministries have proved to be the most fruitful methods of outreach so far in Japan.

Many Japanese people are eager to learn the English language for various reasons. Hundreds of young people go to Japan every summer to teach English and share their faith with their students. Some stay to teach and witness on a year-round basis. Pray for more young people (and older ones too) to take advantage of this wonderful opportunity to share their Christian faith. Pray that their witness may bear much fruit to the glory of God and the extension of His Kingdom.

For information regarding the teaching of English in Japan, you may contact Life International, 448 E. Foothill Blvd., San Dimas, CA 91773.

Japan and Korea

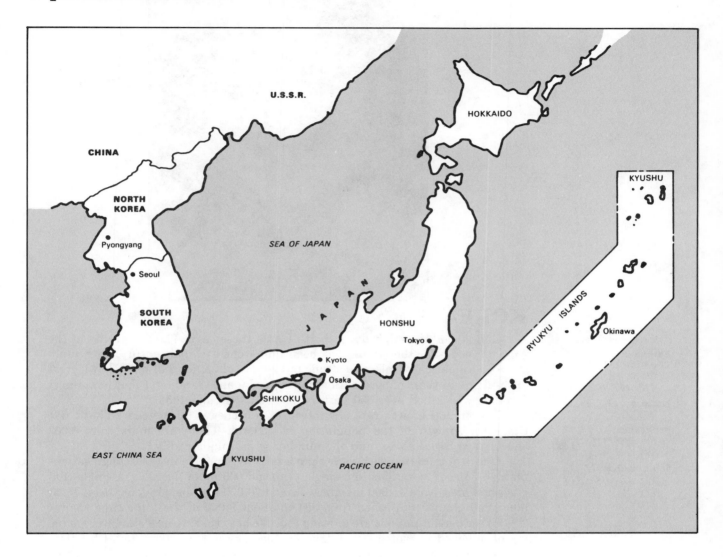

KOREA

God is working mightily in South Korea these days. The receptivity of the Korean people for the Gospel has been unmatched in this century, with rapid growth, dramatic revivals, and strong indigenous churches that have shown great faithfulness in years of persecution under the Japanese and later the Communist invaders who killed over 600 pastors between 1945 and 1951.

The annual growth rate of Protestant churches is ten percent. That's five times the growth of the population in general. There are more than 6,000 churches in Seoul alone, and the number is growing steadily.[3]

One denomination with more than a million members in 3,600 congregations planted 351 congregations in a single year and 500 more the next. A single congregation grew from 15,000 members to over 70,000 members in four years. Their home cell groups multiplied from 394 to about 3,000 in the same time span.

Other denominations are growing too. We hear that six new churches are being established in Korea every day. The country is now about 25% Christian. Another congregation (of a different denomination) has over 500,000 members who jam the 8,10,12 and 2 o'clock Sunday services 8.000 at a time. It is a church of almost sixty full-time ministers and an annual budget of well over a million dollars. This church has added as many as 7,000 new members to its rolls in a single year and has more than 1,300 home churches and 1,300 unpaid pastors or "shepherds." It is in the development of these home churches that we find the story behind the story of this incredible church growth.

The largest Christian gatherings in history took place in Seoul with one million attending both Billy Graham's 1973 Campaign and Campus Crusade's 1974 Explo.

Theological education has made outstanding progress with over 100 seminaries and Bible schools with over 9,000 students. One seminary alone has 1,200 students, It's the largest seminary in Asia.

There is also a growing missionary vision. There are now about 280 Korean missionaries in many lands in both denominational and interdenominational societies, and there are plans to send out many more.

Student work in 97 colleges and universities and among the 190,000 students has made great progress through University Bible Fellowship. The UBF emphasizes Bible study and personal evangelism, and now has workers who have gone out to the USA, Germany, Switzerland and other lands to witness among students. There are many Christian schools all over the country where the Gospel is preached.[4]

Evangelism among the military has resulted in more than half the men in the army being baptized.

Early morning prayer meetings attended by hundreds are still the pattern in many denominations.

Praise God for this tremendous growth, but there is still much to be done. Seventy-five percent of the people are still in the grip of the Evil One.

About 16% of the Koreans are Buddhists, even though Buddhism was suppressed and eclipsed during the Yi dynasty (1392-1910) under which Confucianism became the official religion. Confucianism took on a new life at the time of the Japanese occupation. But it was not until the end of the Korean War in 1954 that it assumed a position of importance in Korean religious and social life.

Confucianism, which is really a system of social ethics more than religion, was introduced into Korea from A.D. 855 and, as stated above, was the state religion from 1392 until 1910. It still encourages the practice of ancestor veneration.

Shamanism is the traditional religion and still the most widely practiced one in Korea. It involves a strong belief in the influence of departed ancestral spirits as well as nature spirits who inhabit trees, rocks, and streams, etc. These spirits must be propitiated or otherwise controlled by individuals or by priests (shamans) to ensure health and success in life's ventures. There's a strong emphasis on exorcism and healing with extensive use of chanting and drums. In 1968 there were more than 7,000 shaman medicine men—nearly a thousand of them in Seoul.

So there is still a great need for evangelism in Korea, still many souls to be won. Praise God, the church is growing five times faster than the general population growth rate. Pray that it will continue to grow at the present rate or even faster in the years ahead.

Cross-References

Animism, *2, 83, 107, 110, 199*

Buddhism, *2, 18, 29, 32, 35, 122, 171, 199*

Confucianism, *29, 35, 122, 154, 171*

Shamanism, *35*

Spiritism, *2, 165*

SUGGESTED READING

ANOINTED FOR BURIAL: CAMBODIA'S LIKE A MIGHTY WIND
By Todd and DeAnne Burke
Plainfield, NJ: Logos International, 1977

A thrilling eyewitness account of the last days of Cambodia. Todd and DeAnne Burke share the powerful testimony of the Khmer people and offer an exciting chronicle of life before the nation fell. They reveal the wonderful intervention of God in Cambodia and offer proof of the power of a simple faith. (259 pp.)

MO BRADLEY AND THAILAND
By Donald C. Lord
Grand Rapids: Wm. B. Eerdmans Publ. Co., 1969

Missionary to Thailand the last 38 years of his life, Mo Bradley made such an impact upon the missionary movement in Thailand that his years there are still referred to as the "Bradley Era" by present missionaries.

INTRODUCING BUDDHISM
By Kenneth S. Latourette
New York: Friendship Press, 1954

The renowned Kenneth Scott Latourette gives background of the Buddhist faith and challenges the reader to see the important differences between Christianity and Buddhism.

SIAM THEN
By William L. Bradley
Pasadena, CA: William Carey Library, 1981

The story of the foreign colony in Bangkok from 1835 through the time Anna Leonowns was governess in the Court of Siam (Anna and the King of Siam) and the years that followed.

BUDDHISM: ITS ESSENCE AND DEVELOPMENT
By Edward Conze
New York: Harper and Row, 1965

This is a most comprehensive yet easily readable account of Buddhism. It is a brilliant piece of work, beautifully written, and dramatically successful in presenting the essentials of Buddhism, from the beginnings to the present Zen schools, in less than 200 pages.

A SHORT HISTORY OF BUDDHISM
By Edward Conze
London: Unwin Paperbacks, 1981

This is a valuable historical survey for the general reader, a lucid and reliable introduction to Buddhism.

ASCENT TO THE TRIBES: PIONEERING IN NORTH THAILAND
By Isobel Kuhn
Chicago: Moody Press, 1956

Isobel's impressions of tribelands soon after she had exchanged China for Thailand as her mission field. In China her beloved Lisu had turned to God in large numbers; would these triumphs be repeated in North Thailand? This abridged account of the initial efforts to evangelize the hill tribes in 1952-53 reveals the formidable challenge of this pioneering task. The final chapters are an up-to-date progress report of planting Christ's Church in each of North Thailand's tribes.

SIAMESE GOLD
By Alex G. Smith
Robesonia, PA: OMF Books

A history of Church Growth in Thailand. This book describes, evaluates and interprets all related historical processes behind the emergence of the Thai Church during successive stages of missionary activity between 1816 and 1982.

THE NEW TRAIL
By Otto Scheuzger
Robesonia, PA: OMF Books

A teen-age boy in a Meo village in Thailand turns from the demon gods to follow the "new trail" of the Jesus way. Authentic village background of the many Hmong refugees in the United States today.

ONCE BITTEN
By Anne J. Townsend
Robesonia, PA: OMF Books

Closely based on the author's own experience in Thailand, she lets us intimately share the life of a missionary doctor, wife, and mother, from the time she arrives in Bangkok as a "raw recruit," until her furlough, and the decision to return to the land she has grown to love. Answers the question, "But what is being a missionary really like?"

SMOKE AWAY
By May Wilson
Robesonia, PA: OMF Books

A Christian boy living in North Thailand sees God's power to change lives, even those of his own parents who smoke opium.

STRATEGY TO MULTIPLY RURAL CHURCHES
By Alex G. Smith
Robesonia, PA: OMF Books.

This central Thailand case study describes years of actual church planting. It is experience, not theory. It should be carefully read by church leaders and missionaries, or aspiring missionaries.

SHIOKARI PASS
By Ayoko Miura
Robesonia, PA: OMF Books

A best selling novel in Japan, acclaimed for dispelling prejudice against Christianity. This love story, based on a real person in her hometown, gives a rare insight into Japanese life and thought. The author's ability to carry her reader into a close affinity with the characters accounts for its popularity.

MULTI-CHANNEL JAPAN
By Hugh Trevor
Robesonia, PA: OMF Books

This book reveals a highly-technical people who are still bound by the ancient Buddhist and Shinto religions, what their spiritual needs are, and our responsibility to share Christ with them. An enlightening booklet!

BUDDHISM AND THE CLAIMS OF CHRIST
By Daniel T. Niles
Richmond, VA: John Knox Press, 1967

REMEMBER CAMBODIA
By Helen Penfold
Robesonia, PA: OMF Books

This Buddhist country has been frequently in the news since its fall to the Communists in 1975. The story of the church there—its dramatic growth in 1970-1975 and continuing outreach in refugee camps and third world countries—is told here from first-hand knowledge.

REFERENCES

1. *Johnstone, Patrick; OPERATION WORLD; Bromeley, Kent, England: Send the Light Publications, p. 130*
2. *Johnstone, Patrick; OPERATION WORLD; Bromeley, Kent, England: Send the Light Publications, p. 115*
3. *Wagner, C. Peter. On the Crest of the Wave. Ventura: Regal Books, 1983. p 28.*
4. *Johnstone, Patrick; OPERATION WORLD; Bromeley, Kent, England: Send the Light Publications.*

THE HINDU WORLD

HINDUISM

The overwhelming majority of India's people—83% of them— are Hindus. Devout Hindus believe that God is in every creature: humans, cows, birds, monkeys, snakes, and even rats. They claim that every living creature has a soul and that every creature that dies may be reborn into another body. This is called "reincarnation". Therefore, it is a sin against the gods to hurt or kill *any* living creature except as a blood sacrifice to a god.

Hindus are said to worship some 330 million gods. *Brahma*, the chief god, is the god of creation; *Shiva* is the god of destruction and reproduction; *Vishnu* is the god of preservation. Vishnu is said to have been reborn on earth many times under the name of *Lord Krishna!*

Another popular idol of Hinduism is Ganesha, the god of prosperity. This idol has a boy's body and an elephant's head. The story of Ganesha is that his stepfather, in a terrible rage, cut off Ganesha's head with a sword, but as his mother screamed in terror, the stepfather ran out of the castle, found an elephant and cut off its head, then placed it on Ganesha's body. So Ganesha is said to have survived every possible misfortune and become immune to bad luck. Today he is worshipped as the god of good luck and prosperity because he is said to have become very rich.

Innumerable demons and ghosts are said to infest the air, the trees, the shrubs, temples, and houses. Only by magic ceremonies conducted by Brahman priests can evil spirits be driven away. Therefore, millions of Hindus spend part of their lives making sacrifices to the gods to prolong life, cure diseases, bring prosperity, or destroy the people that they hate or who have done them wrong.

THE CASTE SYSTEM

The caste system enslaves India to this very day. Into a caste a person is born and in it he dies. There is little chance to escape, for the caste is said to have been ordained by the gods.

Each caste is subservient to the castes above it, and it is considered degrading to a high-caste man if he is a friend to a low-caste person. Each caste stays separate from other castes and keeps its social, political, and economic distance from other castes.

Cross-References
Caste System, *51*
Krishna, *157*
Reincarnation, *29*

Brahmans, the hereditary priest caste, are number one. They are the most privileged people, often the best educated and best informed.

Next highest is the warrior caste, composed of people who enforce religious laws. They are called kshatriyas "KSHAT-re-as" and include many subcastes.

Third in rank are the Vaisyas "VAIS-yas" composed of farmers, merchants, and businessmen.

The fourth caste, called Sudras "SOO-dras" are born to serve the higher castes. Seldom educated, they are usually very poor and helpless with little opportunity to improve their sad plight.

But far, far below the Sudras are a hundred million "outcastes" who are considered so low that they are called "untouchables". They are among the most pitiful people on earth. In some parts of India, an untouchable is considered so low and religiously impure that his very shadow or touch is said to defile a high-caste Hindu, and if his shadow falls on a high-caste Hindu's food, it is considered unfit to eat and must be thrown away.

Untouchables seldom own anything of value, not even a bullock cart.

Untouchables are not permitted to enter Hindu temples, and in many areas their chief employment is carrying out sewage from high-caste people's homes, removing bodies of dead animals, or cleaning up filth and sweeping paths. They are prohibited from using water from high-caste people's wells or even walking across high-caste men's property.

How is it possible for more than 600 million people to be enslaved by the vile beliefs of idol worship and the customs of caste? The chief reason is that Hindus are taught from childhood that they have no choice but to accept their station in life, no matter how low. Caste and Hinduism govern every aspect of life: training, food, employment, social relationships, marriage, and even death.

A Hindu cannot become a Christian without breaking caste. When a Hindu becomes a Christian he is regarded by other Hindus as an outcaste and is treated as such.

HINDU WOMEN

The highest religious duty of a Hindu woman is total submission and obedience to her husband. Hindus seldom provide much education for daughters and most are not allowed to socialize outside their immediate family.

It is said in India, "The parents take care of a son, but only God cares for a daughter." The reason is that sons are regarded as a form of social security because sons incur a debt to their parents for their upbringing and are expected to help them in their old age. Girls cost money, with no expected return, and at marriage, the girl's father is expected to provide a dowry of money or property to the girl's husband. Without a dowry she cannot find a good husband; so daughters are considered a liability.

There have been numerous murders of wives in India, because the girl's father did not provide a sufficient dowry; therefore, her husband decided to kill her and get another wife with a better dowry. It is common practice in India for a girl to drench herself with kerosene and burn herself to death because she was no longer wanted by her husband, and her father refused to take her back. It is also common for husbands to murder their wives and not receive a very severe sentence for it. In 1983, however, a judge did the unheard of thing of sentencing a wife-murderer to hang. Some people were outraged at the severity of the sentence, saying the judge had overturned ancient traditions which have always permitted a man to do as he wishes with his wife.

INDIA

One of the most difficult mission fields throughout the centuries has been India. The responsiveness of the upper and middle caste people has been almost nil, and even among the lower castes and the 100 million outcastes (now called "harijans" or "children of God") the acceptance of the Gospel has not been all that missionaries hoped it would be.

Only about three percent of the entire population of India is professedly Christian—and many of them, sad to say, are third and fourth generation Christians who are not exactly what one would call vibrant Christian witnesses.

Why are there so few Christians in India? Many reasons can be given which apply to all of Asia.

1. **Failure to give people God's Word in their own language.** There are 14 major languages in India and more than 300 others. The Scriptures were never translated into any of these languages until the 18th century. Most people had to wait until the 19th or 20th century before the Scriptures were translated into their mother tongue.

2. **Failure of early Christians to reach out to others.** The overwhelming majority of the people in India never even heard an oral presentation of the Gospel before the 18th century. According to tradition, the Apostle Thomas brought the Gospel to South India in A.D. 52. Whether this is true or not, we know that the Christian Church has been in South India at least since the second century. But the early Christians apparently never carried the Good News about Jesus to other people of central and northern India.

3. **The lack of literacy.** Even if the Scriptures had been translated in those early centuries, very few people could have read them. Even as late as the beginning of the 20th century, 95-98 percent of the people in India and China and other Asiatic countries were unable to read or write.

4. **Doctrinal controversies among Christians .** In the 4th and 5th centuries there were many doctrinal controversies among Christians regarding the divine and human natures of Christ, the ability of sinful man to "cooperate" with the Holy Spirit in his own conversion, and other theological issues.

5. **The decay of the Roman Empire culminating in the fall of Rome in 476.** Gross darkness followed when only one or two percent of Europe was literate and Bibles were scarce, even for those who could read.

6. **Muslim conquests.** The Muslims conquered all of Southwest Asia between 632 and 650 A.D., and made travel to the Far East extremely difficult and hazardous.

7. **Roman Catholic nations ruled the seas.** When the Protestant Reformation began in 1517, the Spanish and Portuguese ruled the seas. This continued until the defeat of the Spanish Armada in 1588.

8. **Wars in Europe.** From 1545 to 1648 the Protestants were defending themselves from Roman Catholic aggression and persecution.

9. **Doctrinal disputes among Protestants. Even the Protestants themselves after the Reformation were embroiled in doctrinal controversy regarding baptism, the Lord's Supper, etc.**

10. **Wrong attitude toward other Peoples of other lands.** Many Protestant Church leaders' attitude in Europe was that we should not do mission work in Africa or Asia because we should not "cast our pearls before swine."

11. **The over emphasis on the doctrine of the sovereignty of God.** They said, "If God wanted the heathen to be saved, He would do it without any help from you or me."

12. **Dangerous and difficult travel.** There were many difficulties and dangers in traveling to distant lands, whether by land or sea. There were no transoceanic steamships until 1838. Before that, a journey from England to India took about six months.

13. **Unhealthful conditions and hostile people in many lands.** Many missionaries died from tropical diseases or were killed within weeks of reaching the field.

14. **Difficulty of communicating with the home base.**

15. **Early contacts with immoral European merchants and military personnel.** These people were thought to be Christians simply because they were Europeans. These unfortunate contacts made Christianity seem unattractive and even repulsive in the eyes of Asian people.

16. **Disrespect of some missionaries for the cultural heritage of others.** An air of superiority on the part of many Europeans (including some missionaries) because of the advanced technology of their own country was prevalent. Also, the imposing of western style clothing, music, art and architecture, church government and other ways of doing things caused many to be unresponsive.

17. **Competition from Ancient, highly developed religious systems** and the belief that their ancient scripture was revealed by God.

18. **Christianity's close ties with Colonialism.** In all of East Asia there is only one country that did not become the victim of Western imperialism. That country was Thailand. Britain, France, Spain, Portugal, Holland, and the United States all had colonies. Missionaries, who were usually the only bilingual people on the scene, often had been drafted by the foreign power to serve as intepreters.

19. **Xenophobia—the fear of anything foreign.**

20. **The exclusive claims of Christianity.** Hindus worship 330 million gods. They are willing to accept Jesus as a reincarnation of Vishnu, but not as the ONLY TRUE GOD AND SAVIOR OF THE WORLD.

21. **Resistance to the teaching that man is by nature sinful.** Followers of the ancient religions found it difficult to accept the Christian teaching that man is by nature sinful and unclean unable to save himself. Ancient philosophers, for example, taught that human nature is essentially good and requires only self-cultivation to bring it to perfection.

22. **Fear of punishment.** Forsaking the religion of one's family and countrymen is never easy. But when 97 to 100 percent of one's countrymen are Hindus or Buddhists or Muslims or any other religion, it is all the more difficult. Converts have generally been scorned and ostracized by their own family members and have become second-class citizens, unable to get a job, unable to marry, unable to vote and not allowed to draw water from the village well. Often they've been brutally beaten or even killed because they have forsaken the god (or the *gods*) of their fathers.

23. **Unbelief.** Many church members don't believe that anyone is going to hell. They say "God is a god of love and wouldn't cast anyone into hell for not believing in Christ, especially if he never had an opportunity to hear the Gospel." If this statement were true, then Christ died in vain.

24. **Lack of love and concern for the lost and indifference to the Lord's command to "make disciples of *all* nations."** Even today most American "Christians" spend many times more on the pleasures of this world than in bringing the Gospel to those who have never heard it before.

These, then, are some of the reasons for the paucity of Christians in India. This list, of course, is not exhaustive but should be sufficient to explain why there are so few followers of Christ in that part of the world. Of all the reasons given perhaps the greatest is the lack of love and concern for those who are dying in their sins and going to a Christless eternity.

THE HISTORY OF CHRISTIANITY IN INDIA

If it is true that the Apostle Thomas was the founder of the Church that bears his name in South India, he apparently did not translate God's Word into the vernacular. When Claudius Buchanan, Chaplain of the East India Company, visited the Mar Thoma Church in 1806, he found that they were using the Syriac Bible, which no one could understand. It is doubtful that even the priests, who read it occasionally in the worship services, could understand what they read.[1]

Whether Thomas was the founder of the Church in India or not, we cannot be sure. We do know that Christianity came to that country at least by the second century. About A.D. 180, Pantaenus, founder of the catechetical school in Alexandria, was sent by the Bishop of the city to India, and there he found Christians and the writing of St. Matthew. However, the land referred to as India might well have been southern Arabia, since the term "India" was used to designate a much larger area than it does today.[2]

According to a Greek Christian traveler named Cosmos, who lived in the sixth century, there was a church in Malabar, the southwest coastal region, and there were a large number of Christians there. The Thomas Christians received bishops from the Nestorian Patriarch in Baghdad. But there seems to have been another Church consisting of Persian traders originally, but who married Indian women and the original Persian element diminished as the percentage of Indian blood increased. Unfortunately, as far as we know, no one born in India was ever consecrated to the episcopate until the seventeenth century, and divine services were always conducted in *Syriac*. As time went on, the people understood less and less of the Syriac service, and many could do little more than recite the venerable words.[3] What a tragedy that they were not given the Word of God in their own language and taught to read it for themselves! There are some 1600 languages in India and no attempt was ever made to translate the Good News of Jesus Christ into any of them for 1700 years.[4] Is it any wonder that so few people in India are Christians today?

Because of the conquest of *Islam* in the seventh and eighth centuries, we hear nothing of the Church in India for hundreds of years. The Muslims controlled the land and sea routes to the Orient, making it impossible for Christian missionaries to travel to the Far East. But a new era began when Vasco de Gama discovered a sea route to India in 1498. The Franciscan priests who accompanied him launched the missionary program of the Catholic Church in that part of Asia.

All of the large religious orders of the *Roman Church* were represented in India, but the Jesuits made the greatest impact. Francis Xavier, the first Jesuit missionary, arrived in Goa on the southwest coast of India in 1542 and worked in that country for three years. Goa, a Portuguese enclave, became the springboard for Xavier's work in Asia.[5]

In the short time that Xavier was in India he founded a college for the training of missionaries. Over a dozen languages were spoken there by students from India, Africa, Malay, Siam, China, Molucca, Ceylon, and Japan. In his later travels, he regularly sent promising youths back to Goa for training. This was the first college for developing Asiatic international leadership.[6]

Xavier worked for some time among the Parava fishing caste along the southeast coast, and with the help of some students from the school of Goa, translated the creeds and prayers of the Church into Tamil, the language spoken by the Paravas. This seems to be the first translation of the creeds or prayers or anything else into an Indian language by Christian missionaries. Another 170 years or more were to pass before the New Testament would be translated into this or any of the languages of that country.[7]

Although the Roman Catholic missionaries translated no Scriptures into Tamil, many thousands of people along the Coromandel (southeast coast) are said to have been converted. But since they were not given the Word of God in their language, how closely they were able to walk with Christ is certainly open to question.

The *first Protestant* work in India was that of Bartholomew Ziegenbalg and Heinrich Plutschau who arrived in 1706. Within seven years, Ziegenbalg had translated the New Testament into the Tamil tongue.[8] This was the first complete translation of the New Testament into any of the languages of India. It was published in 1715.[9] It was only the fifth language in all of Asia that received the Word of God, the others being Hebrew, Syriac, Armenian, and Arabic many centuries before.[10]

Ziegenbalg also began the translation of the Old Testament. This was revised and completed by Benjamin *Schulze* in 1727. This was only the fourth entire Bible to be translated into an Asiatic tongue. Other translations into Tamil followed. Especially noteworthy was the translation by Philip Fabricius of the New Testament in 1772 and the Old Testament in 1796.[11]

We are told that Benjamin Schultze had also started translating the whole Bible into Telugu and the New Testament into Hindustani. Apparently these translations were never published, for the first publication of any portion of Scripture in Telugu, according to *The Book of a Thousand Tongues*, was in 1812, and the complete New Testament in 1818. The first publication of Scriptures in Hindustani was in 1805.[12]

Towering in influence above Ziegenbalg and his colleagues was Christian Fredrich *Schwartz* who arrived in India in 1750 and gave himself tirelessly to the work until he died in 1798. By that time some twenty thousand Christians of varied caste backgrounds were members of the churches that he and his predecessors and colleagues had founded. The finest elements in the Lutheran churches in South India today are descendants of their converts, people who had God's Word in their own language and whose leadership was literate.[13]

The *first* British society organized especially for foreign missionary work was the Baptist Missionary Society, and its first and most illustrious missionary was William Carey (1761-1845). He had received his inspiration largely from the writing of David Brainerd and from the Voyages of Captain Cook.[14]

Carey arrived in India in 1793 and was joined six years later by Joshua Marshman, a teacher, and William Ward, a printer. Together they were known as the "Serampore Trio".[15]

Carey is best remembered for his role as translator. In a period of thirty years, six translations of the entire Bible were completed, Carey himself being responsible for Bengali, Sanskrit, and Marathi. To these were added twenty-three complete New Testaments as well as Bible portions in ten other languages. Some of the "languages", however, were no more than dialects which are no longer spoken. And even though Carey revised the Bengali New Testament eight times, it was unable to hold its own, and has been replaced by other versions.[16]

Other translators were also at work in India. The most notable among them was Henry Martyn, who, like Carey, had received much of his inspiration from the diary of David Brainerd. Martyn arrived in Calcutta in 1806 and died in Persia on his way home to England in 1813 at the age of thirty-one. In just seven years he had completed the New Testament in Urdu, a version which still is the basis of that which is in use today. He had also completed a revision of the Persian Bible and was well underway on the revision of the Arabic.[17]

Cross-References
Arabic Bible, *66*
Bengali, *82*
Carey, William, *18*
Lutheran Church, *115, 151*
Roman Catholic Missions, *31*
Telegu Language, *51*

In 1813 the English parliament forced the East India Company to open its territory to mission work. This resulted in many English missions entering the sub-continent. The Church Missionary Society began work in Madras in 1814. Charles Rhenius, their first missionary, introduced the teacher-catechist system. The church was built around the school in each village, and the school master was also the catechist, responsible to conduct the Sunday worship services.[18]

While these catechists were not highly educated men, they grew in knowledge and in Christian character, and in time became pillars of a great Christian movement. At the time of his death in 1838 there were Christian groups in nearly three hundred villages over an area of about two thousand square miles. Today there are Christian churches in seven hundred villages in the Tirunelveli Diocese, thanks largely to the system worked out by Rhenius.[19]

A new period in the history of Indian missions began in 1830 with the arrival of Alexander Duff. It was Duff's conviction that the time had come to present the Gospel to the cultured sections of the community through higher education in English.

He started a school which opened with just five boys, but it grew to nearly two hundred. Duff's aims were evangelistic as well as educational. When four young men from one of the higher castes were baptized, there was a great uproar. The work was seriously threatened for a time, but gradually it regained the confidence of the public, and the school increased in strength. Duff didn't have many converts. We know of only thirty-three over a period of years. But all of them were of sterling quality, and their descendants became some of the most outstanding Christians in India. Many of them became ordained ministers.[20]

Meanwhile, a constant stream of Scriptures was being issued in many languages. In 1843, for example, Dr. Herlein of the British and Foreign Bible Society toured all over Bengal and the Ganges country distributing sixty thousand Scripture portions. An average of forty thousand copies of Scripture was distributed annually for the next several years. There were versions for hill tribes and special editions of Testaments for educated Indian students. Missionary journeys were made through villages and jungles and also by boat up the rivers where crowds thronged in order to get a copy of the Sacred Word.[21]

But then a tragedy occurred which might easily have wiped out the influence of the Scriptures for many years. That it did not do so is due to the spiritual power of the Bible itself. In *1857* the Indian army mutinied, and the sedition spread over a large area. In the looting and destruction that followed, *huge supplies of Scriptures were burned or scattered.* Books and leaflets were spread far and wide by looters. Some books were found and read by villagers who later asked for a catechist and built themselves a church. In one regiment that fought at the Siege of Delhi, several men were converted by reading some Scriptures they had found in the streets of Delhi.[22]

After the mutiny, the British Government realized more than ever its responsibility toward the people. The churches became alive to the need for evangelization. There was a demand for the Bible everywhere. By this time Books of the Bible were appearing in the languages of the North in Pashto, Kashmiri, and Tibetan. From a chain of hospitals on the Northwest Frontier, Scripture portions were carried great distances to towns and villages where no Christian could go, but where the Word of God could speak for itself.[23]

All over India, Books of the Bible were being read. Between 1854 and 1884 the Madras Auxiliary alone circulated over 2.4 million copies. They were in fifteen different languages. A system of colporteurs were ceaselessly on the move in South India, traveling sixty-five thousand miles a year, visiting a thousand towns and villages. As a result there was a steady growth of the Christian Church throughout the country, along with a desire for education and a better way of life.[24]

People who read the Bible are changed by the Bible. Between 1858 and 1888 several great persons were born in India whose lives were changed by reading the Scriptures, and they proceeded to revolutionize the world in which they lived. One of the most famous of these was a woman.

Ramabai was a Brahmin woman of the highest caste and of great intelligence. Her father recognized her brilliant mind, and taught her, as a child, the holy books of the Hindus in Sanskrit which should not be taught to a woman. For this he was driven into the jungle by the edict of some four hundred Hindu priests and scholars. The family traveled all over India in search of purification and knowledge. Her parents and her sister starved to death during a great famine, and Ramabai and her brother made their way to Calcutta. There she became well known for her unusual gifts. Her powerful exposition of the Hindu Scriptures compelled Hindu scholars to call her Pandita (Mistress of Learning).

Ramabai yearned to help Hindu women who had none of the advantages that she had. She saw the heartbreaking conditions of their lives, their slavery to men, and the abuses of child marriage and widowhood.

She started a campaign for a higher marriage age and for the education of women. No one had ever advocated this before, except for a few missionaries. She searched the Hindu Scriptures in vain for inspiration for this kind of reform. Then she began to read the Bible, and her search was ended.

She became a Christian, and with the help of friends in England and America, founded a home for widows. It grew into a garden city for hundreds of women and children and included schools, dispensaries, gardens, fields, and industries, where Christian love was radiated and the Bible was read at family prayers. She spent the last years of her life translating the Bible into simple Marathi for the women she knew so well. [25]

PEOPLE MOVEMENTS

According to Sherwood Eddy, the various mass movements of the nineteenth century *accounted for eighty percent of the Christians in India.*[26] Involved in these mass movements to Christ were hundreds of thousands of Hindu outcastes who had been denied access to Hindu temples and village wells. Consequently, they had nothing to lose and possibly something to gain by accepting Christianity. Almost all of the people who were brought into the church through mass movements were illiterates except in Andhra Pradesch where some of the high caste Hindus also came forward after the movement was well underway.[27]

There were many mass movements throughout the century beginning between 1795 and 1805 when more than five thousand converts were baptized by Christian Schwartz and others in the extreme south. Later, through Charles Rhenius of the Church Missionary Society, about eleven thousand people were added from the upper class. At least two other mass movements occurred in the same area under the ministries of the Society for the Propation of the Gospel and the London Missionary Society.

There were several other mass movements in Telegu country (now known as Andhra Pradesh). Lutherans saw large mass movements in the coastal area; Anglicans, British Methodists, and Methodist Episcopals in Hyderabad; and Canadian Baptists and the London Missionary Society in Northeastern Andhra.

There were more large people movements to Christ in the north hill country among the Oraons, the Mundas, the Hos, and the Santals, and still others in Central India and in the Punjab in the northwestern part of the country.

Perhaps the largest mass movement was one which started in 1859 among the Chamars in Delhi and spread through Uttar Pradesh, bringing a hundred thousand converts into the Church.

Another mass movement occurred in Northeast India among the Khasis. After the movement was well underway, the Bible was translated into the Khasi language, and the movement to Christ spread throughout the area. Life was transformed and large churches were established. Today forty-seven percent of the tribe is Christian. Mass movements also occurred among the many other hill tribes including the Mizos, the Nagas, the Garos, the Abors, and the Minis. Some of these had been head hunters.

Most of these mass movements have taken place among the outcastes, lower castes of tribal peoples following serious economic conditions or famines or oppression from the higher castes. But it is not correct to say that material or economic gain was the motive that led people to seek membership in the church in these movements.

It must be admitted that mass movements have brought some disadvantages to the Church in India. Because of inadequate training, nominalism has become a major problem. Pagan practices and customs still remained in the lives of large numbers of church members, due mainly to lack of thorough teaching of the Word of God.

For this reason, most of India's Church leaders and many missionaries took a dim view of mass movements. Through much effort, the Indian Christian Church had been raised to a high level of literacy and social acceptance. If it were flooded with thousands of depraved and illiterate people, all that had been accomplished would be undone, and Christianity would be associated to its detriment only with the poorest and least acceptable classes of society.

But Henry Whitehead, bishop of Madras (1899-1923) was convinced that these movements were valid manifestations of the working of the Holy Spirit, and that, although a consecrated Christian life could not be expected of every convert from the beginning, a door was opened through which the Church must enter at all costs. He believed, with good reason, that if enough Christian workers could be supplied, thirty million people of the depressed classes could become Christians within a century.[28]

BIBLE TRANSLATIONS

Of India's 328 languages, 36 have the entire Bible. Another 25 have the New Testament, and another 54 have portions of the New Testament. But the vast majority of the people in the country's 600,000 villages are unable to read whatever Scriptures may have been published in their mother tongue.[29]

CHRISTIAN LITERATURE

Christian literature has played a vital role, directly and indirectly, in the advance of the Gospel in India. During the three year period from 1965 to 1968, nearly fifty-one million Gospel messages in print were distributed by World Literature Crusade, according to Jack McAlister, President of WLC. This endeavor drew 460,000 written decisions from Indians, 71 percent of whom were newly converted. McAlister adds that 80 percent of these decisions were by Hindus.[30]

Bible correspondence courses have also been effective in leading many to Christ. "The Light and Life Bible Correspondence Course" is the most popular. It has been adopted by more than a dozen missions and has been translated into at least twenty-four languages. By 1967, over a million and a half students had enrolled in the course, eighty-five percent of them non-Christians.[31]

In India today there are a number of extraordinary *opportunities for the Bible.* There is religious freedom under the Constitution which removes by law all restrictions against the Bible. There are increasing numbers of literates each year. There is also the challenge of thousands of spiritually displaced persons—

Hindus in Pakistan and Muslims in India—cut off from their co-religionists in either country and looking for a spiritual home which the state in which they live cannot give them. There are millions of intelligent people in both states who find the old religions empty and who are hungry for an adequate spiritual life. We must rush in to fill the vacuum with the Word of Eternal Life, lest we be guilty of a great sin of omission.[32]

Cross-References
Nepal, *4, 5, 17, 55, 59, 91, 100*

While early missionaries did much to train national pastors, evangelists and teachers, *the need for training nationals* is perhaps greater today than ever before, since the government of India is reluctant to grant visas to new missionaries from North America or anywhere else. Even the missionaries from the British Commonwealth, of which India is a part, are finding it more and more difficult to obtain resident visas.

In 1973 there were 1247 North American Protestant missionaries in India. By 1985 there were only 513. The total number of foreign Protestant and Roman Catholic missionaries in India in 1980 was estimated from 2000 to 2500—a considerable decline from 1970 when there were 5768.

Even so, in this land of 785 million people, the number of Christians is growing almost twice as fast as the general population even though the missionary force has declined by forty percent in the past 25 years. There is a growing evangelical voice so that the people are more receptive to the Gospel than ever before.

Thousands of students are studying Scripture through extension courses as well as in forty *seminaries*. One seminary alone, backed by 26 evangelical bodies, is sending out a stream of well-trained evangelical leaders into India and other countries of Asia.

The *missionary vision* of the Indian Church is growing. One mission society has more than forty workers in six fields of India and Nepal. Another has 65 workers in India and three foreign fields. Altogether there are about 600 Indian missionaries in cross-cultural missionary work.[33]

The Spirit of God is moving mightily in India. But there is so very, very much more to be done. Very few of the 600,000 villages of India have any evangelical witness, especially in North India where there's an average of ONE church for every 2000 villages.[34] There are more churches in South India, but for the country as a whole, there's only one pastor for every 400 villages. Most of them are working with the lower castes. Only 17 of India's 3,000 castes and sub-castes have had much opportunity to hear of God's redeeming love.

Praise God for all He is doing in India, But pray that the Lord of harvest will thrust forth laborers into His harvest: pastors, evangelists, Bible teachers, translators, literacy workers, writers, and others skilled in preparing Bible extension courses, so that every person in every village may be able to hear and read the glorious message of Jesus and His love.

A PRAYER FOR INDIA

Almighty God, Merciful Father, You loved India so much that You gave Your only begotten Son to suffer and die for all of India's sins, that whoever believes in Him should not perish, but have everlasting life.

And yet, after all of these centuries, only 3% of the people in this country are believers in Jesus. Many say they believe in Jesus, but they cling to their other hideous "gods". But most of the people have never heard a clear presentation of the glorious message of Your redeeming love.

Father, forgive us for not doing more, for not following Jesus' example of sacrificial love, to proclaim the Word of Life to every person in every city and village of India.

Gracious and loving Father, we pray that you would send your Holy Angels to bind the princes of India, the princes of idolatry and superstition and delusion and all that blinds the eyes of Indian people to the Truth. We pray that Your Word may be proclaimed to all of India's poor, and that it will heal the brokenhearted, deliver those in bondage to Satan, give sight to the spiritually blind, and release the oppressed and downtrodden, that they may know Jesus and the power of His resurrection, and have the peace and joy of knowing their Savior and Lord in this present life, and live and reign with You for all eternity.

O, Father, we pray that You would do something drastic if necessary to deliver India from its bondage. Send angels to proclaim Your Word from heaven in everyone's mother tongue, if that's what it's going to take. Or if persecution or a natural disaster is necessary, so be it, but don't let these people perish in their sins.

Almighty God, nothing is too difficult for You! You can do anything You want to do. And we know that You want all India to be saved. Do whatever is necessary, no matter how drastic, to turn India's millions from darkness to light and from the power of Satan to God, that they may receive forgiveness of sins and a place among those who are sanctified by faith in Jesus.

And Lord, I pray that You'd do something drastic in my own life and in the lives of all who call themselves by Your Name. Pour out Your Holy Spirit upon us, Lord. Give us that power from on high that we must have in order to proclaim Your Word effectively.

And give us, O Lord, the mind of Christ. Who though He was rich, yet for our sakes became poor, that we through His poverty might be rich. Grant that we, like Jesus, may humble ourselves and become obedient even unto death if that's what it will take to bring India to Christ.

O Merciful Father, let Jesus' suffering and death not have been in vain for the vast multitudes in India who have never heard the Greatest Story Ever Told. Grant that we may be willing to do anything You ask us to do. Make us willing to give up our fun and games and every luxury and comfort and everything we don't absolutely have to have in order that India might know Jesus. Grant that we may be willing, and even find joy in sacrificial living and even in suffering persecution for the sake of the cross.

Our Father in heaven, hallowed be Your name in India. Your Kingdom come to India. Your will be done in India as it is in heaven. For we ask it in Jesus' Name. Amen

Christianity in India
Pray for India

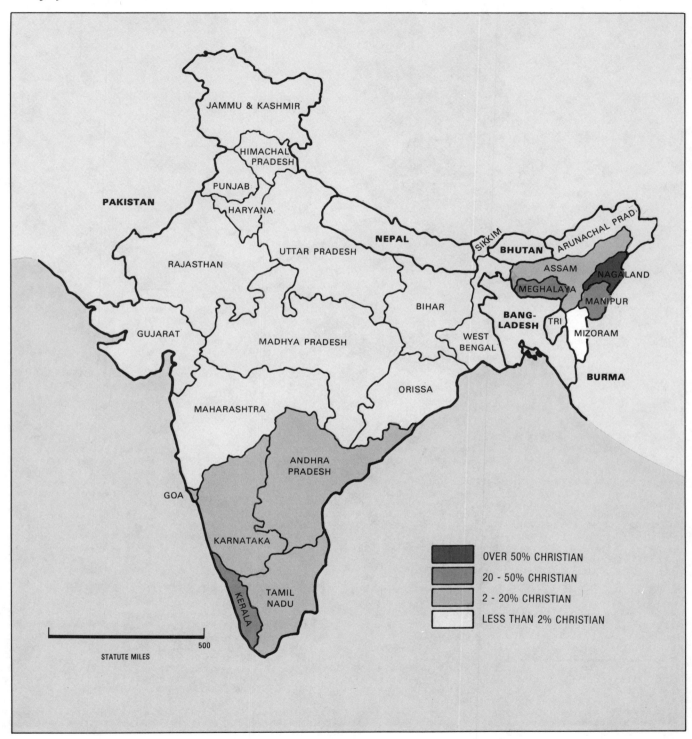

JAMMU & KASHMIR

HIMACHAL PRADESH

PUNJAB

PAKISTAN

HARYANA

NEPAL

SIKKIM

BHUTAN

ARUNACHAL PRAD

UTTAR PRADESH

ASSAM

NAGALAND

RAJASTHAN

MEGHALAYA

MANIPUR

BIHAR

BANG-LADESH

TRI

GUJARAT

MADHYA PRADESH

WEST BENGAL

MIZORAM

BURMA

ORISSA

MAHARASHTRA

ANDHRA PRADESH

GOA

KARNATAKA

KERALA

TAMIL NADU

500

STATUTE MILES

OVER 50% CHRISTIAN

20 - 50% CHRISTIAN

2 - 20% CHRISTIAN

LESS THAN 2% CHRISTIAN

Illiteracy in India
Pray for India

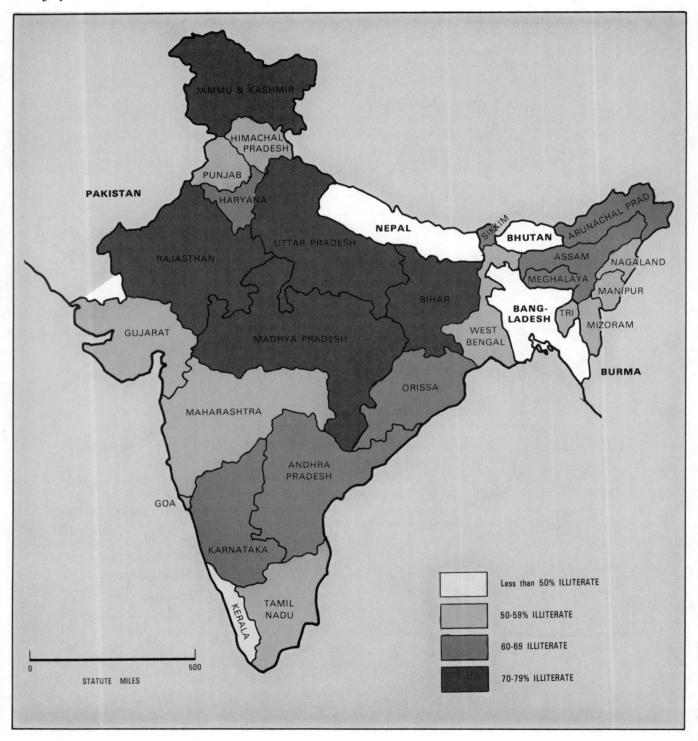

JAMMU & KASHMIR

HIMACHAL PRADESH

PUNJAB

HARYANA

PAKISTAN

NEPAL

UTTAR PRADESH

RAJASTHAN

SIKKIM

BHUTAN

ARUNACHAL PRAD

ASSAM

NAGALAND

MEGHALAYA

MANIPUR

BIHAR

BANG-LADESH

TRI

MIZORAM

GUJARAT

WEST BENGAL

MADHYA PRADESH

BURMA

ORISSA

MAHARASHTRA

ANDHRA PRADESH

GOA

KARNATAKA

TAMIL NADU

KERALA

0   500

STATUTE MILES

Less than 50% ILLITERATE

50-59% ILLITERATE

60-69 ILLITERATE

70-79% ILLITERATE

India's Vital Statistics

STATE	POPULATION (MILLIONS) 1981 FIGURES	AREA (SQ. MI.)	POPULATION DENSITY (SQ. MI.)	% HINDU	% MUSLIM	% CHRISTIAN	% LITERATE	%FEMALE LITERATE	LANGUAGES
ANDHRA PRADESH	53.4	106,855	500	87.0	8.0	4.2	29*	19*	TELEGU, URDU, LABHANI, TULU +25 OTHERS
ASSAM	20.0	30,318	660	72.5	24.5	2.6	35*	24*	ASSAMESE, BONO, RODO KUMAUNI +38 OTHERS
BIHAR	70.0	76,134	1,043	83.4	13.4	1.2	26	14	HINDI, BHOJPURI, MAGAHI, MAITHILI +42 OTHERS
GUJARAT	34.0	75,670	449	89.0	8.0	.4	43	32	GUJARATI, MARWARI, KONKANI, +30 OTHERS
HARYANA	12.8	17,074	750	89.0	4.0	.1	35	22	HINDI, PAHARI, MARWARI, +9 OTHERS
HIMACHAL PRADESH	4.2	21,495	195	96.0	1.4	.1	42	31	HINDI, GADDI, JULAHA +56 OTHERS
JAMMU & KASHMIR	5.9	85,806	69	30.4	65.8	.2	22*	11*	KASHMIRI, DOGRI, GORJI, URDU +30 OTHERS
KARNATAKA	37.0	74,044	500	86.4	10.6	2.1	38	27	KANNADA, URDU HINDI, TAMIL, TELUGU +6 OTHERS
KERALA	25.4	15,005	1,693	59.4	19.5	21.0	69	65	MALAYALAM, TAMIL, TELUGU, HINDI +25 OTHERS
MADHYA PRADESH	52.1	171,000	305	93.7	4.4	.7	28	16	HINDI DIALECTS, MARATHI, GONDI +30 OTHERS
MAHARASHTRA	62.7	118,827	528	82.0	8.4	1.4	47	35	MARATHI, GUJARATI, HINDI, TELUGU +25 OTHERS
MANIPUR	1.4	8,632	162	59.0	7.0	26.0	42	30	MANIPURI +4 OTHERS
MEGHALAYA	1.3	8,683	150	18.0	2.6	47.0	33	29	GARO, JAINTIA, KHASI, MEGHALAYAN
NAGALAND	.8	6,381	125	11.4	—	67.0	42	33	NAGA DIALECTS, ASSAMESE, HINDI
ORISSA	26.3	60,171	437	96.0	1.5	1.7	34	21	ORIYA, KHOND, PANO, SANTAL +22 OTHERS
PUNJAB	16.7	19,400	861	37.0	.3	1.2	41	32	PUNJABI, HINDI, URDU, KULUI +35 OTHERS
RAJASTHAN	34.1	132,130	258	89.0	7.0	.1	24	11	RAJASTHANI, HINDI, BHIL, CHAMAR +16 OTHERS
SIKKIM	.3	2,745	109	69.0	—	.8	34	22	BHUTIA, LEPCHA, NEPALI, SIKKIMESE
TAMIL NADU	48.3	50,220	962	89.0	5.1	5.7	45	34	TAMIL, ADI DRAVIDIAN +29 OTHERS
TRIPURA	2.0	4,045	494	89.0	7.0	1.0	42	31	BENGALI, MANIPURI, TRIPUTI +9 OTHERS
UTTAR PRADESH	110.8	113,673	975	84.0	15.0	.1	27	14	HINDI, URDU, KAMAONI, GAHWALI +84 OTHERS
WEST BENGAL	54.4	33,920	1,604	78.0	2.0	.6	41	30	BENGALI, HINDI, SANTALI, URDU +34 OTHERS

* 1971 STATISTICS, ALL OTHERS ARE FOR 1981. Population figures are from the Oxford School Atlas, Bombay; Oxford University Press, 1982. Religious statistics are from WORLD CHRISTIANITY, South Asia, published by MARC, 1980.

Population of India's Cities, 1981

(From Oxford School Atlas, Bombay: Oxford University Press, 1982)

1. Calcutta	9,165,655		47. Nasik	428,778
2. Bombay	8,227,332		48. Srinagar	423,253
3. Delhi	6,196,414		49. Jullundur	405,709
4. Madras	4,276,635		50. Thana	388,577
5. Bangalore	2,913,537		51. Ajmer	374,750
6. Hyderabad	2,528,198		52. Guntur	367,219
7. Ahmadabad	2,515,195		53. Asansol	365,371
8. Kanpur	1,688,242		54. Kolhapur	351,373
9. Pune (Poona)	1,685,300		55. Moradabad	347,983
10. Nagpur	1,297,977		56. Kota	346,928
11. Lucknow	1,006,538		57. Raipur	338,973
12. Jaipur	1,004,669		58. Warangal	336,018
13. Coimbatore	917,155		59. Cuttack	326,468
14. Patna	916,102		60. Tirunelveli	324,034
15. Surat	912,568		61. Raurkela	321,326
16. Madurai	904,362		62. Aligahr	319,981
17. Indore	827,071		63. Jamnagar	317,037
18. Varanasi (Benares)	793,542		64. Aurangabad	316,244
19. Agra	770,352		65. Bhavnagar	308,194
20. Jabulpur	757,726		66. Gorakhpur	306,399
21. Vadodara	744,043		67. Durgapur	305,838
22. Cochin	685,686		68. Mangalore	305,513
23. Danbad	676,376		69. Belgaum	300,290
24. Bhopal	672,329		70. Saharanpur	294,391
25. Jamshedpur	669,984		71. Dehra Dun	293,628
26. Ulhasnagar	648,149		72. Ujjain	281,878
27. Allahabad	642,420		73. Bikaner	280,366
28. Tiruchchirappalli	607,815		74. Sangli	268,962
29. Ludhiana	606,250		75. Rajahmundry	267,749
30. Vishakhapatnam	594,259		76. Amravati	261,387
31. Amritsar	589,229		77. Pondicherry	251,471
32. Gwalior	559,776		78. Tuticoric	250,673
33. Calicut	546,060		79. Vellore	246,937
34. Vijayawada	544,958		80. Gaha	246,778
35. Meerut	538,461		81. Malegaon	245,769
36. Hubli-Dharwar	526,493		82. Kharagpur	234,931
37. Trivandrum	519,766		83. Jhansi	231,332
38. Salem	515,021		84. Udaipur	229,762
39. Solapur	514,461		85. Kakinada	226,642
40. Ranchi	500,593		86. Akola	225,412
41. Jodhpur	493,609		87. Bhagalpur	221,276
42. Durg-Bhilai	490,158		88. Sagar	207,401
43. Mysore	476,446		89. Patiala	205,849
44. Chandigarh	450,061		90. Rampur	203,491
45. Rajkot	444,156		91. Gauhati	200,377
46. Bareilly	437,801		92. Alleppey	169,934

The Hindu World

650 million Hindus in the world, in 27 different countries, are racially all from the Indian sub-continent. They make up 13% of the world's population.

COUNTRY	HINDU POPULATION	% OF TOTAL POPULATION	OTHER NON-HINDU INDIANS
ASIA			
CENTRAL ASIA:			
INDIA	651,000,000	83%	134,000,000
NEPAL	15,660,000	90%	1,740,000
BANGLADESH	14,574,000	14%	89,426,000
SRI LANKA	2,988,000	18%	11,480,000
PAKISTAN	1,528,000	1.5%	74,860,000
BURMA	754,000	2%	260,000
BHUTAN	350,000	25%	960,000
AFGHANISTAN	57,000	0.5%	25,000
TOTAL:	**686,911,000**		**312,441,000**
SOUTH EAST ASIA			
INDONESIA	5,557,200	3.3%	
MALAYSIA	1,422,000	9%	100,000
FIJI	245,000	35%	90,000
SINGAPORE	182,000	7%	20,000
HONGKONG	55,700	0.1%	1,000
TOTAL:	**7,411,900**		**211,000**
ARABIAN GULF STATES	260,000	5%	100,000
TOTAL FOR ASIA:	**694,582,900 ***		**285,730,000 ***
AFRICA			
EAST:			
Mauritius	500,000	50%	170,000
KENYA	210,000	1%	20,000
TANZANIA	67,200	0.3%	40,000
TOTAL:	**777,200**		**230,000**
SOUTH AFRICA	664,000	2%	280,000
ZAMBIA	17,750	0.25%	—
ZIMBABWE	18,000	0.2%	4,000
TOTAL FOR SOUTH AFRICA:	**699,750**		**284,000**
TOTAL FOR AFRICA:	**1,476,950 ***		**514,000 ***
EUROPE			
GREAT BRITAIN	707,000	1.25%	300,000
HOLLAND	48,000	0.4%	—
TOTAL FOR EUROPE:	**755,000 ***		**300,000 ***
CARIBBEAN			
GUYANA	264,000	33%	140,000
TRINIDAD & TOBAGO	276,000	33%	190,000
SURINAM	128,000	32%	22,000
TOTAL FOR CARIBBEAN:	**668,000 ***		**352,000 ***
NORTH AMERICA			
U.S.A.	48,000	0.02%	9,000
CANADA	51,000	0.2%	12,000
TOTAL FOR NORTH AMERICA:	**99,000 ***		**21,000 ***
*WORLD TOTAL:	**696,581,850**		**313,939,000**

Statistics from the Institute of Hindu Studies, 1605 Elizabeth St., Pasadena, California 91104

SUGGESTED READING

PORTRAIT OF INDIA: *By Bradford Smith. New York: Lippencott, 1962*

An objective look at India from Kashmir to the southern tip—its people, the animals, the means of transportation, the inconceivable red tape of official bureaucracy, the glorious art and architecture, the incredible powers of the yogis and other mystics, the great economic and social problems. All of these things are in the book, and the reader becomes immersed in the colors, sights and sounds of India— the cries of the street vendors, the saffron robes of the holy men, the dust colored rags of the poor people, the splendor of a maharaja's palace, the overwhelming heat.

THE COMPASSIONATE TOUCH: *By Douglas Wead. Minneapolis: Bethany Fellowship 1977*

This is a profoundly moving, unforgettable book. To read it is a wrenching emotional experience. Doug Wead has captured all of the degradation and despair that is Calcutta. But in spite of that, this is not a hopeless book. The stories of lives changed by the remarkable ministry of Mark Buntain will leave you crying with joy and renewed faith in a miracle-working God."

GOD OF THE UNTOUCHABLES: *By Dave Hunt. Old Tappan, NJ: Fleming H. Revell Company, 1976*

This is the account of a real life of a man who saw emptiness in the Eastern religion of his fathers, a man who found that gurus and mantras and exotic customs hold no real promise of hope for anyone, a man who discovered that life has meaning and purpose only when lived in the light of the One who is called God of the untouchables. (156 pp.)

INDIA—PAKISTAN AND THE BORDER LANDS: *By Milton Meyer. Totowa, NJ: Littlefield, Adams and Co., 1968*

One of the leading authorities on the subject discusses one of the oldest most continuous civilizations in the world. Separate chapters cover the history and development of ancient Hindu and Muslim India, India's relationship with the West and the British Crown, Independent India, as well as Pakistan, the Border Lands and the events which have led to the conflicts in recent years. (261 pp.)

ESCAPE INTO THE LIGHT: *By Rabindranath R. Maharaj with Dave Hunt. Eugene, OR: Harvest House Publishers, 1977—published as Death Of A Guru/1984*

Unique revelation of the inward struggles of a Hindu Yogi and guru, and the ultimate triumph over death that he discovered. Challenging and inspiring reading.

THE STORY OF THE CHURCH IN INDIA AND PAKISTAN: *By Stephen Neill. Grand Rapids, MI: William B. Eerdmans Publishing Co., 1970*

Bishop Neill carries his account forward from Thomas Christians to the formation of the United Churches in India. The Church in India had to face Muslim and Hindu antagonism, political and social discrimination as well as interdenominational rivalry. Bishop Neill brings the personalities of the missionary pioneers, martyrs and enemies of the Church vividly alive, portraying not only their successes, but also their failures.

GOD'S TRIBESMAN: *The Rochunga Pudaite Story by James and Marti Hefley. Nashville, TN: Holman Bible Publishers, 1974*

A member of a one time headhunting tribe in India is brought to faith in Christ. He is actively seeking to get a copy of the Bible into the hands of each of the homes of India—beginning with those already able to read it.

SADHU SUNDAR SINGH: *by Cyril Davey. Bromley, Dent, England:Send the Light Books, 1980*

The thrilling story of the sadhu (holy one) who at the age of 16 foresook his family and friends and possessions and all that he had to follow Jesus. Like his Master, he wanted no home and no possessions, but rather to belong to the road—sharing the sufferings of his people, eating with those who would give him shelter, and telling all men of the love of God.

VILLAGE INDIA: *by McKim Marriott et al.. Chicago, The University of Chicago Press, 1955*

Eight villages in seven different linguistic areas and five provinces of India are illuminated by detailed analyses of caste, community, structure, personality, religion, world view, and the current forces of social change.

WILLIAM CAREY: *Biography by Mary Drewery. Grand Rapids, MI:Zondervan Publishing House, 1978*
Mary Drewery's telling of William Carey's life of service to India is an attempt to show the personal side of this missionary statesman. Carey's challenge, "Attempt great things for God and expect great things from God", sparked the modern missions movement.

BEHIND MUD WALLS 1930-1960 With a Sequel: The Village in 1970: *By William and Charlotte Wiser, Berkeley: University of California Press, 1963*

A study of North Indian village life. The Wisers were missionaries in India. Behind mud walls includes their appraisal of village life in 1930, 1960 and 1970. (287 pp.)

HINDUISM: *by Louis Renou, Editor. New York: Washington Square Press, 1961*

This volume presents the spiritual teachings of Hinduism in a wide selection of classical and modern texts. Included are the earliest known hymns, epics and moral treatises, and the writings of more recent authors. Arranged historically with an informative introduction to each selection. (226 pp.)

THE CHURCH TAKES ROOT IN INDIA: *By Basl Matthews. New York: Friendship Press, 1938*

Basil Mathews tries to give a balanced picture of India in transition. As a guest of Indian States and British administrators, of Congressional leaders, Christian missionaries and village pastors, and as a visitor to schools and colleges—he had the privilege of looking on the landscape of India from nearly every possible angle.

REFERENCES

1. McGavran, Grace
1947 **Stories of the Book of Books.** *New York: Friendship Press, page 220*

2. Sinker, Margaret
1953 **The Story of the Bible in India, Pakistan and Ceylon.** *London: British and Foreign Bible Society, page 9.*

3. Neill, Stephen
1970 **A Story of the Christian Church in India and Pakistan.** *Grand Rapids: Eerdmans, page 19.*

4. Kane, J. Herbert
1970 **A Global View of Christian Missions.** *Baltimare: Penguin Books, page 148.*

5. Neill, Stephen
1964 **A History of Christian Missions.** *Baltimore: Penguin Books, page 148.*

6. Mathews, Basil
1952 **Disciples of All Nations.** *London: Oxford Press, page 95.*

7. Watkins, Morris
1978 **Literacy, Bible Reading and Church Growth.** *Pasadena, Wm. Carey Library, page 76.*

8. Neill, Stephen
1970 **A Story of the Christian Church in India and Pakistan.** *Grand Rapids: Eerdmans, page 228-229*

9. Nida, Eugene (ed.)
1972 **The Book of a Thousand Tongues.** *New York: United Bible Societies, p. 418.*

10. North, Eric (ed.)
1938 **The Book of a Thousand Tongues.** *New York: American Bible Society, page 321.*

11. Neill, Stephen
1970 **A Story of the Christian Church in India and Pakistan.** *Grand Rapids: Eerdmans, page 19.*

12. North, Eric (ed.)
1938 **The Book of a Thousand Tongues.** *New York: American Bible Society, page 321.*

13. Mathews, Basil
1952 **Disciples of All Nations.** *London: Oxford Press, page 95.*

14. Sinker, Margaret
1953 **The Story of the Bible in India, Pakistan and Ceylon.** *London: British and Foreign Bible Society, page 18.*

15. Watkins, Morris
1978 **Literacy, Bible Reading and Church Growth.** *Pasadena, Wm. Carey Library, page 114.*

16. Neill, Stephen
1964 **A History of Christian Missions.** *Baltimore: Penguin Books, page 263-264.*

17. Neill, Stephen
1964 **A History of Christian Missions.** *Baltimore: Penguin Books, page 266-267.*

18. Watkins, Morris
1978 **Literacy, Bible Reading and Church Growth.** *Pasadena, Wm. Carey Library, page 114.*

19. Neill, Stephen
1970 **A Story of the Christian Church in India and Pakistan.** *Grand Rapids: Eerdmans, page 19.*

20. Neill, Stephen
1964 **A History of Christian Missions.** *Baltimore: Penguin Books, page 274-275.*

21. Sinker, Margaret
1953 **The Story of the Bible in India, Pakistan and Ceylon.** *London: British and Foreign Bible Society, page 32.*

22. Sinker, Margaret
1953 **The Story of the Bible in India, Pakistan and Ceylon.** *London: British and Foreign Bible Society, page 33.*

23. Sinker, Margaret
1953 **The Story of the Bible in India, Pakistan and Ceylon.** *London: British and Foreign Bible Society, page 36.*

24. Sinker, Margaret
1953 **The Story of the Bible in India, Pakistan and Ceylon.** *London: British and Foreign Bible Society, page 36-37.*

25. Sinker, Margaret
1953 **The Story of the Bible in India, Pakistan and Ceylon.** London: British and Foreign Bible Society, page 39.

26. Kane, J. Herbert
1971 **A Global View of Christian Missions.** Baltimare: Penguin Books, page 122.

27. Williams, Theodore
1975 **India, A Seething Subcontinent.** in Hoke, Donald (ed.) The Church in Asia. Chicago: Moody Press, page 253.

28. Williams, Theodore
1975 **India, A Seething Subcontinent.** in Hoke, Donald (ed.) The Church in Asia. Chicago: Moody Press, page 254-258.

29. Grimes, Barbara (ed.)
1984 **Ethnologue, 10th Edition.** Dallas: Wycliffe Bible Translators, page 395.

30. **ELO Bulletin 1958**: Volume 11, No. 4, page 10.

31. Kane, J. Herbert
1971 **A Global View of Christian Missions.** Baltimare: Penguin Books, page 121.

32. Watkins, Morris
1978 **Literacy, Bible Reading and Church Growth.** Pasadena, Wm. Carey Library, page 175.

33. Johnstone, Patrick
1979 **Operation World.** Bromley, Kent, England: STL Publications, page 109.

34. Johnstone, Patrick
1979 **Operation World.** Bromley, Kent, England: STL Publications, page 110.

THE MUSLIM WORLD

WORLD OF ISLAM

The Muslim World could just as well be called the World of Islam, for that is the name of the religion founded by Mohammed in the 7th century. The word "Islam" means "submission" (to the will of God). The followers of Islam are called Moslems or Muslims, terms that mean "those who submit" (to the will of God).

There are about 850 million Muslims in the world today, about one-sixth of the world's population. The number of Muslims is growing rapidly, despite the fact that tens of thousands of them have been killed, and continue to be killed, in the war between Iran and Iraq.

Muslims overwhelmingly dominate North Africa and the Middle East, Pakistan, Bangladesh, and Indonesia (80-100%) but are also found in large numbers in at least 21 other nations (10-79%).

Islam is a severe but simple religion. Muslims consider it to be an extension of Christianity and Judaism, but they believe the Christian Trinity to be blasphemous, and they deny the deity of Jesus. The Koran is the basic source of Islamic law and ritual. Muslims believe it was dictated to Mohammed by God through the angel Gabriel.

The five pillars of the Islamic faith are: (1) The repetition of their creed, "There is no God but Allah, Mohammed is his prophet." (2) Prayers must be said five times each day at prescribed hours, beginning an hour and a half before sunrise. They may pray privately or at the mosque. A worshiper faces the holy city of Mecca and follows a fixed ritual of recitation and prostration. (3) Almsgiving. Muslims are expected to contribute generously to the religion. The money is used to maintain the mosque and to help the poor and needy. (4) Fasting. Muslims cannot eat or drink during daylight hours of Ramadan, the ninth month of their lunar year. (5) Pilgrimages. Once in his lifetime, every Muslim who is financially and physically able must travel to Mecca to worship. This pilgrimage is called the hadj or hajj. A pilgrim who has made it is called a hajji.

Religious War. Some (but not all) Muslims consider it a sixth obligation to spread Islam by force. This belief is not specifically stated in the Koran.

Islamic Law. The basic ethical code of Islam comes from the Koran. The most important rule is that all Muslims are brothers. The Koran encourages charity, authorizes slavery, and prohibits the drinking of wine, gambling, and eating of pork. A Muslim may have as many as four wives, and divorce is permitted. Divorce is effected by the husband telling his wife three times, "I divorce you."

When Mohammed died, his close associates elected a successor, called a caliph, to take his place as a leader—but not as a prophet. This system was called the "caliphate" and continued until 1924. At present, there is no universal Muslim leader.

THE CHALLENGE OF ISLAM

Perhaps the greatest tragedy in the history of the Christian Church is the failure of the Christians to translate the Word of God into Arabic.

Mohammed (570-632) heard of the one true God whom Christians worshipped, but he had no access to the written Word of God. He learned something about the Christian's God by hearsay from uninstructed or poorly instructed Christians. He seems to have believed he was putting Biblical truth into language his countrymen could understand.[1]

The Quran (Koran) commends Bible reading. But when a Muslim reads it, he finds that it doesn't agree with what he has heard. So he concludes that these writings are not the original Scriptures, but that Jews and Christians have corrupted them.

How tragic that the first book ever written in the Arabic language was the Quran which denies that Jesus is the Son of God who came into the world to save sinners, who died on the cross to pay for our sins and rose from the grave to give us the power over death and give us hope of eternal life through faith in Him.

How tragic that the Word of Christ was not translated into Arabic in those early centuries. Not only have Arabs themselves been kept from the saving knowledge of Jesus Christ, but they soon overran North Africa and Western Asia, conquering even Persia within 20 years after the death of Mohammed. And they tied up the trade routes to India and China for over seven centuries, keeping missionaries from Europe from reaching these lands.

In 642 Alexandria was captured. It wasn't long before the entire land of Egypt was added to the Muslim domain. The advance westward across Africa continued, and in 697 Carthage, once a Christian stronghold, fell into their hands. By 715 the greater part of Spain had fallen to Islam. The Muslim advance was finally checked by Charles Martel at Tours in the very heart of France in 732, almost exactly a hundred years after the death of Mohammed.[2]

Although loss of life was small, the Muslim conquest was a major disaster for the so-called Christian world. The tragedy is that there may never have been any such religion as Islam if the Scriptures had been translated into Arabic and the people had been able to read those Scriptures for themselves. Then, too, if the Berbers of North Africa had been given the Scriptures in their mother tongue, perhaps a much larger percentage of them would have been won for Christ and would not have succumbed to the Muslim advance. But the Berbers not only offered little or no resistance; they actually became allies of the Muslims in their conquest of Spain.[3]

No trace of the North African Church remains, and throughout the Middle East, the lifestyle of the few Christians that Muslims meet will rarely attract anyone to the Gospel of Jesus Christ! Almost all the church members throughout the Middle East are descendents of the Christians of the pre-Muslim era. They are generally decadent and lacking in spiritual life.

About three percent of the people of the Middle East are members of the Eastern Churches; 1.2% are Roman Catholic; and only 3/10ths of one percent are Protestants, and most of them live in the Sudan, south of Egypt. Only about 152,000 Protestant Christians live in Egypt, and only 131,000 can be found in all the other countries of the Middle East.[4]

There are approximately 1300 Christian missionaries in the Middle East from Europe and North America. That is about one missionary for every 170,000 people.[5] No wonder so few Muslims have ever been freed from the bondage of Islam.

Today Islam reigns supreme where once the Christian Church was strong, and this man-made religion has been Christianity's most successful and bitter opponent.

Islam's missionary fervor has greatly increased since the 1974 oil crisis. With vast funds at its disposal, a huge effort is being made to win Europe for Islam and at the same time to end Christian missionary work in Muslim lands.

Paradoxically, Muslims are more open to the Gospel than ever before. This is due to the dramatic political and social changes that are revolutionizing their lives. The teachings of Islam cannot meet the deepest needs of the human heart in these crisis times. Islam is now very divided because of doctrinal differences, attitudes to Communism, Western materialism, and the failure of Muslims to settle national and international problems among themselves and above all, the extraordinary survival and expansion of the little state of Israel. In all this confusion, more Muslims are seeking the truth, but because of perversions of Christianity found in their holy book, the Koran, and because of social pressures, the would-be seeker of the truth is often prevented or hindered from coming to Christ; even if he could find a witnessing Christian to help him.[6]

It is difficult to win Muslims to Christ, for Islam completely misinterprets Christianity and denies its doctrines. So the Muslim is fore-warned and fore-armed against the Gospel, and, in fact, has a built-in prejudice against it. It has been said that to preach the Gospel to the Muslims is to ask the proudest man in the world to accept the thing he hates at the hand of one he despises.

It is also the appalling cost of Christian Discipleship in the Muslim world that creates one of the greatest barriers to the Gospel. The law of apostasy in Islam, generally speaking, is death, though there are only a few places in the world where this would actually take place today. But there are other ways of discouraging one from accepting the Christian faith. A convert will automatically lose his wife and children, be cut off from his job and find it hard, if not impossible, to find another. In fanatical areas, he may be unable to buy or sell in the market, marry or give in marriage, and in the event of death he cannot have a burial place in the local cemetery.

Even so, Muslims are turning to Christ more than ever before. Most of them have been influenced more by reading God's Word than by hearing it. What a tragedy then, that 2/3 of the Muslims of India and the Middle East cannot read.

Pray that more Muslims will learn to read and take advantage of the Bible correspondence courses that are offered by Gospel Missionary Union, North Africa Mission, International Christian Fellowship and others. These courses have been used of the Lord to win more Muslims to Christ than any other means.[7]

Pray for the missionaries in the Middle East and throughout the Muslim world. Discouragement, lack of visible fruit, and the hostility of many can cause some to give up the struggle. Pray for adaptability to new cultures, acceptability among the people, perseverance, and love for the people they seek to win.

Pray for the radio broadcasts to Muslims. Radio is the most effective (and sometimes the only) means of witnessing to Muslims in many areas. The response has been good, especially when followed up by Bible correspondence courses and personal contacts with Christians.[8]

Pray that there might be more and more good evangelistic literature for Muslims. Pray for ex-Muslims engaged in writing these materials, for publishers, and for bookstores and those who seek to get this literature into the hands of those who need it. Pray for more literacy workers, for literature is of little value where people are unable to read.

Pray for national believers. They are few and far between, and much in need of prayer as they live in very difficult circumstances. There is great need for the

Cross-References
Islamic Missions, *105*
Israel, *74, 93, 100, 144*
Literature Ministry, *36, 76, 83, 102, 192*
Radio Broadcasting, *15, 72, 16, 111, 118, 123, 151, 163, 191*

planting and growth of vigorous churches all over the area. Trained leaders are scarce and there is only one Bible School giving instruction in Arabic in the entire world.

Pray for the converts out of Islam, that they may walk closely with the Lord and that they may witness boldly, but tactfully, to win their countrymen to Christ.

Pray for a missionary vision among Arab Christians. Arab missionaries would be more acceptable than Westerners in many lands. There are now about 230 Middle Eastern missionaries, mostly from Egypt, Syria, and Jordan, who are serving the Lord in other Middle Eastern countries. Pray the Lord of the harvest to send forth many more missionaries into the harvest.

Pray for Christian medical workers. This work opens up countries and individual hearts to the Gospel. This is the only way in which missionary work can be done in Yemen, some of the countries bordering the Persian Gulf, and Afghanistan. Pray that this ministry may create more and more opportunities to witness to Muslims. Pray for more Christian medical workers.

Pray for the wider distribution of Gospel recordings and cassette tapes. These are proving to be splendid tools of evangelism and Christian teaching in regions that can never be visited by missionaries.

Pray for the thousands of Muslim students and workers in Europe and in North America who are more accessible than they were in their own country. Pray for all involved in ministering to these people. Pray that converts from this ministry may become effective evangelists when they return home.

Pray for the countless villages and towns that have never welcomed a preacher of the Gospel. Pray especially for Muslim women in many lands who are virtually inaccessible in their prison-like seclusion. Pray for the nomadic tribes of the deserts of North Africa, Arabia, and Iran.

Pray especially for the closed lands of Mauritania, Libya, Saudi Arabia, South Yemen, and Qatar, that they may soon be penetrated by messengers of life and peace through Jesus Christ our Lord.

Pray that there may be a widespread awakening in North America and Europe regarding the Muslim world, that there may be love and compassion and a genuine burden for these people, a real longing to bring them to Christ.

Most of all, *pray* that the Lord will raise up a mighty army of PRAYER WARRIORS to intercede day and night for the Muslim world.

The Muslim World

Please pray for at least one of these countries each day.

COUNTRY	1986 POPULATION (MILLIONS)[1]	%MUSLIM[2]	%PROFESSING CHRISTIAN[3]	%ADULT LITERATE[4]	NORTH AMERICAN MISSIONARIES[5]	PEOPLE PER MISSIONARY[6]
AFGHANISTAN	15.4	99+	—	10 ('84)	7	2,200,000
ALGERIA	22.8	99+	0.8	52 ('84)	10	2,280,000
BAHRAIN	0.4	95.0	2.8	40 ('82)	10	40,000
BANGLADESH	104.1	86.0	.5	25 ('84)	225	462,000
BENIN	4.1	15.0	23.0	11 ('84)	93	44,000
BULGARIA	9.0	10.0	26.0	95 ('83)	0	—
BURKINA FASO	7.1	16.0	8.0	7 ('84)	158	44,936
CAMEROON	10.0	22.0	55.0	65 ('85)	216	46,000
CHAD	5.2	44.0	33.0	17 ('80)	69	75,362
COMOROS	0.5	99.7	0.2	58 ('77)	6	83,333
DJIBOUTI	0.3	90.6	8.7	17 ('85)	0	—
EGYPT	50.5	81.8	6.2	44 ('85)	110	459,000
ETHIOPIA	43.9	31.0	57.0	18 ('85)	145	302,758
GAMBIA	0.8	85.0	3.3	12 ('77)	23	34,782
GHANA	13.6	16.0	63.0	30 ('83)	235	57,872
GUINEA	6.2	68.0	1.3	48 ('83)	13	476,923
GUINEA BISSAU	0.9	38.0	10.0	15 ('85)	9	100,000
GUYANA	0.8	9.0	52.0	86 ('85)	21	38,095
* INDIA	785.0	11.6	3.9	36 ('81)	614	1,213,550
INDONESIA	168.4	89.0	8.5	64 ('81)	1118	150,626
IRAN	46.6	98.0	0.9	48 ('80)	0	—
IRAQ	16.0	96.0	3.0	70 ('84)	0	—
IVORY COAST	10.5	24.0	32.0	41 ('84)	365	28,767
JORDAN	3.7	93.0	5.0	31 ('80)	80	46,250
KENYA	21.0	6.0	73.0	50 ('85)	1,237	16,976
KUWAIT	1.8	95.0	4.0	71 ('85)	6	300,000
LEBANON	2.7	37.0	51.0	75 ('84)	78	34,615
LIBERIA	2.3	21.0	35.0	24 ('84)	412	5,582
LIBYA	3.9	98.0	0.3	60 ('85)	0	—
MALAWI	7.3	16.2	64.5	25 ('85)	159	45,911
MALAYSIA	15.8	49.4	4.8	75 ('83)	104	151,923
MALDIVES	0.2	99+	0.1	80 ('84)	0	—
MALI	7.9	80.0	0.9	10 ('84)	145	54,482
MAURITANIA	1.9	99.4	0.3	17 ('85)	2	950,000
MAURITIUS	1.0	16.4	33.0	79 ('85)	14	71,428
MOROCCO	23.7	99+	0.2	70 ('80)	31	764,516
MOZAMBIQUE	14.0	13.0	40.0	14 ('85)	22	636,363
NIGER	6.7	88.0	0.3	8 ('84)	148	45,270
NIGERIA	105.4	45.0	49.0	30 ('84)	672	156,845
OMAN	1.3	99.0	0.3	20 ('83)	12	108,333
PAKISTAN	101.9	97.0	1.4	24 ('84)	269	378,810
PHILIPPINES	58.1	4.3	94.0	88 ('83)	1758	33,048
QATAR	0.3	92.0	3.3	60 ('85)	0	—

(continued)

The Muslim World (Continued)

COUNTRY	1986 POPULATION (MILLIONS)[1]	%MUSLIM[2]	%PROFESSING CHRISTIAN[3]	%ADULT LITERATE[4]	NORTH AMERICAN MISSIONARIES[5]	PEOPLE PER MISSIONARY[6]
SAUDI ARABIA	11.5	99.0	0.2	24 ('84)	6	1,916,666
SENEGAL	6.9	91.0	5.7	10 ('84)	206	33,495
SIERRA LEONE	3.7	40.0	9.0	15 ('84)	142	26,056
SOMALIA	7.8	100.0	—	5 ('84)	38	205,263
SUDAN	22.9	73.0	6.5	20 ('85)	126	181,746
SURINAME	0.4	13.0	73.0	—	107	3,738
SYRIA	10.5	89.6	5.2	64 ('85)	2	5,250,000
TANZANIA	22.4	32.0	44.0	66 ('84)	252	88,888
TOGO	3.0	17.0	37.0	18 ('84)	111	27,027
TRINIDAD/TOBAGO	1.2	6.5	66.0	93 ('85)	69	17,391
TUNISIA	7.2	99.0	0.1	62 ('84)	9	800,000
TURKEY	52.3	99.0	0.4	70 ('85)	69	757,971
UGANDA	15.2	6.6	78.3	52 ('80)	96	158,333
UNITED ARAB EM.	1.4	97.0	1.3	56 ('85)	45	31,111
U.S.S.R.	280.0	11.0	25.0	99 ('85)	0	—
YEMEN (SOUTH)	2.3	91.0	4.0	39 ('80)	0	—
YEMEN (NORTH)	6.3	100.0	—	20 ('85)	27	233,333
YUGOSLAVIA	23.2	10.0	62.0	90 ('85)	12	1,933,333

* Although India's population is 83% Hindu, its 86 million Muslims make it one of the top four Muslim countries in the world following Indonesia, Pakistan, and Bangladesh.

Pray also for the millions of other Muslims in other countries of Africa, Asia, Europe and the Americas. There are an estimated 817 million Muslims worldwide.

Sources of information:
1. 1986 World Population Data Sheet of the Population Reference Bureau.
2&3. World Christian Encyclopedia (David Barrett Ed.) 1982
4. World Almanac and Book of Facts, 1987
5. Mission Handbook, 13th Edition, 1987
6. Column 1 divided by Column 5

Note: The total population for the 31 countries that are 80% or more Muslim, is 685,200,000. In these countries there are (or were, in 1985) 2604 missionaries, or one for every 263,133 people.

The total population for the 24 countries that are 90% or more Muslim is 363 million. The total number of missionaries in these countries is 833, one for every 435,800 people.

But not all of these missionaries are working with Muslims, and not all are evangelists. There may be only one evangelist for every million or more Muslims. Many are involved in medical work, or community development. Many are working with Hindus (as in Pakistan) or with animistic peoples, or with the few Christians in the land.

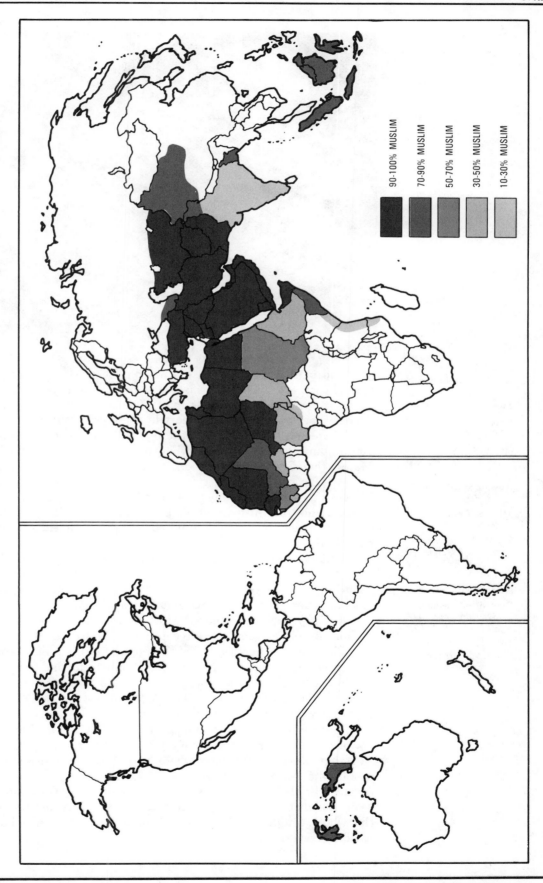

The Muslim World

90-100% MUSLIM
70-90% MUSLIM
50-70% MUSLIM
30-50% MUSLIM
10-30% MUSLIM

THE MIDDLE EAST

God is at work today in the Middle East. Muslims are more open to the Gospel than ever before. This is due to the dramatic political and social changes that are revolutionizing their lives. The teachings of Islam cannot meet the deepest needs of the human heart in these crisis times.

There are now about 230 Middle Eastern missionaries—largely from Egypt, Jordan, and Syria, who are serving the Lord in other Middle Eastern countries. Many other Christians also work in lands closed to normal mission work.[1]

Bible correspondence courses have been used of the Lord to win more Muslims to Christ than any other means. This is especially true of North Africa, Turkey, and Iran.[2] At least 60,000 people in the Middle East are enrolled in Bible correspondence courses, and hundreds are writing in each month professing their faith in Jesus.

Radio is also a very effective means of witnessing to Muslims. In some areas it is the most effective means.[3] Sometimes it is the "only" means. Gospel recordings and cassette tapes are proving effective in evangelism and Christian teaching in regions where missionaries cannot go.

In Egypt, several hundred Muslims are turning to Christ every year. The Nubian people are now more receptive to the Gospel than ever before.

The Coptic Church (13% of the population) is largely nominal. But an extraordinary revival within it has gained momentum and the present leadership is highly educated, articulate and Bible based. The present Patriarch gives weekly Bible studies to 7,000 people. These 5,000,000 Coptic Christians, if revived, could have a decisive impact on the Middle East.

The Christian witness among university students is encouraging. There is now a group in every faculty of Egypt's four big university complexes; even in the Al Azhar Muslim University where Muslim missionaries are trained.

In the Arabian Gulf States (85% Muslim), amazingly enough, there is freedom for all forms of Christian activity, except in Qatar and Kuwait. Pray for a continued open door for Christian work. A strong Arab Church here could affect the whole Middle East, for most countries in the area have some of their nationals working there.

The churches are growing and a considerable number of Indians and Pakistanis are being won to the Lord. There are strong churches in Kuwait, Bahrain, Oman, and the United Arab Emirates. There is considerable interest in Christianity among educated Arab young people.

In Jordan there is a great tolerance for the Christian minority for all forms of Christian activity. The long-lasting Middle East crisis has brought 30 years of suffering to this country, and this has made many Muslims more open to the Gospel. There has been revival in some Christian Churches and many Muslims are being converted. The outreach of believers has increased. More and more young people have been enthusiastic and involved in door-to-door visitation and tract distribution. Jordanian believers are serving the Lord all over the Middle East.

Most other Muslim lands in North Africa and the Middle East are closed to missionaries and hostile to national Christians, but even in such lands as Morocco, the number of believers is increasing more than ever before.

Until recently only about 5% of the people in North Africa and the Middle East were able to read. There is still a high rate of illiteracy. But as more of them learn to read, no doubt more and more people will begin to search the Scripture and be won to Christ. One government censor, objecting to the printing of Christian literature said, "The trouble with these books is that everyone who reads them wants to become a Christian."

Southwest Asia

Saudi Arabia, Syria, Lebanon, Jordan, Israel, Iraq, Iran,
P.D.R. of Yemen, and Afghanistan

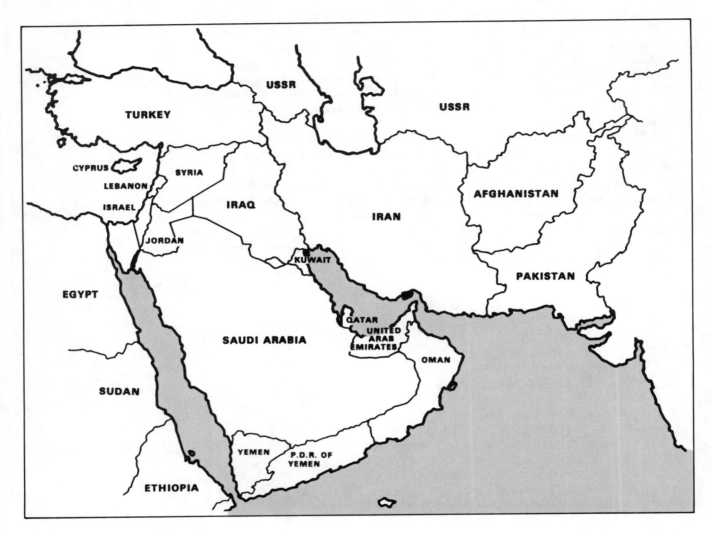

EGYPT

Christianity came to Egypt during the first century A.D. when, accordingly to tradition, St. Mark was the founder of the church at Alexandria.[1] By the end of the second century the church was very strong in Egypt.[2]

Perhaps the best known of all the Christian schools of the early church was the catechetical school in Alexandria, founded about A.D. 180 by Pantaenus. He was followed by Clement, and Clement was followed by the brilliant Origin. The school's primary purpose was the instruction of candidates for Church membership in the principles of the Christian faith. But it also became a center for advanced and creative thought and extensive literary activity.[3]

By the end of the 5th century there was hardly one city of any importance in all of Egypt that was without a bishop.[4] By this time the Scriptures had been translated into three Coptic (Egyptian) dialects, including one from the delta area and one from the southern part of the country.

But the Muslims captured Alexandria in 642 A.D. and within a few years they had overrun all of Egypt, and although Christianity was never totally wiped out, this ancient land has been predominantly Muslim since the 7th century. The Coptic *Orthodox* Church has survived over 1,300 years of Muslim Arab persecution and discrimination. Today about 13% of the total population are members of the Coptic Church, although not more than 10% of them attend services regularly.

The strongest Protestant Church in the Middle East is the Coptic *Evangelical* Church which was begun by three Presbyterian missionaries in 1854. During the past decade, this Coptic Evangelical Church has planted 50 new churches every year.

The churches today are faced with two major problems: conversion to Islam and emigration.

The Coptic Orthodox Church is losing 7,000 professing members every year. The main reasons for these conversions are the difficulties encountered by non-Muslims in finding employment, the desire to obtain positions in the administration, problems associated with mixed marriages (a Muslim woman is not allowed to marry a non-Muslim man), and the possibility of obtaining a divorce in cases where the church will not give permission.

The second problem is emigration, which has until recently affected mostly the other churches, but is now a major factor for Coptic Orthodoxy, also as evidenced by the formation of new Coptic Orthodox parishes in the U.S., Canada, and Australia.[5]

Despite the losses, the Christian community of Egypt (14% of the population) remains by far the most important numerically in the entire Arab world. The 6 million Coptic Christians, if truly revived, could have a tremendous impact on the Middle East.

Eighty-seven percent of Egypt's million people are Muslims, and in recent years the government has contributed much to the renewal of Islam internally and internationally, making Egypt the *major world center for modern Islam.* It established the Supreme Council for Islamic Affairs in 1960 with the purpose of extending Islamic culture in Egypt and overseas. In ten years the Council edited and distributed 8 million copies of works on Islamic culture in 14 languages. It makes financial grants for the construction of mosques and Islamic institutes throughout the world.

The University of Al-Azbar (founded in 973 A.D.) completely reorganized in 1961, has a Department of Culture and Islamic Missions. It has facilities for training 5,000 foreign students and from which numerous missionaries are sent to various countries of Africa, Asia, and Latin America.

Other institutes include Quran House which distributes the Quran (Koran), Radio Cairo which broadcasts daily Muslim religious programs to listeners in many foreign countries, and the Halibi Press which publishes the Quran and other religious books in many languages.

The Bible says "In that day there will be an altar to the Lord in the heart of Egypt, and a monument to the Lord at its border. It will be a sign and witness to the Lord Almighty in the land of Egypt. When they cry out to the Lord because of their oppressors He will send them a Savior and Defender, and He will rescue them. So the Lord will make Himself known to the Egyptians, and in that day they will acknowledge the Lord." (Is. 19:19-21 NIV). Pray that this promise may be fulfilled.

Praise God, there are encouraging signs of Muslims turning to Christ despite legal barriers. Several hundred Muslims are finding new life in Christ every year. But there are millions who have never really had an opportunity to hear a clear presentation of the Gospel, especially among the 2 million Nubians in southern Egypt and the million Bedouins and the Berbers in the western desert, but also among the Egyptian people themselves in Cairo and Alexandria and other cities and villages throughout the land.

There are about 80 missionaries serving in this land of the Nile, and there are more opportunities for the entry of expatriate Christians for service than there has been for many years. Pray for workers. Pray also for the growth of the missionary vision of the Christians in Egypt. Missionaries from Egypt would be more acceptable in other lands than missionaries from Europe or North America. The greatest problem is not the unwillingness of Egyptian believers, but the difficulty of supporting them financially when they go.[6]

Praise God, Christian literature is freely printed and sold, There are ten Christian bookstores in Cairo. Pray for the effective use of this literature and also for the raising up of more local believers who are able to write suitable evangelistic and teaching materials.

TURKEY

Christianity came to Turkey in the very first century through the efforts of the Apostles Paul and Andrew and John and many other great heroes of the faith. Many of the early church councils that were so important in the shaping of doctrine were held in present-day Turkey! Because of the extension of the Roman Empire into Asia, the emperors since Diocletian (284-305) had considered it necessary to have an eastern capital in Asia Minor (Turkey) as well as a western capital in Italy. Before Constantine, various cities had been used. But Constantine built a new capital.

One of the apparent reasons for building this new capital was to create a powerful center for Christianity, to which he had been converted. This could have been difficult to accomplish in the older cities, filled as they were with worshipers of the old pagan gods.

This was the beginning of the Eastern Roman Empire (also called Byzantine Empire or Byzantium after the ancient community that had occupied the site of Constantinople (now Istanbul). The core of the empire was Asia Minor and the Balkan peninsula south of the Danube River. At times the boundaries extended as far as Italy, Mesopotamia, and North Africa.

Centering around the first great city to be founded on Christianity, Byzantium developed the Eastern Orthodox branch of Christianity, converted the Slavic peoples, and defended the faith against Muslim attackers for nearly 800 years, until the Ottoman Turks overran Constantinople in 1453. But long before that date, Muslim invasions weakened the Orthodox hold on the people. The Crusades (1096-1272 A.D.) also did much damage to the cause of Christianity in that part of the world.

Islam's influence continued to grow during the Ottoman Empire which lasted until 1922. Christianity was still a sizeable force of over 20% of the country at the beginning of World War I in 1914. Between 1915 and 1917, however, over 600,000 Armenians and Chaldean Christians were massacred by Turks and over 600,000 more Armenians were deported. In 1923 there was a forced exchange of 1.5 million Greek Orthodox in Turkey for Turkish Muslims in Greece. Since then, through slow but steady emigration, the number of Christians has been steadily decreasing. As late as 1955, sixty of the 80 Greek Orthodox churches in Istanbul were destroyed.

Today only about 6/10 of one percent of Turkey's 52 million people are Christians. Most of them are in Istanbul or in the south eastern part of the country near the Syrian border. A few can be found in Ankara and a few in Ismir (formerly Smyrna). Conversions from Islam are very rare, and children of mixed marriages almost always become Muslim.

The dominant ethnic group is the Turkish people who originated as tribal peoples east of the Caspian Sea and in Northwest China. As their grazing lands became arid, they were forced westward in search of new pastures. In the process they were converted to Islam by Arab and Persian missionaries. They remain one of the few peoples of the Middle East with almost no history of Christian evangelization.

The Turks are a widely scattered people with several dialects. All told, there are an estimated 165 million of them—and 95% of them are Muslims. More Turks actually live outside of Turkey than in the country. There are 38 million in the Soviet Union, 40 million in the Republic of Turkey, 7 million in the People's Republic of China, 7 million in Iran, and 2 million in Afghanistan. Significant numbers of Turks are also found in Bulgaria, Cyprus, Greece, Romania, Syria, Iraq, Yugoslavia, Western Europe and even in Mongolia.

About 7 million of the inhabitants of Turkey (13%) are the Kurds. Although they've inhabited the area for 3,000 years, the homeland of the Kurdish people is divided between five independent countries: mainly Turkey, Iraq and Iran, but also with significant numbers in Syria and the U.S.S.R.

Political factors as well as the natural obstacles of its mountainous terrain have kept the Kurds economically underdeveloped and backward. All but a small minority of them are illiterate, and the governments of Turkey and Iran do not allow the publication of any literature in their language.

In Biblical times, the Kurds were known as the Medes. They once followed the Zoroastrian religion of ancient Persia but most have followed Islam since their conquest by the Arabs in the 7th century. Only one small group of Kurdish Christians is known to exist, and for the most part, the Kurds have had almost no opportunity to hear the Gospel.

Another five percent of Turkey's population are Arabs. Smaller groups include Greeks, Armenians and Bulgarians, The adult literacy rate for Turkey is about 60%, which is high for a Muslim country.

Ninety-nine percent of the people are Muslims. Though Turkey by constitution is a secular state, Islam is on the move. New mosques are being built and Islamic literature is on the increase. The Koran is now available in Turkish. Since 1965 Islam has been taught in the schools.

The Christian minority includes 175,000 Eastern Orthodox, 20,000 Roman Catholics, and 10,000 Protestants. Most of the Protestants are either Armenian or Assyrians. Missionary work is extremely difficult. An embargo on the import of foreign language Scriptures has caused hardship to the small Greek and Armenian Christian communities.

In recent years several outside groups, such as Operation Mobilization, have engaged in widespread distribution of Christian literature and Bible correspondence courses. OM has been responsible for about two-thirds of the Scriptures sold in Turkey. Some of their workers have been arrested and spent time in prison. Some conversions have come through this effort. Pray for these summer teams of young people who distribute the literature. Pray for the recipients of the materials, for interest to write, and for the effectiveness of correspondence courses.

The few Turkish believers need much prayer for they are under constant pressure to leave the Christian faith and return to Islam. There are no Turkish speaking churches, just three or four small and unstable fellowships. They lack a warm fellowship where they can feel at home and can encourage and strengthen one another.

Many converts leave the country because of the difficulties. Pray that more may be willing to suffer for Jesus and be a witness in this land.

Missionaries are not officially permitted, but God has raised up a dedicated force of professionals in universities and hospitals who are contributing much to the establishment of a nucleus of the Turkish Church in the major cities. Many are teaching English as a second language and using their daily contact with their students to share their faith with them. Pray for their continued, fervent but tactful witness, despite much oppostition and even eviction from the country.

PAKISTAN

With the passing of British rule from the Indian subcontinent in 1947, two nations emerged. One was predominantly Hindu, the other predominantly Muslim. But the Muslim state was divided into two parts—East and West Pakistan—separated by nearly 1,000 miles of India. The first few weeks of independence witnessed one of the greatest upheavals in history. Six million Muslims left India for Pakistan, and four million Hindus fled from Pakistan to India. In just two weeks an estimated 500,000 people were killed. That's more than were killed in U.S. military forces in all of World War II.

Shortly after its birth, *Time* magazine characterized Pakistan as "an economic wreck—every tenth person a refugee, the government non-existent and the economy incredibly backward." Since 1947 the history of Pakistan has continued to be turbulent. In a five year period there were six prime ministers. Corruption was so bad that in 1959 the military seized control and sent the politicians home. For ten years the country was ruled by General Ayub Khan until he, too, was deposed after five months of rioting.

In 1971 war broke out between East and West Pakistan, resulting in two separately ruled countries. East Pakistan's name was changed to Bangladesh. We'll hear more about Bangladesh later.

West Pakistan, known now simply as "Pakistan", has continued to see turbulent times. Its greatest problem, perhaps, has been its dispute with India over Kashmir. War has broken out on several occasions. The prolonged dispute has soured Pakistan's national spirit, drained its meager resources, and driven it into the arms of the Peoples Republic of China on the mainland.

Due largely to perennial drought, the people of Pakistan are extremely poor, even by Asian standards. One of the major problems is illiteracy. Only twenty percent of the adult population is able to read and write. Many towns and villages are totally or almost totally blind to the printed page. Muslim Pakistan crowds its more than 99 million people into an area a little larger than Texas. Eighty percent of the nation is rural, living generally in little semi-isolated villages. A family depends upon the fruits of a few small fields for its entire subsistence. Village life is just about the same today as it was a thousand years ago. The average farmer lives in a one or two-room mud and straw home with little or no furniture, no electricity, running water or sanitary facilities.

Purdah, the Muslim custom of secluding women in their homes or behind a veil in public, is still a common practice. Most of the Muslims accept Purdah, believing Allah wishes it and there is no other way.

Life for the city dwelling Pakistani is vastly different from that of the villager. In the city Islam's grip is not as tight, tradition not as important. An increasing number of young people are leaving their villages for exciting but disillusioning city life. Women are shedding their burkas and delving into the professional world.

While millions of Hindus fled from Pakistan in 1947, some remained in their homeland. Today 1.5% of the inhabitants of Pakistan are Hindus. Another 1.5% are Christian. But the vast majority in Pakistan (97%) are Muslims.

Islam is deeply rooted in Pakistani government, culture and way of life. Intricately designed mosques protrude from the heart of every city. The call of the muezzin, the religious leader, triggers the prayer ritual five times a day. Wherever they are, on a street, in the field or upper berth of a train the Muslim places his mat, kneels toward Mecca and prays.

Mohammed, Islam's revered prophet, strongly believed in forcible conversion. Muslims actively propagate their religion. Though a Muslim accepts much

Cross-References

Bangladesh, *6, 34, 55, 59, 65, 69, 81, 85, 92, 100*

China, *4, 7, 9, 29, 31, 34, 91, 100, 116, 121, 215*

East Pakistan, *81*

of the Jewish and Christian background, they believe the Koran is Allah's final word to man. Jesus Christ was a great prophet, they believe, but not as great as their Mohammed.

Response to the Gospel among Muslims has always been slow. One reason for their reluctance to become Christians is the fact that they are often persecuted by their own countrymen and even by the members of their own family when they leave the Muslim faith. Another reason is that few Muslims are prepared to associate with Christians who are usually socially poorer and basically of low-caste Hindu origin. But the greatest reason for their lack of response to the Gospel of Jesus Christ might well be that they just haven't had much opportunity to hear the Word of Life. Ninety percent of the missionaries give most of their time to bringing God's Word to the 3% who are nominal Christians or Hindus. Pray for more missionaries who have a burden for the Muslims and who will be well-equipped to work among them.

There are many, many unevangelized areas such as the Baluchistans in the west with its very small church, and the many warlike Muslim tribes of the Northwest Frontier with Afghanistan. There are many other people groups in isolated valleys of the north that have begun showing interest in the Gospel. These include the Chitral, 15,000; the Hunza, 100,000; the Kohistan 50,000; the Gilgit, 150,000; the Nagiri, 50,000; and the Baltistan 50,000; all of whom are Muslims. There is no permanent Christian work among any of these people and they remain in darkness.

Pray, too, for the nominal Christians, that they would have a greater concern for the evangelization of the Muslims and for their reception in the churches. Cultural and social barriers make it difficult for the believers to be bold because of their low social standing. Leadership training is vital. Pray especially for the developing of TEE (Theological Education by Extension). This is an extremely valuable means of leadership training in Pakistan because of the many small, scattered groups of Christians. The development is hindered by lack of personnel and time to prepare materials in local languages.

There are many opportunities in evangelism, church planting, Bible teaching and in various other ministries. But there's only one missionary in Pakistan for every 330,000 people. Pray for more laborers—especially from Britain and Canada, for workers from these nations need no visas.

BANGLADESH

This impoverished land, formerly known as East Pakistan, is one of the most densely populated countries in the world. Its hundred million inhabitants are jammed into an area no larger than the state of Iowa. Due partly to its over-population, but also because of periodic disasters such as devastating floods and hurricanes, Bangladesh is one of the poorest countries on the face of the earth. There seems to be little hope that the poverty of this unhappy land will ever be substantially alleviated.

With help from India, Bangladesh won its independence from Pakistan in 1971 after very bitter fighting. Instability and corruption have marked the subsequent years, culminating in a coup that brought in the military government in 1976.

Eighty-five percent of the country's inhabitants are Muslims; fourteen percent are Hindus. The remaining one percent are about half Buddhists and half nominal Christians.

Why are there so few Christians? For one thing, Bangladesh is one of the most neglected parts of the non-Christian world, with only one missionary for every 400,000 people.

The first missionaries came to Bangladesh (then part of India) in 1795. But Muslims in Bangladesh, as in Pakistan and the Middle East have always been very resistant to the Gospel. Most of the churches that exist are in the rural areas where illiteracy and poverty are continuing problems. There are a few Bible schools, but graduates cannot always find full-time employment, for the churches are extremely poor. How tragic when eighty percent of this land is still unevangelized.

But Bangladesh is open for the Gospel. Christian aid in times of national disaster has proved to be a dramatic stimulus to church growth in some areas due to the impartial love and sympathy of the Christians, This demonstration of love has led to a surge of people into the tribal churches, to a large number of Hindu inquirers, and a few Muslim converts. There are now about 2000 Muslims and Hindus converted every year.

The church is very small, and half the believers are among the tribal peoples that make up only two percent of the population. These tribal churches have been growing through people movements, and perhaps up to fifteen percent of these people are now Christian though there is much nominalism and lack of understanding of the Gospel.

Only four of the 28 languages have been reduced to writing, and most of these tribes have no Scriptures. The work is growing among the Garos (Baptists), Santalis and Khasi (Lutherans) and several other tribes. But many tribal groups are still unreached, such as the Koch, the Hajong, the Banai, the Murung,and the Mogh.

The overwhelming majority of the inhabitants of Bangladesh speak Bengali which does have the entire Bible and Bible correspondence courses. Bible correspondence courses have proved to be the best way to reach Muslims and Hindus. More than 12,000 papers a month are being processed. Enrollment has more than doubled since 1971. More is being done to personally follow up the students and hold follow-up rallies.

There is an unprecedented demand for Christian literature. The Bible Society reports a tenfold increase in the distribution of Scripture portions. There is also a large increase in sales of all Christian literature. This is largely due to the success of the Bible Correspondence courses and the effective mass distribution of evangelical literature. Unfortunately, the vast majority of the Bengali people are illiterate. If more of them could read, no doubt a lot more of them would be taking the Bible correspondence courses and reading other Christian literature and finding new life in Christ.

Pray that Christians in Bangladesh will devote more time to teaching people to read and using this opportunity to share their faith with their students on a regular basis. Pray also for more Bible translators to translate God's Word into the many languages that are as yet without a single word of Scripture. Pray for more evangelists, church planters, and Bible teachers, for the harvest is great; the souls are precious; the time is short; and the workers are so very, very few.

INDONESIA

Indonesia includes 13,500 islands including Java (one of the most densely populated areas in the world with 1,500 persons per square mile), Sumatra, Kalimantan (most of Borneo), Sulawesi (Celebes), and Irian Jaya (West Irian, the western half of New Guinea). The total land area is 741,101 square miles, about one-fourth that of the 48 contiguous states in the U.S.A. Eighty-four percent of the people are Muslims, 10% are Christians, 3.3% are Hindus (mostly on Bali), and about 1% are animist. The population in 1985 stood at 168,400,000.

One of the most significant movements to Christianity in history occurred recently in this great nation. This is the only country in the world where large numbers of Muslims have turned to Christ. The number of Christians increased 40% in the 1960's and has been increasing steadily since then at a rate of 5.5% annually—about two and a half times the population growth rate. In one recent six-month period, 163 churches were started for former Muslims who were converted by reading Christian ads in Muslim publications.

Evangelical missions have at least 17 first class Bible schools from which a stream of evangelistic teams have gone out all over the country and to other lands. These teams have been the cause of people movements in Irian Jaya (formerly Western New Guinea), Kalimantan (formerly Borneo), South Sumatra, and Java, and of the dramatic revival in Timor. Some have gone to Pakistan, Thailand, and West Africa and have met with great success.

On the island of Timor (pop. 2,500,000), some 200,000 were baptized in a three year period. Now many of these people are carrying the Gospel Message to other islands, to South America, and other parts of the world.

On the large island of Kalimantan with six million inhabitants, a great people movement is in progress among the majority Dayak tribes, with thousands seeking the Lord every year. Strong, nationally-led churches are springing up and are helping to reach out to the many other tribes.

A thriving ethnic church is found among the six million Chinese scattered throughout Indonesia. Twelve percent of the total Chinese population are now Christians and the number is increasing steadily.

The students of Indonesia are a ripe harvest field. There are wonderful opportunities to teach the Bible in primary and secondary schools, and also to witness to the 250,000 university students in 24 universities.

There is a tremendous hunger for evangelistic literature even though most Indonesians are poor readers.

Indonesia

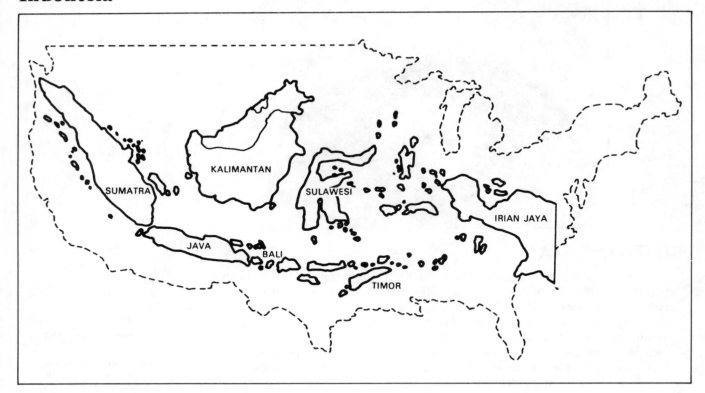

The Spirit of God is moving mightily in Indonesia, but there is still much to be done. While hundreds of thousands of Muslims have come to faith in Jesus Christ, the Church is not fully able to take advantage of the great openness of the Muslim Javanese to the Gospel.

Then too, there are 838 languages in Indonesia. Nine have the entire Bible. Nineteen have the New Testament, and 28 others have Scripture portions. Work is in progress in 33 other languages mostly in Irian Jaya. In most of the languages that do have Scripture, there is very little other Christian literature; national Christian writers are sorely needed. There is also a great need for literacy workers, since 40% of Indonesia's adults and teenagers cannot read.

Praise God for all that He is doing in Indonesia and pray the Lord of harvest to send more laborers into His harvest to take full advantage of the openness of these people to the Gospel.

Literacy in the Muslim World
1900 to 1980

COUNTRY	1900	1950	1975	1980
AFGHANISTAN	0%	4%	12%	13%
ALGERIA	12	18	27	29
BAHRAIN	1	13	41	43
BANGLADESH	5	22	25	25
CHAD	0	3	10	11
COMOROS	0	50	60	61
DJIBOUTI	5	25	35	35
EGYPT	6	21	43	45
GAMBIA	0	3	10	11
GUINEA	6	10	11	11
GUINEA BISSAU	0	4	5	6
INDIA**	6	18	36	37
INDONESIA	9	30	63	64
IRAN	1	10	43	44
IRAQ	3	14	40	41
JORDAN	3	28	45	46
KUWAIT	2	27	60	62
LEBANON	10	60	86	87
MALDIVES	0	20	40	41
MALI	0	2	10	11
MAURITANIA	0	3	16	17
MAYOTTE	0	30	60	62
MOROCCO	3	10	23	24
NIGER	0	0	6	6
NIGERIA	2	11	25	28
OMAN	0	3	20	21
PAKISTAN	4	19	17	17
PALESTINE	13	40	70	72
QATAR	0	5	20	21
SAHARA	2	20	10	10
SAUDIA ARABIA	0	2	12	13
SENEGAL	0	4	12	13
SIERRA LEONE	0	3	10	11
SOMALIA	0	1	5	6
SYRIA	8	32	42	44
TUNISIA	3	14	38	40
TURKEY	4	32	60	62
UNITED ARAB EM.	1	15	25	26
UPPER VOLTA	0	1	11	12
YEMEN, N.	0	1	20	20
YEMEN, S.	0	2	20	21

* All statistics from World Christian Encyclopedia, 1982.

** Though India is predominantly Hindu, there are approximately 80 million Muslims in that country, making it the 4th largest Muslim country in the world.

SUGGESTED READING

TALES OF PERSIA
By William Miller
Toronto: Fellowship of Faith for Muslims

Choice missionary stories beautifully told for children, young and old, by one who served Christ in Iran for 40 years. (Hardback, $5.00)

I DARED TO CALL HIM FATHER
By Bilquis Sheikh
Toronto: Fellowship of Faith for Muslims

A truly unusual testimony of a high-born Pakistani Muslim lady finding Christ and living for Him against great odds. (Hardback, $7.95)

THE WORLD OF ISLAM
By John B. Taylor
New York: Friendship Press, 1979

"A good, factual account of Islam as Muslims might wish it to be presented." (Replaces "Introducing Islam" by J. Christy Wilson.)

THE DAGGER OF ISLAM
By John Laffin
Sphere Books, 1979

"An invaluable guide to the most explosive force on today's scene." Timely and vital reading for everyone. (184 pp., $2.50)

ALEXI AND THE MOUNTAIN TREASURE
By Anita Dyneka
Elgin, IL: David C. Cook Publ. Co. 1979

A story of youthful adventure in a little-known area of Central Asia where Muslims, Communists, and Christians mix. (111 pp.)

A STREET IN MARRAKECH
By Elizabeth Fernea
Doubleday, 1980

A personal encounter with the lives of Moroccan women. (382 pp. $6.25)

MIDDLE EASTERN MUSLIM WOMEN SPEAK
Ed. by Elizabeth Fernea and Basima Bezirgan
University of Texas Press, 1978

"Short biographies and autobiographies of Muslim women from a wide range of backgrounds . . . touching on major Muslim World themes. (413 pp.)

AFGHANISTAN, THE FORBIDDEN HARVEST
By J. Christy Wilson
Elgin, IL: David C. Cook Publ. Co, 1981

The challenging story of God's work in a "closed" fanatically Muslim land. An epic of Christian trial and triumph. (130 pp., $4.95)

TIDE OF THE SUPERNATURAL—A Call to Love the Muslim World
By Kundan L. Massey
Here's Life Publishers, 1980

A stirring and instructive story of God's working in the Islamic Middle East. (184 pp., $4.95)

DR. SA'EED OF IRAN
By Jay Rasooli and Cady Allen
Pasadena, CA: William Carey Library

The thrilling story of a Kurdish doctor, his struggles in turning from Islam to Christianity. A fabulous tale, more absorbing than fiction, yet all of it is true.

INTRODUCTION TO ISLAM
By Aubrey H. Whitehouse
Middle East Christian Outreach

An *excellent* introductory textbook, well designed for student participation. (91 pp.)

WHAT IS THAT IN YOUR HAND?
By Ilaim
Toronto: Fellowship of Faith for Muslims

A unique account of Muslims finding Christ and of the various gifts or talents in the missionary that God uses. ($1.50)

ESCAPE FROM ISLAM
By Hirji-Walji & Jaryl Strong
Wheaton: Tyndale House, 1981

A remarkable conversion story of a devout Muslim, exiled from Idi Amin's Uganda to USA. Gives important insights on a serious Muslim's transition from Islamic to Christian theology.

GUESTS OF THE SHEIK
By Elizabeth Fernea
New York: Doubleday & Company, Inc., 1969

An account of the author's two year stay in a rural village of Iraq. To help her anthropologist husband gather data, Mrs. Fernea assumes the dress and customs of the Iraqi women. She shares in the life of the harem, wearing the veil, learning Iraqi life from the women's point of view. (346 pp.)

LIKE AMIGHTY WIND
By Mel Tari as told to Cliff Dudley
Carol Stream, IL: Creation House, 1972

An account of God's miracles in Indonesia. God's power is revealed in such a way that many who have been held in the power of Satan can see that He alone is Lord. (171 pp.)

THE LIFE AND TIMES OF MUHAMMED
By Sir John Glubb
New York: Stein and Day, 1979

A sound, comprehensive work on the life, times and people of the Prophet. Sir John Glubb has spent more than half his life in Arab countries and writes for the laymen. (416 pp.)

MECCA AND BEYOND
By Edward and Rose Dodd
Boston, MA: The Central Committee on the United Study of Foreign Missions, 1937

A popular book intended for general use in Christian Churches. The authors were children of missionaries to the Muslims. This book presents the Muslim world before the oil discoveries wrought great changes in the Arab culture. (222 pp.)

GOD WAS A STRANGER
By Margaret Kirk
Robesonia, PA: OMF Books

Set in a crisis period of modern Indonesian history, this book tells the story of Chepto, a frustrated teenage boy searching for something worthwhile to do with his life. The lure of Communism ensnares many of his friends. In the midst of all this Chepto finds true meaning in the God who is no longer a stranger.

JAVA SAGA
By David Bentley-Taylor
Robesonia, PA: OMF Books

A comprehensive account of the Church in East Java, chiefly made up of converts from Islam and their descendants. Exciting story of how, in this relatively small area, Evangelicals have won to the faith a larger proportion of the Muslim population than anywhere else in the world.

REFERENCES

1. Watkins, Morris
1978 **Literacy, Bible Reading and Church Growth.** *Pasadena: Wm. Carey Library, page 49.*

2. Neill, Stephen
1964 **A History of Christian Missions.** *Baltimore: Penguin Books, page 63.*

3. Mathews, Basil
1952 **Disciples of All Nations.** *London: Oxford Press, page 43*

4. Johnstone, Patrick
1979 **Operation World.** *Bromley, Kent, England: STL Publications, page 133.*

5. Johnstone, Patrick
1979 **Operation World.** *Bromley, Kent, England: STL Publications, page 133.*

6. Johnstone, Patrick
1979 **Operation World.** *Bromley, Kent, England: STL Publications, page 134.*

7. Johnstone, Patrick
1979 **Operation World.** *Bromley, Kent, England: STL Publications, page 135.*

8. Johnstone, Patrick
1979 **Operation World.** *Bromley, Kent, England: STL Publications, page 135.*

9. Johnstone, Patrick
1979 **Operation World.** *Bromley, Kent, England: STL Publications, page 135.*

Egypt

1. Barret, David (ed.)
1982 **World Christian Encyclopedia.** *New York: Oxford University Press, page 275.*

2. Kane, J. Herbert
1971 **A Global View of Christian Missions.** *Grand Rapids: Baker Book House, page 10.*

3. Latourette, Kenneth Scott
1953 **A History of Christianity.** *New York: Harper & Row, page 147.*

4. Edman, V, Raymond
1949 **The Light in Dark Ages.** *Wheaton, IL: Van Kempen Press, page 76.*

5. Barret, David (ed.)
1982 **World Christian Encyclopedia.** *New York: Oxford University Press, page 275.*

6. Johnstone, Patrick
1979 **Operation World.** *Bromley, Kent, England: STL Publications, page 138.012*

TRANSLATION NEEDS

More than 3,200 different people groups—mostly in Africa, Asia, and the South Pacific—speak languages that have never been written down. They are, therefore, without a single word of Scripture in their mother tongue. Many of the speakers of these languages have been educated in the national or official language of their country—English, French, or Spanish, for example—and are able to read the Bible in that language. But there are an estimated 150 to 200 million people who can't read the official language or any other language that has even one chapter of the Gospel of Jesus Christ.

While many of these 3,200 languages are spoken by only a few hundred people, or in some cases less than a hundred people, it is also true that many of these Bibleless languages are spoken by hundreds of thousands or even millions of people.

Of the 5445 languages spoken in the world, 233 have the complete and adequate Bible, another 501 have an adequate New Testament, and 900 have some portion of God's Word. That leaves 3771 without any Scripture at all or less than the Gospel of Mark. Translators are working, however, in most of the languages that have portions of Scripture, and other linguists have recently begun the study of languages to reduce them to writing. Altogether, work is progressing in at least 980 languages.

Nevertheless, there are still at least 3000 languages that have never been written down and where no linguists have even begun to study the language.

About 1200 of these unwritten languages are spoken in Africa, another 1200 in Asia, 600 in the South Pacific and 200 in the Americas. That's a total of some 3600 languages worldwide that have never been written down, or have just recently been written down and have less than one book of the New Testament.

Many of these languages are spoken in countries that are closed to traditional kinds of missionary work, and in other countries the work of translation and literacy work and evangelism is greatly hampered by uncooperative or even hostile people, including Communist guerrillas in some instances. Even where the Bibleless people are friendly, there are the linguistic, cultural, and social barriers that must be overcome.

But there is good reason to hope that all of the unwritten languages of the world will be written down and will have at least the basic teachings of Christianity in print by the end of this century—if the Lord does not return before then. Many countries are wide open to the Gospel and are welcoming missionaries and cooperating with them in every way. Other governments are not really interested in the Gospel, but when linguists come with the proposal to analyze unwritten languages and teach their people to read and to prepare literature that will make them more healthful, more helpful, more productive, and more responsible citizens of their country—these linguists are warmly received.

At least 6,400 more linguists are needed—two for each of the 3,200 unwritten languages. But, especially in the larger people groups, it would be much better if there were at least three teams of workers—one team to concentrate on language analysis and translation, one team to concentrate on preparing literacy materials and teaching people to read and training national writers, and another team to concentrate on evangelism and church planting and training the ministry. Actually, three teams (six workers) should be the absolute minimum in a people group of just a few thousand people.

In addition to the teams that are working directly with a particular people group, many supportive workers are needed. Airplane pilots are needed to carry teams to remote jungle and mountain villages. Airplane and auto mechanics, teachers for the missionaries' children, buyers, bookkeepers, builders, printers, graphic artists, and many others must be found to perform these services so that the translators, literacy workers, and evangelists can concentrate on the work that they were sent to do. At least 12,000 workers are needed to give the Scriptures to these 3,200 people groups, train good leadership, and plant vibrant Christian churches among them. PRAY THE LORD OF HARVEST TO SEND FORTH LABORERS INTO HIS HARVEST!

Countries Ranked by Translation Need

	TOTAL LIVING LANGUAGES	DEFINITE NEED	POTENTIAL NEED	TOTAL DEFINITE AND POTENTIAL
Indonesia	583	69	385	464
Papua New Guinea	695	155	284	439
Nigeria	408	47	267	314
India	328	19	194	213
Cameroon	233	33	115	148
Zaire	192	24	114	138
Sudan	137	16	81	97
Tanzania	115	18	65	83
Chad	112	33	48	81
USSR	138	30	51	81
Vanuatu	107	2	78	80
China	115	45	32	77
Ethiopia	96	17	41	58
Burma	90	20	37	57
Laos	70	14	39	53
Mexico	236	33	20	37
Nepal	76	14	39	53
Brazil	152		42	50
Vietnam	62	28	17	45
Australia	121	2	42	44
Congo	55	6	35	41
Central African Republic	54	2	33	35
Malaysia, Sarawak	39	3	31	34
Malaysia, Sabah	50	12	21	33
Afghanistan	47	5	27	32
Pakistan	50	5	27	32
Philippines	151	10	22	32
Gabon	38	2	27	29
Benin	51	7	21	28
New Caledonia	39	5	23	28
Thailand	61	18	10	28
Ivory Coast	68	13	13	26
Solomon Islands	62	12	14	26
Ghana	60	4	20	24
Peru	86	8	15	23
Upper Volta	50	4	19	23
Iran	31	5	17	22
Kenya	55	2	20	22
Senegal	32	9	13	22
Togo	42	4	16	20
USA	158	6	12	18
Angola	30	2	14	16
Uganda	43	5	11	16
Guatemala	57	4	11	15
Malaysia, Malaya	28	1	14	15
Botswana	18	1	13	14
Colombia	75	6	8	14
Liberia	31	4	9	13

Source: Wycliffe Bible Translators' Ethnologue, 1984

Countries Ranked by Translation Need (Continued)

	TOTAL LIVING LANGUAGES	DEFINITE NEED	POTENTIAL NEED	TOTAL DEFINITE AND POTENTIAL
Guinea Bissau	19	6	5	11
Iraq	18	2	9	11
Italy	21	0	10	10
Kampuchea	14	5	5	10
Mali	21	3	7	10
Bangladesh	33	5	4	9
Mozambique	23	4	5	9
Paraguay	21	3	6	9
Algeria	15	0	8	8
Canada	70	3	5	8
Guinea	20	4	3	7
Micronesia	15	2	5	7
Niger	14	4	3	7
Turkey	30	2	5	7
Zambia	31	2	5	7
Equador	22	5	1	6
Gambia	13	5	1	6
Germany, West	11	0	6	6
Libya	8	2	4	6
South Africa	28	0	6	6
Argentina	21	3	2	5
Equatorial Guinea	9	1	4	5
France	18	1	4	5
Greece	15	0	5	5
Mongolia	9	4	1	5
Sierra Leone	20	4	1	5
Bhutan	7	1	3	4
Fiji	7	1	3	4
Sweden	9	0	4	4
Taiwan	14	4	0	4
Tunisia	6	0	4	4
Venezuela	37	1	3	4
Yugoslavia	16	0	4	4
Zimbabwe	19	1	3	4
Bolivia	38	2	1	3
Costa Rica	8	0	3	3
Egypt	6	0	3	3
French Polynesia	7	2	1	3
Malawi	13	0	3	3
Mauritania	5	2	1	3
Namibia	17	0	3	3
Norway	7	0	3	3
Oman	5	1	2	3
Poland	7	0	3	3
Saudi Arabia	3	0	3	3
South Yemen	5	0	3	3
Belize	9	0	2	2
Brunei	12	0	2	2
Cook Islands	5	0	2	2
Czechoslovakia	8	0	2	2

Source: Wycliffe Bible Translators' Ethnologue, 1984

Countries Ranked by Translation Need (Continued)

	TOTAL LIVING LANGUAGES	DEFINITE NEED	POTENTIAL NEED	TOTAL DEFINITE AND POTENTIAL
Finland	7	2	0	2
French Guiana	9	1	1	2
Israel	9	0	2	2
Kuwait	2	0	2	2
Monaco	3	0	2	2
Nicaragua	6	1	1	2
Surinam	16	1	1	2
Tonga	4	0	2	2
United Arab Emirates	2	0	2	2
Wallis and Futana	3	1	1	2
Anguilla	2	0	1	1
Antigua	2	0	1	1
Austria	7	0	1	1
Bahamas	2	0	1	1
Bahrain	3	0	1	1
Barbados	2	0	1	1
Belgium	7	0	1	1
British Indian Ocean Territory	4	0	1	1
British West Indies	2	0	1	1
Bulgaria	7	0	1	1
Chile	7	0	1	1
Cyprus	4	0	1	1
Denmark	5	0	1	1
Djibouti	4	0	1	1
Dominica	2	1	0	1
Dominican Republic	3	0	1	1
Grenada	2	0	1	1
Guyana	12	1	0	1
Haiti	3	1	0	1
Honduras	10	1	0	1
Hungary	6	0	1	1
Jamaica	2	0	1	1
Lesotho	4	0	1	1
Luxembourg	3	0	1	1
Macau	3	0	1	1
Maldives	1	1	0	1
Martinique	2	0	1	1
Morocco	5	0	1	1
Netherlands	3	0	1	1
Norfolk Island	2	0	1	
Panama	12	0	1	1
Pitcairn	3	0	1	1
Portugal	3	0	1	1
Qatar	3	0	1	1
Romania	13	0	1	1
Rwanda	3	0	1	1
Sao Tome e Principe	2	0	1	1
Somalia	5	0	1	1
Spain	5	0	1	1
Sri Lanka	5	0	1	1

Source: Wycliffe Bible Translators' Ethnologue, 1984

Countries Ranked by Translation Need (Continued)

	TOTAL LIVING LANGUAGES	DEFINITE NEED	POTENTIAL NEED	TOTAL DEFINITE AND POTENTIAL
St. Kitts-Nevis	2	0	1	1
St. Lucia	2	1	0	1
St. Vincent and the Grenadines	2	0	1	1
Syria	8	0	1	1
Tokelau	2	0	1	1
Trinidad and Tobago	3	0	1	1
U.S. Virgin Islands	5	0	1	1
Yemen	2	0	1	1

Source: Wycliffe Bible Translators' Ethnologue, 1984

Languages spoken in more than one country are counted in each country for purposes of this table.

'Potential Need' Includes 'Probable', 'Possible', and Unlikely Need' categories; all needing further survey.

These needs do not include the 'Needs Revision' catagory.

Note: By adding all the languages listed in column one, we get a total of 7766, which is 2321 more than the total living languages in the world. This is because many languages are listed for several countries. English, for example, is listed 74 times. The same holds true for the other three columns.

Bible Translation Status Estimates for Living Languages of the World, 1984

AREA	DEFINITE NEED	NT OR BIBLE NEEDS REVISION	PROBABLE NEED	POSSIBLE NEED	UNLIKELY NEED	ADEQUATELY BILINGUAL	NEARLY EXTINCT	TRANSLATION OF NT IN PROGRESS	HAS ADEQUATE NT	HAS ADEQUATE BIBLE	TOTALS	PORTIONS OF NT
NORTH AMERICA	38	2	1	33	0	114	56	99	74	2	419	(104)
CENTRAL AMERICA	5	0	0	13	0	1	4	33	17	0	73	(33)
CARIBBEAN	2	0	1	4	0	0	1	1	1	1	11	(1)
SOUTH AMERICA	32	2	2	70	5	26	29	143	59	0	368	(98)
AFRICA	221	18	67	851	41	17	13	250	152	97	1727	(226)
EUROPE	0	1	4	26	0	4	1	8	4	35	83	(23)
MIDDLE EAST	3	3	1	28	0	1	1	2	1	6	45	(3)
ASIA	244	20	40	880	4	39	12	240	109	78	1666	(239)
PACIFIC	176	21	16	392	4	37	16	176	82	14	934	(145)
AUSTRALIA	2	0	1	33	7	3	43	28	2	0	119	(28)
TOTALS	723	66	133	2330	61	242	176	980	501	233	5445	(900)

Each language is counted only once even if spoken in more than one country. Languages which have portions are mainly those with translation in progress.

Source: Wycliffe Bible Translators' Ethnologue, 1984

Bible Translation Status of Languages of the World (5445 Languages)

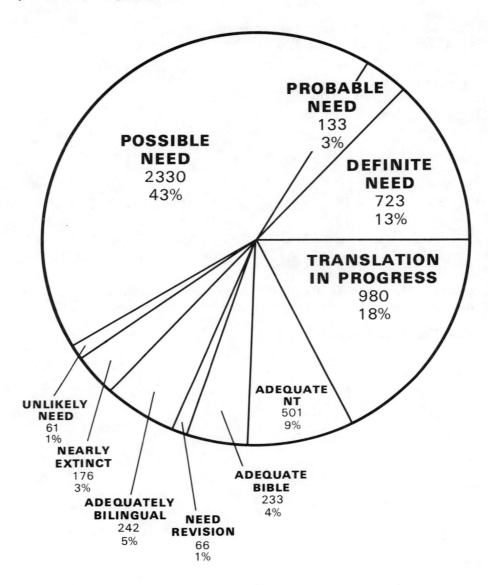

Total languages with some Scripture: 1634=30%

Scripture Portions only: 900=17%

Total Definite and Potential Need: 3247=60%
    (Potential includes Probable, Possible, and Unlikely languages still needing survey evaluation)

Each language is counted only once, even if spoken in more than one country.

Source: Wycliffe Bible Translators' Ethnologue, 1984

Geographical Distribution of Living Languages
(5445 Languages)

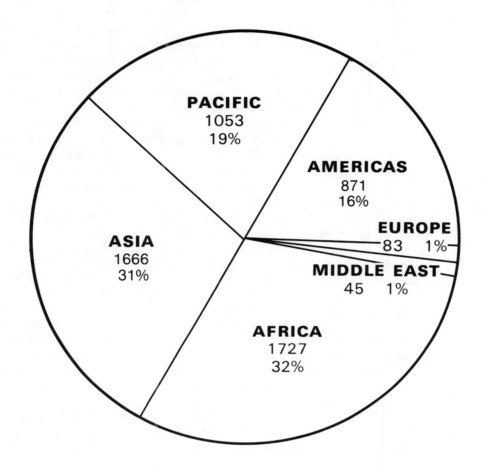

THE ILLITERATE WORLD

In addition to the 3,200 people groups that speak languages that have never been written down, there are hundreds of millions of adults and teenagers that can't read their own language, even though it has been written down for decades or even centuries. Some authorities estimate that 1.4 billion people over 12 years of age are unable to read or write. Ninety-seven percent of these people have some Scripture in their mother tongue. Most of them have the entire Bible or at least the New Testament. Millions of them have many other Christian books and magazines in their language. But what good does it do them if they can't read?

We have often heard, and know from personal experience, that one literate person can read the Bible or a Gospel tract to his illiterate friends and relatives, and that many of them will come to faith in Jesus. Praise God!

But we can't be satisfied with that. A billion illiterate unbelievers cannot be won to Christ in this manner, for there are hundreds of thousands of villages in the world where absolutely *no one* can read and where there is no Christian witness at all. The whole continent of Asia, with its 2.7 billion people, is less than three percent Christian. The Middle East (from Morocco to Afghanistan) is less than one percent Christian. If the Word of eternal life is ever going to make a significant impact upon these multitudes, thousands upon thousands of national pastors, teachers, evangelists, and writers must be trained.

But there can be no thorough training where people cannot read. And throughout the Muslim and Hindu and Buddhist worlds there are two to three million villages where no one, or almost no one, can read.

Some people say that the job is too big, we'll never teach everyone, or even a small fraction of the people, to read. "Besides," they say, "we can reach everyone with the radio and with TV." But that is just wishful thinking. These people are extremely poor. Very few of them have radios. In India there's only one radio for every 50 people. Villages have no electricity, and they can't afford batteries, so even if they were given the radios, they couldn't listen to them very long. But even if they could listen to the radio every day, they may never hear a gospel broadcast in their own language. Or a villager might hear the Good News about Jesus and he might hear about a Bible correspondence course that is being offered. But if he can't read and write, what good would it do to know about such a course? On the other hand, if he could read, he would be doubly blessed by having a radio and hearing about the Bible correspondence course and being able to take advantage of this opportunity.

We are not speaking against the radio. God forbid! We praise God for every Gospel and TV broadcast and for every Gospel film and cassette tape. But what we are saying is that these wonderful aids to the proclamation of God's Word are not enough for the planting of strong and vibrant Christian churches in the millions of villages where none currently exist and where there is not even one resident Gospel witness.

We should continue, yes, increase our use of radio and TV, films and cassettes in every language on earth. But even that will require at least some people in every language who can read the Scriptures and write scripts in their mother tongue.

Meanwhile, we must train all the pastors and teachers and evangelists and authors that we can possibly train, and we can't train them thoroughly unless they can read.

Even that is not enough. Every Christian ought to have the privilege of reading God's Word for himself. Indeed, if Christians are to grow in their faith, if they are to resist all the onslaughts of Satan, if they are to teach God's Word diligently to their children, if they are to comfort and edify one another, and if they are to be effective witnesses for Christ and shine as lights in this crooked and perverse generation, *they must read the Word of God daily*—that His Word may dwell in them richly.

Obviously it's going to take an army of very dedicated linguists to prepare all the literacy materials and all the Bible lessons and other Christian literature and to train all the national workers needed. It's a staggering need, but it is possible, for with God *all* things are possible. Pray the Lord of the harvest to send forth laborers into His harvest.

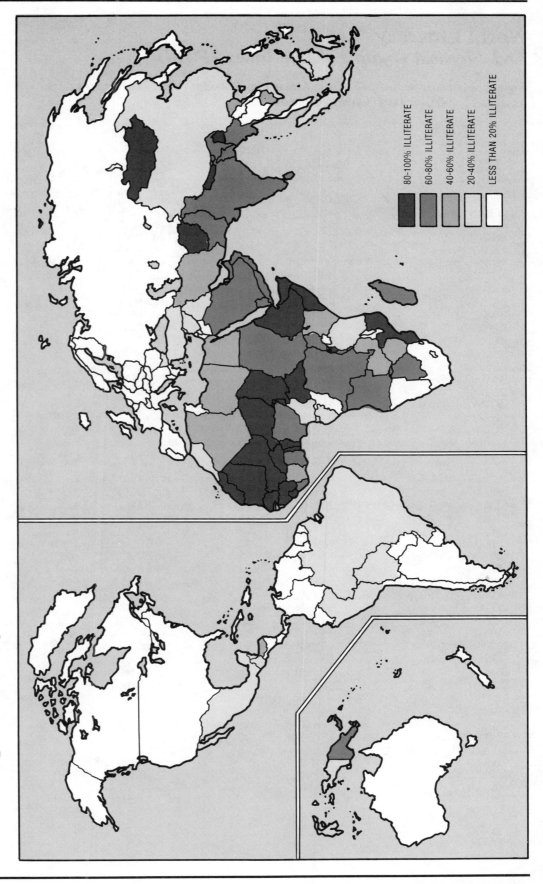

World Map of Illiteracy – 1987

80-100% ILLITERATE
60-80% ILLITERATE
40-60% ILLITERATE
20-40% ILLITERATE
LESS THAN 20% ILLITERATE

World Litteracy
And Physical Quality of Life Index (PQLI)

Figures obtained from the 1987 World Almanac and Book of Facts. The literacy rate is for ages 15 and over (at the year indicated).

COUNTRY	LITERACY (1987)	PERCENT 5-12 IN SCHOOL	COUNTRY	LITERACY (1987)	PERCENT 5-12 IN SCHOOL
AFGHANISTAN	10	13	FRANCE	99 ('84)	68
ALBANIA	75	—	GABON	65 ('85)	71
ALGERIA	52	55	GAMBIA	12 ('82)	17
ANGOLA	28	—	GERMANY E.	99 ('85)	66
ARGENTINA	94	59	GERMANY W.	99 ('85)	69
AUSTRALIA	100	73	GHANA	30 ('83)	45
AUSTRIA	98	65	GREECE	96 ('85)	69
BAHAMAS	93	—	GUATEMALA	48 ('84)	18
BAHRAIN	40 ('82)	60	GUINEA	48 ('83)	18
BANGLADESH	25 ('84)	35	GUINEA-BISSAU	15 ('85)	—
BARBADOS	99 ('84)	75	GUYANA	86 ('85)	62
BELGIUM	98 ('85)	58	HAITI	20 ('84)	32
BELIZE	80 ('85)	—	HONDURAS	55 ('84)	42
BENIN	11 ('84)	29	HUNGARY	98 ('83)	55
BHUTAN	10 ('85)	—	ICELAND	36 ('84)	70
BOLIVIA	75 ('83)	58	INDIA	36 (81')	42
BOTSWANA	35 ('85)	49	INDONESIA	64 ('81)	39
*BRAZIL	7 6 ('85)	51	IRAN	48 ('80)	51
BULGARIA	95 ('83)	57	IRAQ	70 ('84)	60
BURMA	78 ('84)	40	IRELAND	99 ('84)	72
BURUNDI	30 ('85)	10	ISRAEL	88 ('84)	62
CAMBODIA	48 ('80)	40	ITALY	98 ('84)	62
CAMEROON	65 ('85)	49	*IVORY COAST	41 ('84)	37
CANADA	99 ('85)	76	JAMAICA	76 ('84)	63
CENTRAL AFRICAN EMPIRE	20 ('83)	37	JAPAN	99 ('85)	71
CHAD	17 ('80)	16	JORDAN	31 ('80)	56
CHILE	90 ('83)	72	KENYA	50 ('85)	57
CHINA, (PRC)	75 ('84)	65	KIRIBATI	90 ('80)	
CHINA, (TAIWAN)	85	65	KOREA, N.	99 ('84)	61
COLOMBIA	82 ('81)	54	KOREA, S.	92 ('83)	65
COMOROS	15 ('85)	—	KUWAIT	71 ('85)	68
CONGO, PEOPLES REPUBLIC	80 ('80)	75	LAOS	50 ('81)	35
COSTA RICA	90 ('82)	58	LEBANON	75 ('84)	69
CUBA	96 ('85)	92	LESOTHO	65 ('84)	58
CYPRUS	99 ('84)	54	LIBERIA	24 ('84)	33
CZECHOSLOVAKIA	99 ('81)	60	LIBYA	60 ('85)	79
DENMARK	99 ('83)	70	LIECHTENSTEIN	100 ('86)	—
DJIBOUTI	17 ('85)	—	LUXEMBOURG	100 ('83)	59
DOMINICAN REPUBLIC	62 ('81)	51	MADAGASCAR	53 ('84)	48
DOMINICA	80	—	MALAWI	25 ('85)	32
ECUADOR	90 ('84)	60	MALAYSIA	75 ('83)	60
EGYPT	44 ('85)	44	MALDIVES	85 ('84)	40
EL SALVADOR	62 ('85)	50	MALI	10 ('84)	14
EQUAT. GUINEA	55 ('84)	45	MALTA	90 ('85)	69
ETHIOPIA	18 ('85)	12	MAURITANIA	17 ('85)	15
FIJI ISLANDS	80 ('85)	74	MAURITIUS	79 ('85)	63
FINLAND	99 ('85)	71	MEXICO	74 ('83)	64

World Literacy (Continued)
AND PHYSICAL QUALITY OF LIFE INDEX (PQLI) (continued)

COUNTRY	LITERACY (1987)	PERCENT 5-12 IN SCHOOL	COUNTRY	LITERACY (1987)	PERCENT 5-12 IN SCHOOL
MONGOLIA	89 ('83)	56	SPAIN	97 ('85)	66
MOROCCO	70 ('80)	29	SRI LANKA	87 ('85)	47
MOZAMBIQUE	14 ('85)	20	SUDAN	20 ('85)	26
NEPAL	23 ('81)	22	SURINAM	65 ('84)	—
NETHERLANDS	99 ('85)	63	SWAZILAND	65 ('85)	72
NEW ZEALAND	99 ('84)	81	SWEDEN	99 ('84)	72
NICARAGUA	87 ('83)	43	SWITZERLAND	99	62
NIGER	8 ('84)	11	SYRIA	65 ('85)	59
NIGERIA	25-35 ('84)	22	TAIWAN	89 '83)	—
NORWAY	100 ('84)	69	TANZANIA	66 ('84)	36
OMAN	20 ('83)	25	THAILAND	86 ('85)	47
PAKISTAN	24 ('84)	27	TOGO	18 ('84)	55
PANAMA	87 ('85)	68	TONGA	93 ('85)	—
PAPUA NEW GUINEA	25 ('84)	28	TRINIDAD & TOBAGO	93 ('85)	48
PARAGUAY	83 ('84)	52	TUNISIA	62 ('84)	50
PERU	72 ('78)	62	TURKEY	70 ('85)	49
PHILIPPINES	88 ('85)	55	TUVALU	96 ('79)	—
POLAND	98 ('85)	54	UGANDA	52 ('80)	27
PORTUGAL	80 ('85)	62	USSR	99 ('85)	58
QATAR	60 ('85)	60	UNITED ARAB EMIRATES	56 ('85)	35
ROMANIA	98 ('83)	64	UNITED KING.	99 ('84)	83
RWANDA	37 ('85)	27	UNITED STATES OF AMERICA	99 ('85)	85
ST. CHRISTOPHER & NEVIS	90 ('84)	—	UPPER VOLTA (BURKINA FASO)	7 ('84)	7
ST. LUCIA	78 ('84)	—	URUGUAY	94 ('82)	60
ST. VINCENT & GRENADINES	85 ('81)	—	VENEZUELA	85 ('84)	58
SAN MARINO	97 ('85)	—	VIETNAM	78 ('78)	62
SAO TOME & PRINCIPE	50 ('85)	—	W. SAMOA	90 ('83)	—
SAUDI ARABIA	24 ('84)	36	YEMEN, ARAB R.	20 ('85)	15
SENEGAL	10 ('84)	21	YEMEN, SOUTH	39 ('85)	80
SEYCHELLES	60 ('83)	—	YUGOSLAVIA	90 ('85)	60
SIERRA LEONE	84 ('85)	24	ZAIRE	28 ('85)	45
SINGAPORE	85 ('85)	59	ZAMBIA	54 ('84)	52
SOLOMON IS.	13 ('80)	—	ZIMBABWE	50 ('85)	39
SOMALIA	5 ('84)	19			
SOUTH AFRICA	98 ('82)	61			

Advantages of Literature
(Over the spoken word)

1. It can be secured and studied in secret.
2. It gets undivided attention in quiet hours.
3. It leaps language barriers and race tensions that often hamper personal contact.
4. It goes where the missionary cannot go.
5. It lives after spoken words are lost.
6. It is the most economical way of carrying out Christ's Great Commission.
7. It never needs a furlough.
8. It never gets sick.
9. It always speaks the language of the people without an accent.
10. It goes into the homes of the people and keeps repeating its message until they understand.
11. It is often more convincing than the spoken word. New literates especially have a tendency to believe everything they read.
12. Illiterates will often believe Scriptures when read to them before they will believe the testimony of another illiterate.

Advantages of a Literacy Program

1. It opens the door to the country. Government leaders know that literacy is the key to social and economic development.
2. It opens the door to various ethnic groups, once inside the country, for basically the same reason.
3. It opens the door to the individual heart.
4. It enables the church to train the ministry adequately through correspondence courses, theological education by extension, and in residence schools.
5. It provides Christians with an outlet for meaningful service and witness.
6. The ability to read helps church members grow spiritually and witness more effectively.
7. The ability of the laymen to read can help prevent false teaching in the church.
8. Literacy can help train strong national church leaders and build a strong national missionary church.
9. Scripture reading as a functional substitute can be used for spiritual gain.
10. Bible reading helps parents bring up their children in the nurture and admonition of the Lord.
11. Bible reading can help avoid syncretism.
12. Bible reading can help avoid materialism.

Those taught to read in church-oriented literacy programs are more easily drawn into other church activities. Participants in the literacy classes find it easy to invite family members and friends, thus utilizing "web relationships" for church growth.

Christian literature produced by national authors can speak in the culture of the people addressed. It can minister to the felt needs of the people in that culture. For example, if the people have a great fear of evil spirits, the literature could emphasize Christ's power over evil spirits. The missionary and the national author together could have a tremendous influence for Christ through such literature.

Africa—1984

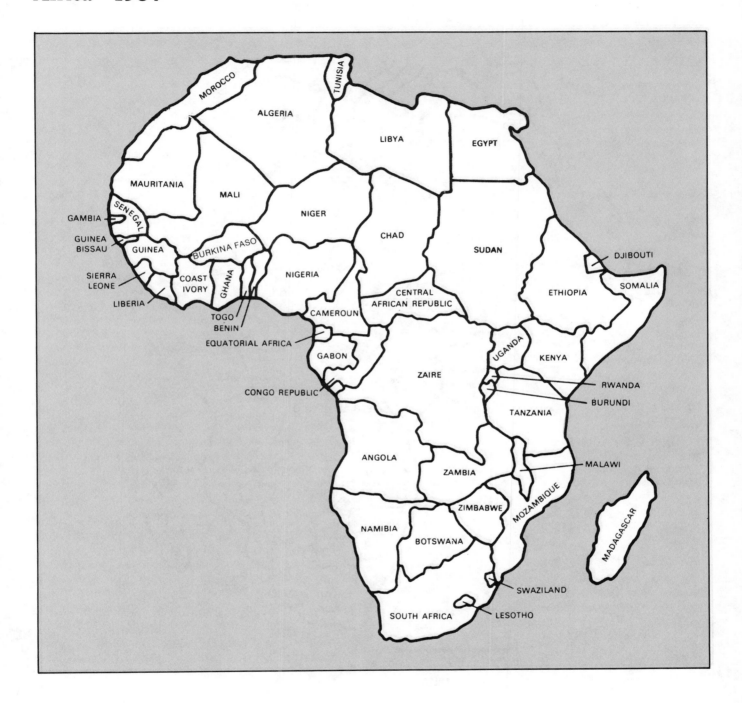

Africa—1914

TANGIER
IFNI
RIO DE ORO
MOROCCO
ALGERIA
TUNISIA
LIBYA
EGYPT
FRENCH WEST AFRICA
ERITREA
FR SOMALILAND
SOMALILAND PROT.
ANGLO
EGYPTIAN
SUDAN
GAMBIA
PORTUGUESE
GUINEA
SIERRA LEONE
LIBERIA
GOLD COAST
TOGO
RIO MUNI
NIGERIA
KAMERUN
EQUITORIAL AFRICA
ABYSSINIA
IT. SOMALILAND
FRENCH
UGANDA
PROT
EAST
AFRICA
PROT.
BELGIAN CONGO
GERMAN
EAST
AFRICA
NYASALAND PROT.
ANGOLA
RHODESIA
MOZAMBIQUE
MADAGASCAR
GERMAN
SOUTH-
WEST
AFRICA
BECHUA
NALAND
PROT.
SWAZILAND
UNION OF
SOUTH
AFRICA
BASUTOLAND

0   500   1000
STATUTE MILES

WEST AFRICA

At the beginning of this century only 8% of Africa was Christian; today 34% (52% South of the Sahara). In the midst of revolutionary change, insurmountable problems, and great insecurity, there is an unparalleled hunger for God's Word.

In Nigeria, Africa's most populous country, much is being done through training in some 40 seminaries and Bible Schools and through theological education by extension in many of the country's 395 languages. Bible teaching or Islamic teaching is compulsory in all Nigerian Schools. All children have to decide between Christianity and Islam.

The harrowing experiences of the civil war (1967-70) brought revival and a great spiritual deepening. One church doubled its membership to 240,000 in five years, and these people are reaching out to less evangelized tribes.

In the Middle Belt of Nigeria, many denominations experienced 400% growth over a period of ten years.

Nigerian churches now have at least 900 missionary couples in crosscultural mission work, in their own country and in Ghana, Benin, Chad, and Niger.

The well known Muslim Fulani (5,000,000 of them) are mostly nomadic cattle raisers that wander all over sub-Saharan Africa from Senegal to the Cameroon. Efforts to win these people are bearing fruit. There are now several hundred believers among them in Nigeria and several hundred more in Benin.

In the Ivory Coast there are unlimited opportunities for evangelism. The Church is growing at the rate of 25%-30% per year.

In Ghana, response to full page Christian ads in a popular newspaper has been excellent. The African Christian Press is now well known all over Africa for the excellent Christian literature which they produce, written by African authors.

In Guinea (less than 2% Christian), the Church has developed and matured greatly since the expulsion of most missionaries. In three tribes there is a mighty work of the Spirit in progress and hundreds are being converted each year and the tempo is accelerating.

The church is growing rapidly in Liberia and Sierra Leone as many tribes are receiving God's Word in their own language for the first time. The impact of Radio ELWA, located in Monrovia, has been immense, with an average of 6,000 letters per month from Liberia alone. Broadcasts in 46 languages are also prepared in studios in 3 other countries.

Burkino Faso (Upper Volta) is wide open to the Gospel. There are no restrictions on mission work.

Even in the Senegal (89% Muslim), Mali (77% Muslim), and Niger (87% Muslim) the Protestant Church is growing. The honesty, hard work, and love manifested by the Christians during the recent famines has given an unprecedented opening for these people.

Praise the Lord for the increase and pray for missionaries skilled in language analysis, Bible translation, literacy work, and in training the ministry by extension.

NIGERIA

Back in the 1840s and 1850s when the first missionaries came to Nigeria, this country (and all of West Africa for that matter) soon became known as the "White Man's Grave". Many missionaries died from malaria and other tropical diseases within a few months. Others had to return to their homeland, broken in health. But new missionaries kept coming, and because they did, there are millions of Christians in that land today where for centuries there had only been gross darkness and bondage to Satan.

There was almost constant tribal warfare. When a chief died several prisoners from an enemy tribe would be sacrificed and eaten. Sometimes the chiefs entire family would be buried with him to serve him in the future life. Sometimes they would even be buried alive.

In some tribes, when a mother died in childbirth, it was believed that the baby had an evil spirit, so it was thrown into the bush to die. If a woman gave birth to twins, it was believed that one of them was the child of the devil. Not knowing which one it was, both infants were killed. The mother of the twins was not permitted to get water from the area, and no one would have anything to do with her. These unfortunate mothers often committed suicide.

These evil practices continued into the 20th century and may still take place in some of the more remote parts of the country.

But thanks be to God, Satan's stronghold is being shattered and souls liberated from his dominion Today about 49% of Nigeria's 108 million people are Christians.

Another 45% are Muslims. For several years the Muslims were winning 14 animistic people to Islam for every one that was won to Christ. But all that has changed in recent years, and Christianity is growing faster than Islam and much faster than the general population growth rate.

Nigeria is by far the most populous country in all of Africa. In fact, there are more people in Nigeria than in all other countries of West Africa combined. About 2/3 of these people live in the southern 1/2 of the country, in the rain-soaked, insect-infested, fever ridden forests near the coast. The northern part of the country is desert and semidesert. Most of the people in the north are Muslims. There are also many Muslims in the southwest and a few in the southeast.

One of the most famous of all missionaries to Africa was Mary Slessor who labored in Southeastern Nigeria for 40 years (1875-1915). Known as the "White Queen of Calabar" her heroism is unmatched in the annals of missionary history.

Her influence over native chiefs, her administration of justice, and her success in abolishing intertribal warfare have made her a legend even to this day. Many other missionaries labored long and hard before Mary's arrival and during the same years, but at the turn of the century only 1% of Nigeria's 16 million people were Christian. By 1930 the country was still only about 5% Christian. But today, total church membership has risen to 48% and is growing more rapidly than ever.

Church growth has been slowest in the Muslim north, but mission work never got started there until 1901. In fact, it was the 1920s before work could be established in such northern centers as Jos and Kano. Even then there were many restrictions. But by the grace of God many souls have been won to Christ in this region and today the response to the Gospel is greater than ever.

The Republic of Nigeria received its independence from Great Britain in 1960. It was better prepared for independence than any other country in Africa, but political coups and counter-coups and assassinations marred the first decade of self rule. A bloody massacre of 500,000 Ibos, mostly in the north, sent 2,000,000 Ibos from all parts of Nigeria back to their own region in the southeast. The secession of the eastern region (Biafra) in 1967 set off a civil war that lasted two and a half years and cost the Ibos and other tribes a hundred thousand civilian lives, mostly from starvation. Although they suffered so much during the war, many of them in their hunger and poverty turned to the Lord. The Assemblies of God reported 60 new churches during the two and a half years that missionaries were excluded. The Sudan Interior Mission churches, mostly in the northern part of the country, doubled during the war, and have increased several times since then. The Qua Iboe Church in the southeastern part of the country doubled its membership in five years.

Hausa, with some 25-30 million speakers, is the major language of northern Nigeria. Iboe is the predominant language in the southeast and Yoruba is predominant in the southwest. Each of these languages is the mother tongue for some 12-15 million people. But there are another 392 languages spoken in Nigeria, some by a million or more people, some by 5000 or less. Only 9 languages have the entire Bible. Another 20 languages have the entire New Testament, and there are Scripture portions in an additional 62 languages. Work is in progress in 52 languages. Even if these 52 languages are included with the 62 that have some Scripture portions, more than 250 people groups are without a single word of God in their mother tongue and have no hope of getting any very soon. Pray for more translators, and pray for those working now, that they may translate God's Word accurately and clearly—that it may make the same impact on the hearers today that the original Scriptures made on the original hearers.

Pray, too, for adult literacy workers, for 75% of the adults and teenagers in Nigeria are not able to read their own or any other language. Hundreds of villages are almost totally illiterate. The situation is not improving very fast, for only 37% of the children of school age are in school.

Those who do attend school must study the Bible or the Koran, for Bible teaching or Islamic teaching is compulsory in all the schools. All children who attend school will have to choose between Christianity and Islam. Both Christians and Muslims are making a great effort to train teachers to take advantage of this opportunity. Pray that more Christians would go into the teaching ministry, that they may make full use of this chance to win young people.

Pray also for the training of more pastors and evangelists and Christian writers, for the need for more workers and for better-trained workers is far greater than the present supply. Pray especially for more evangelists to take advantage of the increasing interest in the Gospel among the Fulani and other Muslims in the north.

EAST AFRICA

All over Africa, south of the Sahara, Christianity is growing at a phenomenal rate. In Kenya there is more freedom to preach the Gospel than ever before, and the Church has grown dramatically. Over 70% of the population now claims to be Christian. Most of the Protestant churches are evangelical and evangelistic with mature Christian leaders.

In Tanzania, there is freedom to witness despite the growing influence of Socialism. For the first time, nearly the entire population can be relatively easily and freely evangelized. The hearts of the people are open to the Gospel as never before, and provision has been made in each village for the building of a church. The town churches are overflowing, and there is a marked hunger for God's Word in these days.

In Uganda, in spite of bitter persecution in recent years, 78% of the inhabitants of this land profess Christianity. Nominal adherence to petty legalisms that were creeping in have been partially swept away by the harsh time recently experienced. There are reports of full churches and of renewed outbreaks of revival in some areas.

In Rwanda, where Communist influence was once great, the door is open to the Gospel, and there is a spontaneous movement of the Holy Spirit in the Church. Many prayer meetings are springing up all over the country, nourished by the Scriptures and centered on Jesus.

In Ethiopia, the Protestant Church has grown dramatically during the last few years, especially in the south and southwest among the pagan tribes. Revivals, great people movements, the use of "New Life for All" and church growth principles gave the rapid increase in spite of wars, persecutions, famines, and wide-spread illiteracy. The missionary outreach of the national believers has played a vital role in taking the Gospel to hitherto unreached tribes. Hundreds of believers have gone out and planted new churches with great sacrifice and suffering—often in areas hundreds of miles from their home.

Many missions have done much relief work in the severe famines that have impoverished large areas of the country. This has opened up some areas in the unevangelized north to the Gospel, and has also opened some hearts among Muslims in the east.

The Gospel of John has recently been translated into Afars and is making a favorable impact on these Muslim people in Ethiopia and neighboring Djibouti.

Somalis, formerly very resistant to the Gospel, have been more opened to the Word of Life due to relief given by missionaries in the recent severe famine.

With hundreds of new church groups springing up in East Africa every week, there is a very critical need for well-trained church leaders. Otherwise the blind will be leading the blind. There is also a tremendous need for Bible translators, literacy workers, national writers, and others skilled in preparing Bible extension courses and in training the ministry by extension. Pray the Lord of harvest that He will thrust forth laborers into His harvest.

KENYA

Kenya, straddling the equator in East Africa, is the best known country on that continent. It is a land of big game animals where adventure-loving people like to go on safari. It is a beautiful land, especially in the south where 85% of the people live.

Kenya is about twice the size of Nevada and has a population approaching 20 million. With a growth rate of 4.1% per year, *Kenya is the fastest growing country in the entire world.*

At the turn of this century, 56 years after the first Christian missionaries arrived, there were only 2000 Christians in Kenya. Today, 70% of the population call themselves Christians. These include many Protestant groups, Roman Catholic, Anglicans, Eastern Orthodox, and others.

Twenty-three percent of the people still follow African traditional religious practices. They believe that there is a god who created all things, but that he went away somewhere and forgot all about them, or doesn't care. They believe every sickness, every disaster, every serious problem is due to the disfavor of the spirits of their ancestors or of evil spirits, of whom the world is full. Whenever there's a flood or drought or epidemic or any serious trouble, they sacrifice a goat or a chicken or some other animal to appease the spirits, so that they will go away and leave them alone. They live in constant fear of witchcraft and the spirit world.

Another seven percent of the people of Kenya are Muslims. They believe that Jesus was a great teacher and a great prophet, but nothing more, Most of them live in the northeast, near Somalia which is almost 100% Muslim, or along the shores of the Indian Ocean, or in the Tana River area.

About 12% of the people of Kenya belong to people groups that have had little or no opportunity to hear the Gospel. These include many of the Muslims mentioned above and the tribal peoples in the north, central, and northwestern part of the country—like the Pokot, the Turkana, and the Samburu.

Swahili is the official language of Kenya. English is also widely spoken. But altogether 44 languages are spoken in Kenya. Eleven of them have the entire Bible, another dozen have the New Testament, and four others have at least some Scripture portions, but 17 languages have never even been written down.

Many of those who do have the Scripture in their own language cannot read it for themselves. Sixty percent of the people in Kenya over 15 years of age never learned to read and write, so the Bible is of little value to them. It's difficult to stay in tune with God and be faithful to His Word when you can't read His Word daily. Many of the pastors and other church leaders in the more remote areas are barely literate themselves. How can an illiterate person know if the pastor is teaching and preaching God's word in truth and purity when they are barely literate themselves. A great deal of literacy work has yet to be done in order for churches to be "strong in the Lord" and have a vibrant Christian outreach.

Much progress is being made. There are many seminaries and Bible schools in Kenya, and many are studying God's Word through Bible correspondence and extension courses. Many of the Kenyans themselves are reaching out to other people groups, preaching the Word of Christ and planting churches. But there is still much to be done, still room for pioneer missionaries from North America and other lands—especially for those who can write down tribal languages or teach people to read their own language, once it has been written down.

SOUTH AND CENTRAL AFRICA

South Africa is 43% Protestant and growing steadily. The missionary vision of the Church is strong despite the country's political isolation. There are many outstanding ministers and theologians and fine people of prayer in the several churches of South Africa. There are now about 1,620 South Africans in cross—cultural mission work, about 1/6 of them are working in nine other lands.

There has been a dramatic openness to the Gospel among the Hindu people who number 763,000 in South Africa. About 13% of them have been won to Christ. About 1/5 of all Christian converts out of Hinduism in the world live in South Africa. Pray that there may be a growth of concern for the evangelization of India, Mauritius, and Hindus in other lands.

Much is done in producing evangelistic and Christian growth literature by such as All Nations Gospel Publishers who send large quantities of Gospel literature all over the world. Many Christian programs are produced by the South African Broadcasting Corporation and by the new Trans World Radio station in Swaziland.

In Zaire (85% Christian) there is an evangelical witness in nearly every tribe and district. The churches have been growing fast and the "New Life for All" campaign was very effective in getting the Gospel into unreached and difficult areas, and many new churches were planted.

There is a growing missionary vision among the believers. Some Christian workers have been sent out by the national church to work among the Sudan Zande who live a 500 mile bicycle ride away.

In Malawi there is peace and freedom to preach the Gospel, and there is a great interest and hunger for the things of God with many coming to the Lord whenever the Gospel is preached.

Even in Mozambique, where a hard-line Marxist regime is determined to destroy all religious "superstitions", God has been raising up a witness in the center and in the north. The Lomwe Church has grown dramatically to 25,000 members with missionary outreach to several tribes. Missionaries in South Tanzania have seen many Mozambique Maconde refugees turning to the Lord. Many or them have returned to evangelize their own people in their homeland. There is a considerable witness from the strong churches in Malawi to areas around the borders of Mozambique.

The great need in South and Central Africa is for well trained leaders and Christian writers. Bible translators and literacy workers are also desperately needed. Praise the Lord for all He is doing in Africa, and pray that the above needs may soon be met.

SUGGESTED READING

BRUCHKO: *By Bruce Olson. Ventura, CA: Regals Books, 1980*

Considered one of the greatest missionary books ever written, this tale of adventure and challenge tells the story of a courageous youth who goes to a murderous Indian tribe in South America, and brings them to faith in Christ. A beautiful example of conquering love. (formerly "For this Cross I'll Kill You".

THROUGH GATES OF SPLENDOR: *By Elisabeth Elliot. Wheaton, IL:Tyndale House Publishers, 1981*

Through Gates of Splendor is the account of five missionaries who were martyred in Ecuador in 1956 while trying to reach the Auca Indians for Christ.

MANUEL: *By Hugh Steven. Old Tappan, NJ: Fleming H. Revell Company, 1970*

A Totonac Indian achieves academic honors and wide recognition, then returns to his own people in the mountains of Mexico. Manuel's contact with an American Bible Translator in his own village led him to faith in Christ and to a life of service as a teacher of his own people. (127 pp.)

GOD'S TRIBESMAN: *By James and Marti Hefley. Nashville, TN: Holman Bible Publishers, 1974*

A member of a one time head-huntinging tribe in India is brought to faith in Christ. He is actively seeking to get a copy of the Bible into the hands of each of the homes of India, beginning with those already able to read it.

DAVID BRAINERD His Message for Today: *By Oswald J. Smith. London: Marshall, Morgan & Scott, Lrd, 1949*

The Pastor of The Peoples Church in Toronto has edited the diary of David Brainerd, missionary to the American Indians. His diary has blessed and challenged many people who have been greatly used of God in reaching unreached peoples. (95 pp.)

DAVID LIVINGSTONE: *By Hubert Livingstone Wilson. New York: George Doran Company*

A historical account of David Livingstone's explorations and missionary endeavors in Africa. For adults and children.

JUNGLE PILOT: *By Russel Hitt. New York: Harper and Brothers, 1959*

The life and witness of Nate Saint—the inventive genius of Operation Auca. Nate Saint and four other missionaries were martyred in Ecuador trying to Reach the Auca Indians for the Savior.

INTO THE GLORY: *By Jamie Buckingham. Plainfield, NJ: Logos International, 1974*

The miracle-filled story of the Jungle Aviation and Radio Service—taking Wycliffe Bible Translators to the earth's remotest regions.

LORDS OF THE EARTH
By Don Richardson
Ventura: Regal Books

The fascinating story of the Yali cannibals who serve hateful gods, and of missionary Stan Dale who dared to enter their domain.

INTRODUCING ANIMISM: *By Eugene Nida and William Smalley. New York: Friendship Press, 1959*

Animism is not a unified faith but is an assortment of primitive religious beliefs and practices that are found in various parts of the world. The only common denominator among animists is a false concept of the spirit world. Even in countries where the Gospel has been preached for years, there are remnants of animistic beliefs and practices. Animistic peoples have been among those most readily receptive to the Gospel of Christ.

PEACE CHILD
By Don Richardson
Ventura: Regal Books, 1974

The gripping account of how God's Peace Child found acceptance among the treacherous Sawi people whose own legends also told of a "peace child". (288 pp.

TWO THOUSAND TONGUES TO GO
By Ethel Wallis and Mary Bennett
New York: Harper & Brothers, 1959

Chronicles the beginnings of Wycliffe Bible Translators from the Cakchiquel Indians in Guatemala to the world-wide challenge of the tribes without God's Word in *their* languages. (308 pp.)

ROARING LION
By Robert Peterson
Robesonia, PA: OMF Books, 1984

In every age of missionary experience, demon possession has been a reality. The author gives first-hand evidence of demon possession in Borneo, and the power of God to deliver from it. He writes to forewarn and to forearm the reader with Scripture on the subject.

FEAR IN THE LONG HOUSE
By Jenny Bray
Robesonia, PA: OMF Books, 1984

"My son," said the old man, eyeing Ding's flushed and angry face. "the spirits are our rulers, they are strong and powerful." And because of the omens, crops were poor, fishing was banned, and huntsmen had to turn back. A teen-age boy's struggle from fear of spirits to faith in Christ.

ETERNITY IN THEIR HEARTS
By Don Richardson
Ventura: Regal Books

King Solomon's statement that God has set eternity in the hearts of men is proven through fascinating examples of how God enabled different pagan peoples to understand the meaning of the gospel.

DEMON GODS OF THORNY RIVER
By Robert Peterson
Robesonia, PA: OMF Books, 1984

This story of a Chinese immigrant family in West Borneo vividly portrays the intense fear that dominates those in slavery to evil spirits and pagan beliefs. Much is mere superstition but more is the actual frightful activity of demons. After the miracle of "new birth" the Lin family finds freedom.

DRUNK BEFORE DAWN
By Shirley Lee
Robesonia, PA: OMF Books, 1984

The jubilee story of the Borneo Evangelical Mission. Many of the tribal people of Borneo were often "drunk before dawn" until the Gospel of Christ reached them in the 1930s. Forty years later another new dawn came as God moved among them in revival.

COMMUNISM

There are now 1,600,000,000 (1984) people under communist tyranny, which means that just over one-third of the world's population is now ruled by 50,000,000 Communist Party members. In two years (1975-1976), seven countries were seized by the communists. Communist advances continue in lands where the governments are inclined toward Marxism but not wholly committed to either the Russian or Chinese form of communism. These include Benin, Guinea, Guinea-Bissau, Madagascar, Sao Tome and Principe, Cape Verde Islands, Algeria, and Iraq.[1]

Ruthless promotion of wars, revolutions, guerrilla movements, together with subversion and propaganda, have brought many nations under the shadow of a communist takeover—in fact, the world itself is threatened by this tyranny.

The expansion of communism has taken place within only the last 70 years, but everywhere it has gone it has been accompanied by untold misery and death for millions. After careful investigation, the U.S. Senate Internal Security Subcommittee reported that 35 to 45 million people were killed in the Soviet Union and another 34 to 63 million were murdered in Communist China. Some estimate that 150,000,000 people worldwide have been killed directly or indirectly in the wake of this Satanic advance.

Before the Revolution, Moscow, with a population of 750,000 had over 2000 churches. Today, with a population of 7,000,000, only 20 churches are open. and if it were not for Moscow's function as a show-case for foreign visitors, not many of these would be open either.

The Roman Catholic Church in Russia numbered about 6,000,000 in 1917. Its organization was completely destroyed by the Communists.

A large percentage of the 2,100,000 Germans who lived in Russia in 1917 were Lutherans. The Lutheran Church at that time had 539 parishes with 1,828 churches and 230 pastors. Her organization was destroyed without a trace. The churches were turned into movie houses, clubs, party centers, and stables.

More than 100,000 Volga Germans perished during the civil war and the great famine. In the autumn and winter of 1929, many were dragged off to Siberia where most of them died owing to the terrible conditions. Of the Black Sea Germans (224,000 Lutherans, 195,000 Roman Catholics, 104,000 Mennonites before World War I), practically the whole male population was arrested during the purges of 1937 and 1938. When Hitler attacked the Soviet Union in 1941, most of the male Volga Germans were sent to concentration camps or were shot outright.

Communism and Christianity are incompatible. Christianity is the only ideology with mass appeal that has been able to withstand communism and even expand under its persecution. Hence the communist's bitter hatred of the Gospel. Communism's vain hope that Christianity would die with its advent has proved to be foolish. With the possible exception of Albania, the number of believers with a living faith has increased in every country coming under communism. Although the communists have officially proclaimed religious freedom, in practice they have sought to destroy all forms of religion that they could not control. The advances of the Gospel have been many— particularly the movement of the Holy Spirit among communist-indoctrinated young people, touches of revival in different places, and rapid growth of the churches in Romania and USSR where the persecution has been most severe.

Conditions vary widely between the different countries and even within the countries. There are, basically, four different situations: 1) Lands where organized Christianity has been blotted out and the Church forced to go completely "underground." This is so in North Korea, Laos, Cambodia, Mongolia and Albania. 2) Lands with strict control of registered churches, a situation that has led to compromise on the part of some Christian leaders and to the multiplication of unregistered or "underground" churches. This is the case in the USSR, Romania, China, Bulgaria, Czechoslovakia, Vietnam, Zanzibar, South Yemen, Angola and Mozambique. 3) Lands with limited freedom to worship, but where believers are persecuted through job discrimination, economic hardship or lack of opportunity for education, as in Cuba, East Germany, Hungary, and Yugoslavia. 4) Lands with considerable freedom and little persecution at present as in Poland and East Germany.[23]

The hard-line countries such as the USSR practice every kind of cruelty on Christians. Many are sent to prison; others are deprived of parental rights, exiled, thrown out of work, heavily fined, or committed to mental institutions for such "crimes" as teaching children about the Lord, evangelizing, distributing literature, attending prayer meetings, etc. Persecution has markedly increased in nearly all countries following the communist victories in Asia and Africa (since 1975) and even after the signing of the 1975 Helsinki Agreement which, among other things, guaranteed religious freedom.

Communists are opposed not only to Christianity but to all religions. In 1950 the Chinese Reds came into Tibet with the avowed purpose of wiping out the Buddhist religion. They systematically tortured and murdered the religious leaders, and humiliated and degraded them before they put them to death. In fact, mass executions were carried out in which fake charges were made in front of people who had been forced to attend these assemblies. Brutal tortures were then carried out in front of the people before the victims were put to death. Children were removed from parental and religious influences and hauled off by the truckload to China to be systematically brainwashed and raised as communists. By these mass deportations and by indiscriminate killing of older people, the communists have changed the face of Tibet; they have exterminated its religion, destroyed its culture and even the people's identity—all in the name of "liberating" Tibet.[2]

WORLD CONQUEST, THE COMMUNIST GOAL

It's no secret, except perhaps to the liberal news media in the United States, that the Communist goal is world conquest, no matter how many people are killed in the process. The closing sentences of the Communist Manifesto (1848) declare the Communist dedication to world revolution:

"The Communists everywhere support every revolutionary movement against the existing social and political order of things...They openly declare that their ends can be attained only by the forcible overthrow of all existing social conditions.

"Let the ruling classes tremble at a Communist revolution. The proletarians have nothing to lose but their chains. They have a world to win." (Basic writings on Politics and Philosophy, Marx and Engels, p.41).

The Communists say their victory is certain because the average American is so intellectually lazy, intoxicated with entertainment, limited in his horizon, and inherently selfish that he won't have the conviction or dedication to do that which is necessary to stop it.

A French Communist once said: "The Gospel of Jesus Christ is more powerful than our Marxist doctrine, yet we will beat you Christians. You give only a little time and hardly any money; we Communists keep only what is necessary of our salaries and give the rest for propaganda. We consecrate all of our free time. How can anyone believe the Gospel if you do not sacrifice to spread it? We will win because we believe in our message and will sacrifice even our lives. You Christians are afraid to soil your hands."[3]

How do the communists gain control? Scores of books on the market suggest that communists first attempt to teach the people their definition of "democracy." They indicate they have come to "liberate" the people. They pose as friends; they may double or triple the food rations to gain the confidence of the people. And then, the curtain falls. There may be mass executions first of leaders—lawyers, judges, clergymen, and government officials. Then there may be a period of quiet and rest. Just when the people begin to think that the communist government is perhaps becoming benign, maybe even beginning to look out for their interests, again the curtain falls with another wave of arrests. Thousands of people may be unjustly accused and publicly executed. Eventually no significant leadership remains and there is little resistance. With no arms to defend themselves, the people become helpless slaves of their communist masters.

Unfortunately, the spiritual and moral decline of the West has greatly assisted the expansion of communism.

Thank God, there were many true believers in Russia when the communists took over in 1917. And even though the communists have tried to prevent it, the Word of God has been getting into Russia ever since. People are being converted in large numbers, including some who are well known and very influential.

There have been some remarkable conversions to Christ in recent years—Kosygin's wife, Solzhenitsyn, and some of the most brilliant writers and scientists that Russia has produced.

Even though people under 18 years of age are forbidden to attend church services, the churches carry on and are usually packed at every meeting.

Many evangelicals, however, refused to accept these limitaions and broke away to form their own unrecognized group, or independent churches. These churches are growing rapidly and spreading all over the country. On them falls the full weight of Communist persecution.

Despite restrictions against evangelistic work and youth work, young people are turning to the Lord in large numbers. Many villages with only 2 or 3 believers a couple of years ago now have 50 to 100. There are reports of a move of the Spirit in the Baltic States (Estonia, Latvia, and Lithuania) and Armenia.

There are ten missionary radio stations that surround Russia, broadcasting about 243 hours per week to the USSR. One out of every 2 people in the USSR has a radio, and millions listen in. Some believe that there have been over a million people converted through these broadcasts and many new churches planted as a result in hitherto unevangelized places.

The Romanian people are also very hungry for the Word of God. Intense atheistic propaganda and severe persecution have only stimulated their interest and refined the Church. Every year there are reports of many thousands of baptisms in the evangelical churches.

There has been a remarkable people movement among the Gypsies in Romania. Many thousands of them have been converted since 1972.

In Poland the Roman Catholic Church is too strong for the Communists to dominate or destroy, so there is more religious freedom than in any other Communist state. The Protestants have more freedom than they've had for centuries because they are considered a counterbalance to the Roman Catholics.

We praise God for every Christian convert in the Soviet Union and other Communist lands around the world. But we must remember that there is still much bitter persecution in these lands. In fact, the persecution of believers is increasing in ferocity.[4] A vast organization is being built up to coordinate the destruction of the "underground" church.

We must continue to pray every day for the suffering Christians and their leaders who face constant harassment from the authorities who have infiltrated into both official and underground groups. Pray that their faith may be strong, and that their witness may win many to the Lord.

Pray for all the suffering peoples who don't know the Lord, that they may see the barrenness and the failure of Communism and turn to Christ. Pray that the leaders in the Soviet Union and China and all Communist countries may turn to the Lord for their own sakes, and that the Gospel may be published and spread unhindered to every people group in their own language from East Berlin and Prague and Budapest to Vladivostok, Saigon and Beijing and in every Communist dominated land.

Countries of the Communist World

(Except for "Peoples Republic of China")

Region or Country	Population, 1986	Primary Religion
EUROPE		
[1]Afghanistan	—	Muslim
[1]Albania	3.0	Muslim
[2]Bulgaria	9.0	Eastern Orthodox
[2]Czechoslovakia	15.5	Roman Catholic
[3]East Germany	16.7	Protestant
[3]Hungary	10.6	Roman Catholic
[4]Poland	37.5	Roman Catholic
[2]Romania	22.8	Russian Orthodox
[3]Yugoslavia	23.2	Orthodox Catholics, controlled by government
[2]U.S.S.R.	280.0	Russian Orthodox, about 10 million Protestants
Total for Europe	**418.3**	
ASIA (Excluding Peoples' Republic of China)		
Burma	37.7	Buddhist
[1]Kampuchea (Cambodia)	6.4	Buddhist
[1]Korea, North	20.5	Previously Buddhist/Harshest repression of all religions
[1]Laos	3.7	Buddhist
[1]Mongolia	1.9	Previously Buddhist, all religions now repressed
[2]Vietnam	62.0	Buddhist
[2]Yemen, South	2.3	
Total for Asia	**134.5**	
AFRICA		
[2]Angola	8.2	Roman Catholic
[4]Congo (Brazzaville)	1.8	Roman Catholic
[?]Equat. Guinea	0.4	Roman Catholic, but all churches closed
[?]Ethiopia	43.9	Ethiopian Orthodox
[2]Mozambique	14.0	Catholic/Government committed to destruction of all religions
[2]Zanzibar	0.5	—
Total for Africa	**68.8**	
LATIN AMERICA		
[3]Cuba	10.2	Roman Catholic
[?]Nicaragua	3.3	
Total for Latin America	**13.5**	

The advance continues with Thailand, Namibia (S.W. Africa), and Zimbabwe (S. Rhodesia) under direct military attack. There are other lands with Marxist inclined governments, but they are not wholly committed to Russian or Chinese Communism. These include Berli (3.9 million), Guinea (6.2 million), Guinea Bissau (0.9 million), Madagascar (10.3 million), Sao Tome and Principe (0.1 million), Cape Verde Island (0.3 million), Somalia (7.8 million), Algeria (22.8 million), and Iraq (16.0 million).

Due to revolutions, guerrilla movements, subversion, and propaganda, many other nations are severely threatened by a Communist takeover.

[1] Organized Christianity has been blotted out and the Church is completely underground.
[2] Strict control of registered churches, leading to multiplication of underground churches.
[3] Limited freedom of worship, but believers are discriminated against.
[4] Considerable freedom of worship with little persecution.

Statistics from World Population Data Sheet of the Population Reference Bureau, 1986.

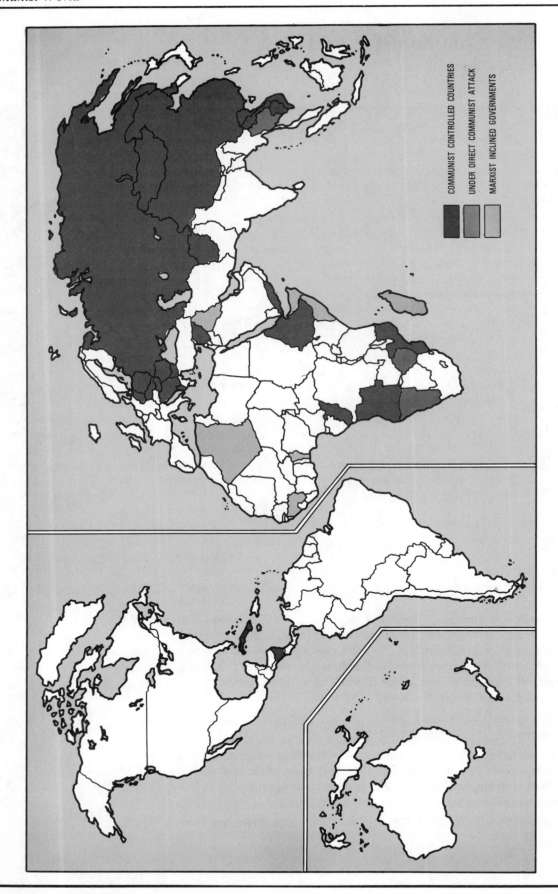

COMMUNIST CONTROLLED COUNTRIES

UNDER DIRECT COMMUNIST ATTACK

MARXIST INCLINED GOVERNMENTS

The Communist World

COMMUNISM AROUND THE WORLD

IN CHINA

On October 1st, 1949 Mao Zedong proclaimed the establishment of the People's Republic of China. The 27 years that followed were marked by three great disasters.

The first disaster was the Hundred Flowers Movement launched in 1956. By that time Chairman Mao felt confident enough of his control over the country to encourage freedom of speech. That year-long movement ended in accusations of treason for those who dared to express their opinions. Many who spoke were critical of Mao and the Party. Ostracism of some and execution of others followed for those who dared to speak—and those who dared do what they were told not to do. Communism had reared its ugly head.[5]

The second great disaster was the so-called "Great Leap Forward" which began in 1957. This was an attempt to almost instantaneously collectivize all of China's agriculture and industry. It was a complete failure. As late as 1984, China's Statistics Bureau reported that "between 1959 and 1962 more than 10 million people died needlessly of the famine and natural disasters that followed Mao's experiment with collectivization."[6] Western observers place the figure much higher. They estimate that the number who died needlessly was between 15 and 30 million! One respected China scholar, Father Ladony, puts the figure at 50 million. Eventually Mao was forced to call off the disastrous experiment.

Then came the last, and by far the worst, of the Three Disasters imposed by Chairman Mao. The so-called "Cultural Revolution" lasted 10 tumultuous years, from 1966 to 1976. During those ten years of uncontrolled violence, millions were slaughtered. The latest figure released by Beijing was 22 million! And the economic development of the country was set back perhaps a quarter of a century. Education was severely disrupted. Millions of young people were sent to the countryside to work on communes. As a result, virtually a whole generation lost its opportunity for schooling, and this in a country that has always venerated scholarship. Mao would not be forgiven. The future of millions of youth was doomed.

A turning point came in September, 1976 when Chairman Mao died. In October the Gang of Four (which included Mao's wife) who had tried to perpetuate the Cultural Revolution, were arrested, and Hua Guofeng was named Mao's successor. In July, 1977, Deng Xiaoping was restored to all his posts following his vilification by Mao. He set to work immediately to get the desperately needed restoration underway. However, the sudden turn of events had left the Chinese people bewildered and disillusioned.

Politically, Deng is a survivor, having been twice purged. Ideologically, he is a communist, but as a Chinese, his commitment is toward modernization of China by almost any means. This is what had gotten him into trouble with Mao. He was too pragmatic. His pragmatism took preference over ideology.

Deng set out to transform the Communist Party into his own image. That dramatic and relentless process is still underway.

Then Deng launched the Four Modernizations Movement to accomplish the goals of making China a modern, powerful, socialist country by the end of the century. This included the modernization of industry, agriculture, science-technology, and the military. Substantial progress has been made. In just six years, China has transformed herself from one of the poorer third-world nations into what is being called a "candidate superpower." This has been accomplished by junking the policies of the Cultural Revolution and pragmatically pursuing the goals of modernization. The result has been not only to change the ideology, which the Chinese Communist Party has always insisted should be at the heart of economic theory, but also many of the policies as well. At this writing, Deng Xaioping is still guiding China's obvious turn to the "right." Communism now has a different face.

Although the standard of living has changed but little for the masses of peasants, there does seem to be enough food to go around in most areas of China. Chinese peasants are glad to be rid of the communes. They are now being given a plot of ground and a freer hand in their own affairs. The result has been a striking increase in agricultural production. Factory workers are benefiting as technocrats replace the inept ideological leadership of the past. Practices similar to capitalism have dramatically raised production. Consequently many people have more money. Education is improving, and the military is being modernized. The standard of living is gradually creeping upward. An occasional farmer is able to buy a car; a few have private telephones. Materialism, while touching only a few of the Chinese peasants, has invaded the city in a big way. Consequently, each wave of foreign tourists is able to see the evidences of material progress.

But material progress is not enough. The people want and expect human rights, personal liberty, and religious freedom. In these three areas Communist China has failed miserably. China's constitution pays lip service to these inalienable rights. But the fact remains that only the Party and the State have rights. Everyone else is subject to them. The list of miseries which this has caused is unending. People are still arrested, imprisoned, and even executed without legal representation. An appeal against a sentence in China merely means that the prisoner is not repentant, and thus is really asking for further and swifter punishment. And, if you don't have the right family background, no court of law in China can help you.

It is the entire moral fabric of China that has suffered most from Communism. With the rooting out of Confucianism went all the moral guidelines that have enabled China to perpetuate itself longer than any civilization in history. Communism has not provided a substitute. Instead, treachery and lying are endemic to the system. Systematic lying prevails. The people no longer believe anything the State says or promises. In return, the people have learned that they must lie to survive. What a tragedy! Honesty was once a hallmark of Chinese culture.

China's present policies regarding religious freedom are also a travesty. There is **no religious freedom in China.** Communism cannot permit freedom. It can and does permit some practice of religion, but it cannot and does not permit freedom of religion. This is a very important distinction.

Tourists visiting China see open churches and conclude there is religious freedom in China. Not so! All religion is carefully controlled by the State. The State controls where the church meets, who does the preaching, and what the people read. For instance, the Bibles which the State has printed in China are all in the Traditional Script—a script that is not taught in the schools. Thus, it is difficult for young people to read and understand the Bible. This, of course, is intentional. Bibles in the Simplified Script are frowned upon, lest the young people read and believe. In fact, it is illegal to evangelize young people. For them there is not even freedom to practice religion.

What hope is there for China? Many believe that the Chinese culture will gradually reassert itself. Some say, "China will change Communism more than Communism will change China." But it will take time. There are some encouraging signs that this process has already begun. Perhaps the worst is over. We pray that it is.

IN MONGOLIA

Mongolia has virtually been a satellite state of the U.S.S.R. since the proclamation of a People's Republic in 1921. All religions have been suppressed. Buddhism was the national religion, but only one monastery remains active. There is no evidence that there are any national Christians, and it is almost impossible to get new Bibles into the land from the free world.[7]

IN KOREA

Liberation from the Japanese in 1945 did not result in a free united Korea due to Russian objections. A communist puppet government was installed in the North, and a democratic government in the South. The North invaded the South in 1949. The war dragged on until 1953. The large and well-equipped Korean Communist forces continue to threaten a second invasion of the South. The government of Kim Il Sung, the communist dictator, is one of the most oppressive in the world.

The government harshly represses all religions. Nowhere has the Christian Church been more violently oppressed than here. During and after the Korean War, many thousands of pastors and believers were murdered. Nearly all believers have fled to the South.

The remaining Christians are forced to worship in great secrecy. There are occasional reports of the discovery of a group of believers and their subsequent imprisonment and martyrdom. We ought to be praying daily for these few remaining believers and for their witness.

A little Christian literature still finds its way into North Korea in various and ingenious ways. Pray that more of the written Word may penetrate this benighted land.

Radio is the only direct way to reach the people. We need to pray for the broadcasts from TEAM (The Evangelical Alliance Mission) and FEBA (Far East Broadcasting Association) stations in South Korea. Pray that people may hear these programs and believe.[8]

IN VIETNAM

The tragic 30-year Vietnam war ended in April of 1975 with the complete victory of the Communist North over the Western aligned South. This communist-ruled nation is strenuously working to gain political control over all of Indochina, Thailand, and beyond.

The government has very strict control of Catholics and Protestants in the North. There is still relative freedom in the South, but future government action is likely to be harsh.

The subjugation of the South by the communists was followed by a systematic looting in Saigon of the vast military and consumer goods left by the U.S.A. Poverty and famine as well as the sending of over one million politically "unreliable" people to "re-education camps" has driven many to despair and suicide.

The present situation for the believers in the South is not yet one of severe persecution. Yet, about 50 pastors have been killed, many believers are in prison, and all suffer the economic hardships of the whole population. Yet churches are free to meet, Christian workers to minister, and Bibles are sold.

The believers in the North are free to meet together, but pastors are strictly controlled as to what they preach and are forced to report to the communists on their own activities and on the activities of their members. The few Christians are under great pressure through the seven-day week and the use of Sundays for indoctrination classes. And, of course, there is discrimination against believers in education and employment.

The young people face severe trials in Vietnam—not the least of which is the permission granted the Viet Cong soldiers to take any unmarried girl in marriage. Pray that the Christian girls find Christian husbands.[9]

Cross-References

Far East Broadcasting Co., *15*

Korea, *4, 11, 17, 29, 37, 38, 100*

North Korea, *7, 17, 37, 100, 116, 119*

Persecution, *11, 14, 38, 77, 80, 109, 116, 129, 143*

Radio Broadcasting, *15, 67, 72, 106, 111, 118, 151, 163, 191*

South Korea, *17, 23, 31, 37, 38, 100, 177*

Vietnam, *5, 7, 17, 31, 34, 91, 101, 116, 119*

IN CAMBODIA

Just before the communist victory in 1975, the capital city of Pnomh Penh had a population of 2.5 million people (swollen with many refugees). The communists immediately and brutally drove out the entire population, young and old, sick and dying, into the jungles—many to their deaths.

The most drastic and radical revolutionary changes were immediately put into effect. There is now no money, no private land or private possessions. The entire country is a vast forced labor camp.

The communist leaders have ruthlessly destroyed all links with the past. All birth and death records and graveyards have been destroyed, family names cancelled and family life deliberately broken up. The entire army of the defeated government , all teachers, former government employees, those with secondary education and above were brutally murdered. Reliable estimates by world news organizations say two million Cambodians may have been killed in purges.[10] Marxist leaders predict another three million may be liquidated to complete the building of their "pure society." In the relationship of murders to population, Hitler, Stalin, and Mao Zedong must take a back seat to the Cambodian Marxists.

The persecuted Christians have been scattered all over the country and probably all the leaders and older Christians have been martyred except for a few who managed to escape to Thailand. Nearly all the Christian literature in the country has been destroyed. The believers are few, very young in the faith, and most without the comfort of God's Word or any fellowship.

By the end of 1976, about 60,000 had managed to flee from their homeland. The great majority of escapees died or were killed before reaching Thailand.[11]

IN LAOS

The Rightist government of Laos collapsed in 1975 before the Communist Pathet Lao forces and massive military aid and direction from North Vietnam. The land is virtually a satellite state of Vietnam that is being mobilized for the subjugation of free Thailand.

The Laotian people are under the iron heel of Communism. The whole nation is being forcibly indoctrinated in Communism, with even Christians being compelled to lead indoctrination classes.

The Protestant Church among the Lao is very weak, lacking in effective leadership and largely illiterate. Humanly speaking, this Church has little chance of surviving the onslaughts of communism. Pray that the fires of persecution may refine the small company of believers into an effective soul-winning force. Most of the strongest leaders have had to flee for their lives.[12]

The persecution of the believers in Laos is building in intensity. All land, buildings, crops, and livestock have been nationalized, and there is starvation. A very close watch is kept on Christians, though services continue in two churches. All others have been closed. Many young people have been drafted into the army. Some pastors are in prison. All evangelism is strictly forbidden. The only two Bible schools in existence before the communist takeover are now closed. There are few radios in the land, and these are closely watched by the communists. There is little electricity, and batteries are almost unobtainable. Thus, not very many are able to hear the Gospel broadcasts of the FEBC in Manila.[13]

IN MOZAMBIQUE

Mozambique was stirred by the independence fever that swept Africa in the 1950s and '60s. Nationals pressed Portugal for promises of freedom but to no avail. Freedom fighters asked western democracies for help. But the U.S. and Britain had commitments to Portugal through the NATO alliance. To their chagrin, the nationalists saw western arms going to Portugal. They turned to communist countries for arms!

The Mozambique independence movement was backed by Protestants who had suffered much under the Portuguese. Some pastors even joined the Mozambique Liberation Front (FRELIMO), the leading organization crusading for freedom. But while most Protestant missionaries sympathized, their denominations in the U.S. and Britain adopted a hands-off policy.

In 1971 members of the White Fathers Catholic missionary order denounced their church in Mozambique for its identification with Portuguese rule. Portuguese authorities immediately ordered them out of the country.

From this time on the Portuguese government began arresting church leaders, both Catholic and Protestant, suspected of rebel sympathies.

On June 13 and 14, 1972, Portuguese security police arrested several hundred Mozambiquans including about twenty members and leaders of the Presbyterian church. No official cause was given for the arrests. Some of the church leaders were aged and in need of medical attention, but were denied permission to take any medicines with them. They were ferried to an infamous detention camp for political prisoners near Lourenco Marques, the capital.

The following New Year's Eve, Presbyterian church authorities announced the release of 37 of their churchmen from the dread prison. They regretted that no information was available about the fate of the several hundred other prisoners that had been arrested with the Presbyterians.

Bitter fighting continued in Mozambique until a military coup in Lisbon overthrew the government of Portugal. The new Portuguese government quickly granted Mozambique provisional independence in 1974. A year later Mozambique gained full independence. The head of FRELIMO, Samora Machel, became the country's first president.

For a while there was cheering by Mozambique Christians. But the jubilation soon faded when President Machel called for development of a Marxist state and announced that the government was taking over the private ownership of homes.

Further government actions cast a deeper pall. Several Catholic priests were deported. Members of ten denominations were arrested and charged as plotters against the state. Infant baptism was banned.[14]

In 1979 the president openly appealed for an "all-out war on churches." The destruction of all religious "superstitions" was expedited by closure of churches and harassment of Christians.

No form of evangelism is allowed. Baptism and church attendance is illegal for anyone under 18 years of age. It is illegal to "influence young people religiously" and Christian literature cannot any longer be imported or printed or even distributed or read in public. The number of meetings has had to be reduced, and all known believers are closely watched. There are a number of believers in prison or in harsh and primitive labor camps euphemistically called "re-education centers."

There are persistent rumors that all children over five years old will soon be removed from parents and sent to training camps.

Thus Mozambique, like every other communist land, is in desperate need of our prayers. Pray for the conversion of the communist leaders, that the Gospel may have free course throughout this land that has suffered so much for centuries, first under the Portuguese, and now under the national communists.

IN ETHIOPIA

It is possible that more Christians have died in the 20th century in Ethiopia than in any other nation of black Africa. Ethiopia has the longest history of political independence of any country in Africa and is the only country in black Africa with a Christian heritage. But today, both the historic Ethiopian Orthodox Church and the vigorous evangelical congregations are struggling against a militant Marxism that threatens to spread to neighboring countries.[15]

On September 12, 1974, a coalition of Ethiopian army officers overthrew the government. They deposed Haile Selassie, ending his 58 years of rule, arrested 200 of the emperor's closest associates, and announced a "war on feudalism." Selassie died the following year.

A 120-man military committee, led by Lt. Gen. Aman Andom, took power. General Andom was deposed less than three months later, and many of his supporters executed. The new leader Brig. Gen. Benti was installed November 28, 1974. About 26 months later, on February 3, 1977, General Benti was killed. A few days later a new government headed by Lt. Col. Mengistu Mariam emerged. The colonel took on dictatorial powers and proclaimed the formation of a Soviet-style "People's Democratic Republic."

For over seven hundred years Ethiopia and neighboring Somalia had quarreled over the Ogaden desert region. In July, 1977, Ogaden guerrillas, supported by Somalian planes, launched a major campaign to take control of the Ogaden and annex it to Somalia. The guerrillas advanced rapidly until the Soviet Union and Cuba intervened on the side of Ethiopia. The Soviets sent massive military aid and advisers and the Cubans sent troops. Somalia responded by canceling its "treaty of friendship" with Russia, ordering 6000 Russian advisers out, and breaking diplomatic relations with Cuba.

Inside Ethiopia the Soviet/Cuban-supported Mengistu regime embarked on a reign of terror. Up to 150 assassinations and executions occurred every day. The new Marxist government passed out guns to civilian supporters so they could join in the murder of political opponents. Military officers began using dynamite for mass killings to save bullets. The Swedish Save the Children Federation reported that at one time 1000 children had been massacred and their bodies left in the streets to be ravaged by hyenas and vultures.

In a short time Ethiopia expelled 300 U.S. consular and trade officials and shut down U.S. aid agencies. Western news correspondents were also ordered out of the country.[16]

Most missionaries were gone by the end of 1977. Mission leaders cited political turmoil and insurmountable restrictions on their work.

After the missionaries left, a Lutheran mission leader from Germany was allowed to visit Addis Ababa. He returned home to report about ten percent of the population of the capital living behind prison bars in "appalling conditions." The Reverend Johannes Hasselhorn, mission secretary of the Evangelical Lutheran Church of Hanover, also stated that "priests and other church workers are hunted down like dogs." The Ethiopian Church, with which Lutheran missionaries had worked, he said, was unable to make plans "even five minutes in advance," because its members can never predict "what might happen tomorrow."

At this time the future of Ethiopia looks grim from a human perspective. But the missionaries who were forced to leave are remembering another time, during the Italian occupation (1936-41), when the Ethiopian church grew by leaps and bounds. Pray that it will happen again, that the blood of the martyrs will become the seed of the church, and that for everyone who dies for his faith a hundred more may be born again to take his place.

IN FORMER PORTUGUESE POSSESSIONS

Portugal was the first of the European colonial powers in Africa and among the worst. Tiny Portuguese Guinea on the western bulge of Africa was claimed in 1446, Mozambique on the southeast coast in 1483, and Angola on the southwest coast in the 1500s. Portugal had hoped to exploit Angola's rich lodes of gold and silver, but the greatest riches came from slaves. This cruel traffic in human cargo continued long after foreign pressure forced Portugal to pass a law abolishing slavery in 1869. Under a new "contract labor law" African adult males were required to work for Portuguese employers who could deduct from their paycheck the cost of fines, rent, overdue taxes, or any other cleverly devised charge. Employers could also send their contract laborers to neighboring countries. In this way hundreds of thousands were sent to toil in South Africa's sweltering mines. They were given no choice. Any African not under contract could be arrested for vagrancy.[17] Is it any wonder that these people longed for independence and freedom from these cruel taskmasters?

Because of the harsh treatment, disease, immorality, drunkenness, and ignorance pervaded the colonies.

In all of this, church and state were intertwined. At the height of the slave trade, Catholic bishops blessed cargoes of chained Africans departing for Portuguese Brazil. Catholic institutions were provided labor pools. A single monastery in Luanda, the capital of Angola, had at one time 12,000 slaves.

Catholic authorities tried to block the entry of Protestant missionaries. Missionaries managed to enter Angola in 1878 and Mozambique in 1880, but it was not until 1939 that the first evangelical workers were allowed to enter Portuguese Guinea. The evangelical witness met with great success in Angola and Mozambique, but in both countries the Church developed through severe restrictions and, at times, bitter persecution.

IN ANGOLA

Angola is the tragedy of Mozambique and worse: it is a history of some 450 years of oppression by Portugal, seen in 70% illiteracy, rampant disease, abject misery and discrimination, and religious intolerance by the state-aligned Catholic Church (Hefley, 1981:411).

Because of the oppression of the Portuguese, three nationalist movements fought for fifteen years to achieve independence in 1975. After all these years of savage fighting, while western countries refused to intervene, the Communist-backed MPLA faction (Popular Movement for Liberation of Angola) gained the upper hand and won control of the capital, Luanda, as well as other major cities. But the war did not stop. Soldiers of the other two factions (FINLA and UNITA) mounted a guerrilla war against MPLA. The 750,000 Angolan refugees that had been in Zaire returned, only to face starvation. Christian relief groups were unable to obtain agreements from the three revolutionary movements to bring in supplies.

The Future of Christianity under Marxism

Agostinho Neto, head of the MPLA is apparently bent on the destruction of the church in Angola. He declared, "No (Communist) Party member can be a church member, and no church member can be a member of the Party." He went on to say, "Twenty years from now we expect no churches to exist in Angola."[18]

Nevertheless, Neto has permitted a surprising amount of religious freedom "in this period of transition to scientific socialism." Churches function freely, except in areas where bush fighting continues. Hundreds of people are reportedly being baptized every Sunday. Bibles are still being sold. Church leaders can travel and hold conferences.

Some of the foreign missionaries expelled by the Portuguese have been allowed to return.

Cuban troops remain in Angola. Neto's MPLA government strongly supports Soviet-Cuban policies in the rest of Africa. If MPLA is successful in holding off the rival groups, Angola could become as repressive as the Soviet Union toward evangelical Christianity. Angolan believers watch, pray, and work, knowing that many who are living now may be the martyrs of the future.[21]

IN CUBA

Castro's revolution brought communists to power in 1959. While the Roman Catholic hierarchy slept, Castro and his followers were busy arresting political opponents and putting them on trial with trumped-up charges. Many had fought in the Cuban Revolution with Castro. Their only crime was objecting to their leader's leftist turn. Hundreds of these political prisoners were either executed or imprisoned in Morro Castle, the fortress at the entrance to Havana Harbor. Thousands of Cubans had been tried on lesser charges. Some lost their property and went to prison simply because their last name happened to be the same as someone in the deposed Batista government.[22]

On July 17, 1960, a mass was celebrated in the Havana Cathedral for victims of communism. Those in attendance sang, "Viva Cristo Rey" (Long Live Christ the King) and waved handkerchiefs. Outside, a communist mob was waiting for mass to end. Fights and beatings ensued, with scores of worshipers picked up by the police. Three weeks later the Catholic bishops signed a collective message stating, "Catholicism and communism . . . are totally opposed and can never be reconciled . . . The majority of the Cuban people, which is catholic, is against materialistic and atheistic communism. Only by deceit or coercion could the Cuban people be led into a communist regime . . ."

Castro's militiamen responded by raiding churches, convents and schools. Soldiers profaned altars, smashed statues and relics, stole chalices and jeweled crucifixes. Some got drunk on sacramental wine, staged mock weddings, then danced through the streets, holding up sacred vessels. Others donned clerical cloth and consorted with known prostitutes in public.

After the ill-fated Bay of Pigs invasion on April 17, 1961, Castro's militia rounded up Catholic priests, including four of the country's bishops, and others suspected of opposing the regime. In Havana alone twenty thousand were arrested in just a few days.

Following a religious demonstration in September, 1961, Castro decreed that religious demonstrations would never again be allowed in Cuba. Any priests who did not pledge loyalty to the government would lose their citizenship and be deported. Shortly after this, a hundred priests were herded on board a ship in the middle of the night and deported to the U.S.A. Over 2,000 nuns also left Cuba during this time. Some went voluntarily. Most were expelled. The forced exodus left only about 400 priests and nuns to serve Cuba's Catholics.

Later in the year Castro quit pretending. "I am a Marxist-Leninist and I will be a Marxist-Leninist to the last day of my life," he declared on television.

Most Protestants had favored the Revolution.

Before Castro's declaration that he was a Marxist-Leninist, the Protestant minority sympathized with the announced aims of the revolution. Many cheered Castro's land distribution policies. But when it became obvious that Cuba was becoming a communist state, the seeds of discontent were sown. As the government tightened controls, thousands of Protestants fled to Florida.

But the Protestants didn't experience any overt persecution yet. They were small and divided. Their churches didn't operate large institutions or own large sections of land, as did the Catholics. There was little for Castro to confiscate.

But in March of 1964 Castro openly attacked certain "Protestant sects." This signaled a wave of persecution and government legislation over church affairs similar to what had happened in the Eastern European satellites of the Soviet Union.

The law limited religious activities to church buildings and to traditional schedules. Special services could not be held on weekday nights, except Wednesday. Only persons above legal age could become church members. Youth under fifteen, unless accompanied by a parent, were forbidden to enter churches.

Church construction was stopped and some buildings were confiscated. About a hundred churches were closed. Theological students were drafted or sent to labor camps. Radio preaching and the distribution of Christian literature was outlawed. In 1965 police arrested 53 Baptists simultaneously. Thirty-four of them were tried and sentenced for offenses ranging from espionage to "twisting biblical texts for the purpose of ideological diversionism."[19]

An Uneasy Detente.

An uneasy detente now exists between the Christians and the Castro communist government. There has been a relaxation in the enforcement of anti-religion laws. Most, if not all, of the pastors that were imprisoned have been released.

Castro and other Cuban communists deny that they are enemies of religion. However, the policies of international Marxism that they have adopted indicate that this is mere propaganda intended to deceive the public. Their ultimate goal is to stamp out religious faith. At present it is not in their best interests for the advancement of communism to violently oppose religious activities or to make martyrs of those who will not submit.[20]

IN NICARAGUA

In his televised address to the nation, urging humanitarian and military aid for the "Contra" forces in Nicaragua, President Reagan referred to the torture of the Protestant preacher, Prudencio Baltodano, by the Nicaraguan communists. The following report gives the details.

Prudencio Baltodano, a Protestant preacher from a poor rural section of Nicaragua, recently survived brutal torture at the hands of the communist Sandinistas. Though left for dead, his bleeding body tied to a tree, he miraculously survived and was able to escape.

Lying on his back in a room he shares with four others, Prudencia spoke to reporters about his ordeal. The top of his head was bandaged, covering the wounds left by the Sandinistas when they cut off his ears. A large scar ran down his throat. Terrorists, wishing to kill him "without wasting a bullet," had used a bayonet.

Prudencio was a peasant farmer who had never been involved in politics in any way. In the late 1970s he started preaching the Gospel in the rural areas of southern Nicaragua where he lived. Though he considered himself a humble, hardworking man with no political sophistication, he found some of the projects of the Sandinista government very disturbing.

He told reporters, "I did not agree with the literacy program being used by the government because the communists used it to turn people against God. In my village they had a Cuban teacher in charge of the children's education. In her teaching procedure she would make a comparison between what God could give to children and what the government could give them. She would do her demonstration with pieces of candy. She would tell the children to close their eyes and ask God for candy. Then she would ask them to open their eyes and look at their empty hands.

"Then she would go over the instructions again but this time the children were told to ask her for the candy. When they opened their eyes, they would see a piece of candy in their hands."

Pastor Baltodano then told of the circumstances that led to his capture and then torture at the hands of the Sandinistas.

"After harsh combat between the Contras and the Sandinistas, the Contras left the area where I lived and preached, leaving the Sandinistas in charge of the village. The Sandinistas proceeded to arrest plenty of people, among them a pastor named Miguel Flores. He was taken, tied up, his nose cut off, his eyes put out, his face was cut up, his ears were cut off, and he was tied up and left to die.

"I fled to the mountains with another man and about forty women and children. At two in the afternoon the next day, our group was surrounded by Sandinista forces.

"The soldiers ordered the women to go home and not to worry. Then my friend and I were ordered to get undressed, and the soldiers ordered us to put on the uniform that the freedom fighters used. This was so they could claim we were counter-revolutionary soldiers.

"One of the soldiers said, 'You are an evangelical pastor, preacher. You are one of the ones that go around convincing the peasants to join the Contras.'

"I told them that was not true and that the only convincing I was doing was trying to convince people to come to God and Christ.

"A soldier told me, **'Pastors and preachers are our enemies. We don't believe in God. In case you're interested, we are communists.'** Then he pointed to another soldier and said, 'This is God.'

"Turning back to me, he said, 'Start to pray and see if your God will save you.'"

Pastor Baltodana then went on to describe the torture he went through and how he managed to escape after he had been left for dead.

This is just one of many stories coming out of Nicaragua about innocent people being tortured and murdered by the communist Sandinistas.

SUGGESTED READING

VANYA: *By Mhrna Grant. Ventura: Regal Books, 1983*
"A gripping story of a young Soviet soldier's witness for Christ and God's miraculous powers at work in his life of persecution, A "MUST" for everyone concerned about the persecuted Church in Russia. Published in many languages. ($5.95)

IRINA'S STORY: *By Hermann Hartfeld. Minneapolis: Bethany*
The compelling, true story of Irina, a Russian Christian, and a love stronger than terror—love for God and love for a pastor in the underground Church.

WHERE CHRIST IS STILL TORTURED: *By Richard Wurmbrand. Torrance, CA: Diane Books Publishing Co. 1982*
In this book Richard Wurmbrand brings the story of persecuted Christians up to date. Persecution continues to tighten its grip on Christian Churches in lands ruled by atheists and tyrants. It is only the Holy Spirit who enables them to survive and flourish in the face of discrimination, oppression, torture, and murder. Nor is it Christians alone who are so treated. What is the response of the Western Church? Does it understand what is happening? Where Christ is Still Tortured helps Christians to be able recognize and fight their enemy. (160 pp)

EAST WIND: *By Ruth Hunt. Grands Rapids, MI: Zondervan Publishing House, 1976*
Maria Zeitner Linke, survivor of nine years of imprisonment in the death camps and prisons of Stalin's Russia following World War II, tells her story. She writes "only one who has felt the nearness of death can truly be grateful for each new day, no matter how much it might bring." East Wind is a powerful book. Historically its scope is broad. Spiritually its impact is tremendous. It will be a long time before another story will move you as much as Maria's.(240 pages)

IN THE PRESENCE OF MINE ENEMIES: *By Howard and Phyllis Rutledge with Mel and Lyla White. Charlotte, NC: Fleming H. Revell Co., 1973*
The heroic story of a former POW and his wife and the faith that sustained them. Howard Rutledge was a POW for seven years in North Vietnam.

BEYOND THE WALL: *By Hank Paulson with Don Richardson. Ventura, CA:Regal Books, 1982*
Beyond the Wall shows how the Communist philosophy has tried to stamp out religion throughout the Eastern European Communist nations. The strategy of the Communist rulers is to infiltrate churches to weaken them from within—in order not to make heroes and martyrs. But heroes there are, and you'll meet them and weep and rejoice with them and learn from their courageousness in following Christ. (172 pp $4.95)

CHRISTIANS UNDER THE HAMMER AND SICKLE: *By Wunrich Scheffbuch. Grand Rapids, MI: Zondervan Publishing House, 1972*
The book details the plight of evangelical believers in Russia as their faith is tested by fines, imprisonment, loss of jobs and educational opportunities, forcible removal of children and the strain of seeing fellow believers crack under relentless official pressure. The book cites actual documents and includes photographs, a list of prisoners and a comprehensive chronology of events.

PETER DYNAMITE: *By Norman Rohrer and Peter Deyneka, Jr. Grand Rapids, MI: Baker Book House, 1975*

Peter Dynamite is an apt pseudonym for Peter Deyneka, Sr., a Russian born peasant who converted to Christ in his youth while in America. His spiritual life has demonstrated the dunamis (power) of the Holy Spirit at work. God has used him to bring thousands to faith in Christ from among his native Slavic Peoples. Must reading for every believer. Theodore Epp, Director, Back To The Bible Broadcast. (192 pp.)

TORTURED FOR HIS FAITH: *By Haralan Popov. Grand Rapids, MI: Zondervan Publishing House, 1970*

Tortured For His Faith presents a courageous pastor's thirteen years of torture and imprisonment—and his fight to keep faith alive in prisons and his Communist homeland. He writes to debunk the spreading myth that Communism is "mellowing" toward religion and that the practices of the past, while bad, are over. Actually Christianity is being attacked more severely behind the IRON curtain than ever before. (140 pp.)

Communist World References

1. Johnstone, Patrick. *OPERATION WORLD. Bromeley, Kent, England: Send the Light Publications,* p. 70.
2. Neipp, Paul, *COMMUNISM IS TOTAL TYRANNY. Ridgecrest, CA: Through to Victory, p. 1.*
3. Osborne, T.L. *WHAT SHALL WE DO? Tulsa, OK: T.L. Osborne.*
4. Johnstone, Patrick. *OPERATION WORLD. Bromeley, Kent, England: Send the Light Publications,* p. 84.
5. *ASIAN REPORT. Hong Kong: Asian Outreach.*
6. *ASIAN REPORT. Hong Kong: Asian Outreach.*
7. Johnstone, Patrick. *OPERATION WORLD. Bromeley, Kent, England: Send the Light Publications,* 1979:91-92.
8. Johnstone, Patrick. *OPERATION WORLD. Bromeley, Kent, England: Send the Light Publications,* 1979:91.
9. Johnstone, Patrick. *OPERATION WORLD. Bromeley, Kent, England: Send the Light Publications,* 1979:93-95.
10. Hefley, James C. *BY THEIR BLOOD: Christian Martyrs of the Twentieth Century. Milford, MI: Mott Media, 1979:140*
11. Johnstone, Patrick. *OPERATION WORLD. Bromeley, Kent, England: Send the Light Publications,* 1979:86-87.
12. Johnstone, Patrick. *OPERATION WORLD. Bromeley, Kent, England: Send the Light Publications,* 1979:92-93.
13. Johnstone, Patrick. *OPERATION WORLD. Bromeley, Kent, England: Send the Light Publications,* 1979:92-93.
14. Hefley, James C. *BY THEIR BLOOD: Christian Martyrs of the Twentieth Century. Milford, MI: Mott Media, 1979:411.*
15. Hefley, James C. *BY THEIR BLOOD: Christian Martyrs of the Twentieth Century. Milford, MI: Mott Media, 1979:358.*
16. Hefley, James C. *BY THEIR BLOOD: Christian Martyrs of the Twentieth Century. Milford, MI: Mott Media, 1979:373.*
17. Hefley, James C. *BY THEIR BLOOD: Christian Martyrs of the Twentieth Century. Milford, MI: Mott Media, 1979:406.*
18. Hefley, James C. *BY THEIR BLOOD: Christian Martyrs of the Twentieth Century. Milford, MI: Mott Media, 1979:417.*
19. Hefley, James C. *BY THEIR BLOOD: Christian Martyrs of the Twentieth Century. Milford, MI: Mott Media, 1979:513.*
20. Hefley, James C. *BY THEIR BLOOD: Christian Martyrs of the Twentieth Century. Milford, MI: Mott Media, 1979:514.*
21. Hefley, James C. *BY THEIR BLOOD: Christian Martyrs of the Twentieth Century. Milford, MI: Mott Media, 1979:417.*
22. Hefley, James C. *BY THEIR BLOOD: Christian Martyrs of the Twentieth Century. Milford, MI: Mott Media, 1979:509.*
23. Johnstone, Patrick. *OPERATION WORLD. Bromeley, Kent, England: Send the Light Publications.* 1982:89.

THE SO-CALLED CHRISTIAN WORLD

UNDERSTANDING THE SO-CALLED CHRISTIAN WORLD

By the "So-called Christian World" we mean all of the Western Hemisphere, Western Europe, Australia, New Zealand, and the Philippines—lands which have been nominally Christian for centuries. Most of these are the nations which emerged from the Roman Empire, nations often referred to as "western," nations which were at the forefront of technological development throughout the industrial revolution. It is among these nations that the Gospel first took hold. It is from the eldest of these nations, in their colonial expansions, that Christianity was carried from the 15th through the 19th centuries. These are the lands that are more Christian than Muslim or Hindu or Buddhist or some other Oriental religion—lands thought by most Asians and Africans to be Christian.

Many countries in Africa have a higher percentage of Christians than there are in the United States. Gabon and Nambia are both 96% Christian; the United States, 88%. Zaire is 94% nominal Christian; The Congo, 93%; Lesotho, 92%; Angola, 90%; Equatorial Guinea, 89%. Sixteen other countries in Africa are more than 50% Christian. But most of these have been predominantly Christian in only recent years, so we have not included them in the So-called Christian World.

Some have asked us why we don't call it the "Christian World" rather than the "So-called Christian World." The reason, of course, is that not all who profess to be Christian are truly Christian.

Many cultists profess to be Christians, yet deny the Lord who bought them, claiming that He is some kind of lesser god and could not have made full satisfaction for our sins or that He was no god at all, just a good man, a great teacher, a miracle worker, but nothing more. They deny the basic Christian doctrine that Jesus is the only way to eternal life (John 14:6, John 3:36, Acts 4:12, I John 5:12), that all have sinned and come short of the glory of God, being justified freely by His grace through the redemption that is in Jesus Christ (Rom. 3:23-24).

Millions of others belong to churches that officially teach this basic truth, and they honor Christ with their lips, but their heart is far from Him (Matt. 15:18). Some of them prophesy in the name of Jesus, and in His name cast out devils, and do many wonderful works. But they shall never enter into the kingdom of heaven. The Lord will say to them, "I never knew you; depart from Me, you that work iniquity" (Matt. 7:21-23).

Jesus said, "By their fruits you shall know them" (Matt. 7:16,20). While speaking specifically of false prophets, these words apply to *all* professing Christians. And we don't see much fruit of the Spirit (Gal. 5:22,23) among millions of church members today. The vast majority of church goers seldom read the Bible, pray only for themselves, hardly ever witness, and give less than 3% of their income to the glory of God and the extension of His kingdom.

In the meantime, these so-called Christian countries have become so immoral as to defy description. Prostitution, homosexuality, pornography, rape, incest, drug addiction, alcoholism, child molestation, bestiality, and every kind of sexual perversion imaginable portrayed in books and even on the screen, not to mention the million or more unborn babies that are murdered every year.

Add to all of this immorality, the fighting between Catholics and Protestants that the world has witnessed down through the centuries and even today in Ireland, the Crusades against the Muslims in the 12th and 13th centuries (which haven't been forgotten by them), the discrimination and bigotry seen in so-called Christian lands, the Satanism, the humanistic atheism taught in our public schools, the injustice in our courts, the total disregard of authority on the part of so many, and what do we have? Certainly not a Christian nation! And where will you find conditions any better in

Cross-References
Alcoholism, *127*
Christian World, *3*
Immorality, *127*
So-Called Christian World, *3, 7*

this so-called Christian world? Certainly not in Mexico or Panama or Brazil or France or any other country you can name in Latin America or Western Europe or anywhere else.

Judeo–Christian World

This is another name that might be used for the area we identify as the "so-called Christian world." The roots of our faith are in Judaism. The gentile and the Jew co-existed. Today, even though there is a Jewish nation, Israel, there are Jews dispersed world-wide, with most still residing within the so-called Christian world.

THE UNITED STATES

While it's true that the overwhelming majority of the people in the United States are NOMINAL Christians (40% Protestant, 30% Roman Catholic), it is also true that a very small percentage of these professing Christians are really committed to exalting Christ, even in their own country, much less in the regions beyond.

Americans spend 700 times as much of their money on recreation and luxuries and on sinful and harmful pursuits as they give to world evangelization. They spend 60 times as much on alcoholic beverages, 30 times as much on tobacco, and 15 times as much on their pets as on the proclamation of the Gospel of Jesus Christ in other lands, as we were commanded to do.

Another $80 billion is spent annually on cocaine, marijuana, and other *mind-destroying drugs,* for which much of the money was obtained through armed robbery and cold-blooded murder. In some communities, half the high school students are on dope. Even in elementary schools, many children are already "hooked". And a very alarming number of our military service-men—on whom we depend for protection—are also drug addicts.

In addition to the drug problem, 20 million drunks in the United States are responsible for the slaughter of 25,000 people on our highways every year and the mangling of thousands of others. Alcoholics who don't actually kill anyone often destroy their own families in one way or another and cost taxpayers millions of dollars every year for rehabilitation programs and imprisonment.

With all this alcoholism and dope addiction—together with the light sentences for dope peddling and violent crimes (such as a five year sentence for two murders), it should come as no surprise to anyone that the United States has the *highest crime rate in the entire world.*

Since our supreme court can't even define *obscenity,* we now have no censorship of films and literature. Anything goes! All kinds of sex acts are portrayed on the screen, even on some TV channels, as well as in literature. Some of the very wealthiest people in the U.S. are pornographers. Because of all this portrayal of illicit sex and sex perversion, we've been reading with horror about the increasing number of forcible rapes (an estimated 82,000 in 1980) including gang rapes and the raping of elderly women and small children. And, of course, thousands of rapes go

Cross-References
United States, *7, 172, 176*
USA, *23, 59, 91, 101, 200, 204*

unreported. Then, too, homosexuals flaunt their perversion and arrogantly demand their "rights."

Prostitution is another big business in the United States. In a recent year, 89,000 arrests were made for this activity, probably a very small percentage of those who make this their profession. But little is said on TV or anywhere else against this evil practice. It is just accepted as another way of life.

Public schools in the U.S. have become little more than battle grounds. Teachers are not allowed to discipline children. Consequently little is taught. Increasing numbers of young people are graduating from high school who can't even read simple directions or fill out an application form without help.

What they *do* learn is that there are no absolutes, no right or wrong, do whatever you think is right and makes you feel good. They are taught evolution which denies the existence of God and all moral values. If there's no God, who's to say what's right and wrong?

Is it any wonder that there's little or no respect for teachers or law enforcement officers or any kind of authority? This country is rushing headlong into anarchy, where everyone does what is right in his own eyes and very little of what he does is right in the sight of God.

Anti-Christian humanism is spreading throughout Europe and North America. This philosophy has corrupted every part of our culture—art, music, social values, morality, and theology. It has also spawned Communism which is determined to wipe out Christianity. The resulting moral collapse of the West has brought these lands into their tragic, spiritually bankrupt state in the face of the most determined opposition it has ever had to face. People now speak of the decadent civilization of the West, the de-Christianizing of Europe, or even the post-Christian era.

Largely because of this atheistic, humanistic teaching in our schools and the sexual permissiveness in this country and the misguided judges on our supreme court, there are now *4,000 murders in the United States every day*—one murder every 21 seconds—one and a half million murders every year. The reference is to the legal murder of unborn children through abortion.

Add to this all the other murders (23,000 per year), kidnapping, cursing and beating of parents, astrology, witchcraft, spiritism, affliction of widows and orphans, blasphemy (all of which were punishable by death in the Old Testament) and add the armed robbery, arson, vandalism, wife beating, child abuse, gambling, forgery, embezzlement, lying, cheating, slandering, perjury, orgies, debauchery and all the other indescribably wicked and lewd conduct—it is quite obvious that the U.S. is anything but a Christian country.

One of the tragic things about all this corruption in the United States is the fact that these evil-doers are thought to be Christians by the peoples of Asia and Africa. After all, they do come from Christian countries, don't they? So when they see these Americans and Europeans behaving the way they do, they think that they are behaving like Christians, and who wants a religion like that? No wonder Americans have been looked upon for many years as "foreign devils." *PROBABLY THE GREATEST HINDRANCE TO THE GOSPEL OF JESUS CHRIST* now, as down through the centuries, has been the conduct of *people who called themselves Christians, or were thought to be Christians* simply because they came from a supposedly Christian country.

WHY DOESN'T GOD DESTROY AMERICA? God destroyed the entire earth once because of wickedness. "He saw how great man's wickedness has become, and that every inclination of the thoughts of his heart was only evil all the time (Gen. 6:5). So He wiped man off the face of the earth except for Noah and his family.

God destroyed Sodom and Gomorrah because of their sexual perversion (Jude 7) and because they were arrogant, overfed, and unconcerned; they didn't help the poor and needy. They were haughty and did detestable things (Ezekiel 16:49-50).

Cross-References
Stewardship, *194, 197, 210*

Jesus told His disciples that it will be more bearable for Sodom and Gomorrah on the day of judgement than for people who would not listen to their message concerning the Kingdom (Matt. 10:15) and would not repent (Matt. 11:24).

People in the U.S. have had far more opportunity to hear and read the Word of God than anyone ever had in Sodom or Gomorrah or anywhere else. But millions trample the Word of God under foot, defying and blaspheming Him, rejecting His Son who died for them and rose again, and arrogantly parade their shameful deeds for all to see. Millions of others could not be accused of any acts of violence or sex perversion, but like the Sodomites, are arrogant, overfed, and unconcerned about the poor and needy and do nothing to glorify God in their own land or in the regions beyond.

Millions go to church every Sunday, but they rob God every week (Mal. 3:8) giving little or nothing for the advancement of the kingdom. (The average church member in the U.S. gives less than 3% of his income for all church purposes, and only 5% of that amount is used for foreign missions). That's 15/100ths of one percent of the average church member's income used to make disciples of all nations as Christ commanded. Anyone who knows the good he ought to do, and doesn't do it sins (James 4:17).

In 1981, the per capita income in the U.S. was over $10,000. If the average Protestant church member gave 10% of his income for all church purposes, the total for the 70 million Protestants would be 70 billion dollars (70 million × $10,000 × 10%) instead of the $24 billion that was actually given. And if just half of that $70 billion were given to world missions, there would have been $35 billion, instead of just one billion dollars given for preaching the Gospel in other lands. And there would still be 60% more for exalting Christ in our own land than was used for this purpose in 1981).

So, since even the average church member in this country has rebelled against God and has steadfastly refused to obey His Great Commission to "make disciples of all people" (Matt. 28:19), and have little or no concern for the poor and needy in other lands (especially the *spiritually* poor and needy), WHY DOESN'T HE DESTROY AMERICA as He destroyed Sodom and Gomorrah?

A *possible answer* is that there are still *more missionaries* sent out from this country than from any other. Of the 81,000 missionaries sent to other peoples in 1979, 55,000 of them were sent from the U.S. and Canada.

As God would have spared Sodom for the sake of ten righteous people (out of a total of perhaps 10,000) so He is sparing the U.S. for the sake of the ten—that is, the "one-tenth of one percent" of the inhabitants of this land who love the Lord with all their heart and soul and keep His commandments. Truly, righteousness *does* exalt a nation (Prov. 14:34).

Praise God for those who are truly Christian. Pray for a great revival throughout the U.S. and Canada and the Western world, for the sake of those who are revived and for their own country, for the sake of the whole world, and for Jesus' sake—that His suffering and dying for them will not have been in vain.

God said, "If my people who call themselves by My name, will humble themselves and pray and seek My face and turn from their wicked ways—then I will hear from heaven, and will forgive their sin, and will heal their land" (II Chron. 7:14).

THAT IS OUR ONLY HOPE!

But if we forsake His decrees and commands and serve other gods (money, sex, or whatever) no doubt He will pulverize this nation like He did Sodom and Gomorrah, or He will scatter us as He did His own people Israel or permit us to be enslaved by the Communists as so many millions of others have been in Eastern Europe and Asia and parts of Africa. Worst of all, the children of the kingdom shall be cast out into outer darkness where there shall be weeping and gnashing of teeth (for all eternity).

If we continue this immoral downward plunge and continue to trample the Good News of Jesus Christ underfoot, then, as Jesus told the Jews, the Kingdom of God will be taken from you and given to a nation bringing forth the fruits thereof.

Pray for our nation and for the Western so-called Christian World. Pray for the political leaders and for the church leaders. Pray for the Lord's richest blessing on all those who proclaim His Word in truth and purity and sincerity. Pray for Christian teachers in our public and private schools and for Christian leaders in government and other places of influence. Pray for revival to sweep these nominal Christian countries from border to border, from coast to coast.

Jimmy and Carol Owens in the book *If MY People...* listed some suggestions for prayer taken from Derek Prince:

1. The first ministry and outreach of believers meeting together in regular fellowship is *prayer*.
2. The first specific topic for prayer is the *government*.
3. We are to pray for *good government*.
4. God desires all men to have the truth of the gospel preached to them.
5. Good government *facilitates* the preaching of the gospel while bad government *hinders* it.
6. Therefore good government is the will of God.

The Owens also have a suggested prayer list:

1. *Sins of the Nation*: Continue to confess the sins of the nation as the Holy Spirit brings them to your attention. Ask for God's forgiveness and mercy.
2. *Government Officials* from the national to local levels. Pray for their salvation and for God's guidance for them. Pray for them by name, if possible. Ask God to remove the ungodly and corrupt and replace them with people of His choice.
3. *Your City:* In Jeremiah 29:7, God spoke to His people who were living in captivity in Babylon. The Lord told them to settle down there and "occupy" in the midst of their enemies. He gave them prayer responsibility for their city.
4. *Courts:* Pray that justice will be done for all men. Ask for righteous judges who will make decisions which are in line with God's will.
5. *Law Enforcement Agencies:* Pray for the salvation of many law officers. Pray for their protection from violence.
6. *Violence:* Pray against spirits of violence in your city and in the nation. Speak against and bind up these spirits who stir up terrorists and anarchists. Take authority over them in the name of Jesus Christ.
7. *The Media:* Pray that people of integrity be placed in the news media. Pray diligently against pornography in all phases of the media. Speak against the spirits of lust that stir up this activity.
8. *The Economy:* Pray for those who exert great influence over the national (and international) economy, such as business leaders, international banking concerns and labor unions. Ask God to raise up people of His own choice to positions of leadership. Bring them under the influence of the kingdom of leadership.
9. *Schools:* Pray that God will raise Christian teachers and officials in our school systems. Speak out in prayer and in public against the encroachment of occult influences in our schools.

10. *Families:* Pray for your own, your neighbors and those in your church. Ask God to save the lost, to heal relationships, to "turn the hearts of the parents to the children and the hearts of the children to their parents" (Mal. 4:6).

11. *Areas of Special Need:* World economy and food shortages, for example. Use your newspaper and newscasts as guidelines for prayer. Pray as you listen to the news. It's a good way to keep your government officials under a constant covering of prayer.

12. *Revival:* Pray for a great ingathering of those who don't know the Lord, and an outpouring of God's love and power in the Church.

13. *The Hungry:* Pray for them as you would for your own family. Fasting will help you identify with them in their hunger. Ask God to show you how to help in practical ways.

14. *Your Church:* Pray for your fellow Christians and their needs, and pray for your pastor! He needs your prayer support.

15. *Principalities and Powers:* Pray together as a church against the ruling spirits in your nation. Pray and believe for the over-ruling power of God to begin functioning in these areas. Establish the kingdom of God in your national government through intercession and spiritual warfare.

Cross-References
Campus Ministry, *155*
Los Angeles, *146, 150, 154*

THE NEEDS AND THE OPPORTUNITIES FOR CROSS CULTURAL MINISTRY IN THE UNITED STATES

While Protestant Christianity is spreading rapidly in Africa and Latin America and in some parts of Asia, Protestantism is definitely shrinking in the United States, from 67% of the populace in 1900 to a projected 33% by the end of the century.

Meanwhile the Lord is bringing people from nearly every land and tongue to our shores—and to our very doorstep. Twenty percent (32.4 million) of the people in this country speak languages other than English (1983). The Los Angeles police department uses 42 languages in its work.

In 1984 there were 339,000 international students in the U.S. from 181 different countries. Eighty-four colleges had more than 500 international students enrolled. Sixty percent of these foreign students are from Asia, 15% from Latin America, 13% from Africa, and 8% from Europe.

Ten thousand of these international students are from the People's Republic of China. It is estimated that this number will double in the next year or two, providing Americans with perhaps one of the best opportunities for Chinese evangelism in this decade (Watchman on the Great Wall, Oct., 1981, page 6).

Mark Hanna of International Students Incorporated reports that fewer than one-half of one percent of all Protestant missionaries are working among international students, who constitute one of the greatest missionary opportunities of the century. These internationals will be among the top leaders of the world in the next twenty to twenty five years. Many will return to countries that are closed to traditional mission work and/or to resistant peoples. Tragically, less than one-fourth of one percent of these international students are being effectively reached with the Gospel of Jesus Christ.[1]

In addition to these foreign students, hundreds of thousands of immigrants and refugees are coming to the U.S. every year. And their numbers will continue to increase because the U.S. government allows 700,000 immigrants to enter legally every year. In addition, hundreds of thousands or even a million or more enter illegally every twelve months.

In 1984 there were 14 million ethnics living in the U.S. in addition to the 28 million blacks, 16 million Hispanics, 7 million Jews, and 1.4 million American Indians. These 14 million include 2.7 million Vietnamese, a million Chinese, 700,000 Japanese, 775,000 Filipinos, 665,000 Cubans, 600,000 Haitians, 335,000 Koreans, 120,000 Thais, another 120,000 Laotians, and thousands from virtually every country in Asia, Africa, and Latin America. Yes, God certainly is bringing the world to our very door. What a tragedy, what a terrible sin of omission if we neglect to do all we can to evangelize these people!

ETHNIC GROUPS WITHIN THE U.S.A.

THE JEWS

Many Christians are not concerned about winning the Jews to Christ. They seem to think that the Jews are beyond hope, that they will never accept Jesus as their Lord and Savior. But God is not willing that any should perish (2 Pet. 3:9), nor is He finished with the Jew (Rom. 11:1). St. Paul asks, "Did they stumble so as to fall beyond recovery? Not at all! Rather, because of their transgressions, salvation has come to the Gentiles to make Israel envious. But if their transgression means riches for the world, and their loss means riches for the Gentiles, how much greater riches will their fulness bring? (Rom. 11:11-13). And if they do not persist in unbelief, they will be grafted in, for God is able to graft them in again.

St. Paul goes on to say, "Israel has experienced hardening *in part* until the full number of the Gentiles has come in. And so all Israel shall be saved (Rom. 11:25,26). As far as election is concerned, they are loved on account of the patriarchs, for God's gift and his call are irrevocable. Just as you who were at one time disobedient to God have now received mercy as a result of their disobedience, so they too have now become disobedient in order that they too may now receive mercy as a result of God's mercy to you. For God has bound all men over to disobedience so that He may have mercy on them all. Oh the depth of the riches of the wisdom and knowledge of God! How unsearchable his judgments and His paths beyond tracing out!" (Rom 11:11,12,25,26,28-33).

No, God is not finished with the Jew. This should be obvious not only from Scripture, but through the history of the Jews from the first century to the present. These people have gone through long, intense, terrible suffering for more than 19 centuries and are still fighting for their existence today. Ever since the destruction of Jerusalem in 70 A.D., that place has been a tale of horror and blood. The Jews, scattered throughout the world, have been the object of extermination in one country after another. Repeatedly they have been brought to the verge of annihilation. Their sufferings as "Christ-killers" during the Middle Ages were unbelievable.

Much of the persecution of the Jews has been at the hands of so-called Christian nations or their leaders. It is said that John Chrysostom, an early Church Father, preached that God hates the Jew, and the Christians should also hate them because the Jew was the Christ killer. Actually, we are all responsible for the suffering and death of our Savior. We are all sinners, and Christ Jesus came into the world to save sinners. He was wounded for *our* transgressions (Isa. 53:6). It was *our* sins that nailed Him to the cross.

The Roman Catholic church banished Jews from the Vatican State in the 13th and 16th centuries. The Inquisitors sought to force the Jewish Marronos in Spain to live like Christians for 300 years until they were finally expelled from that country in 1492.

Is it any wonder, then, that a mistrust of Christians and a deeply rooted prejudice against Christianity possess the soul of the Jewish people when they have suffered such ill treatment at the instigation of churchmen!

For three centuries Protestant churches did nothing to evangelize the Jews. The first mission established to evangelize them was founded in England in 1809.

The colonial churches in the new world had little concern for the spiritual welfare of the growing number of Jewish emigrants who were fleeing to America for asylum from various countries of the world. It was not until 1885 that the American

Cross-References

England, *7, 166*

Judaism, *199*

Persecution, *11, 14, 38, 77, 80, 109, 116, 123, 129*

Roman Catholic Church, *118, 148, 150, 162, 169, 199*

Messianic Fellowship was established under the name, "Chicago Hebrew Mission." A decade later in New York City the American Board of Missions to the Jews began work among the largest concentration of Jews in the world. But the greatest concern for Jewish evangelism in the U.S. is a 20th century phenomenon.

By 1970 there were 50 mission societies and over 400 missionaries to the seven million Jews in the United States. That's one missionary for every fifteen thousand Jews. But these missionaries are not evenly distributed. One-third of the Jews in this country live in New York City, but only 44 missionaries work in that city; each missionary, therefore, has a mission field of 45,000 Jews.

Hundreds of cities have no missionaries at all. Boston, for example, has 170,000 Jews and not a single missionary (Parvin 1985:160). Obviously much more needs to be done to evangelize the Jewish people in the United States. The same is true throughout the world.

Every Christian should be concerned and should be witnessing to Jews whenever he has an opportunity, and he should be praying for them all the time and also praying for the peace of Jerusalem (Ps. 122:6).

Worldwide there are about 17 million Jews including 3.2 million in Israel, seven million in North America, 4 million in Russia, half a million in Britain, and a like number in France and in Argentina. While many societies work specifically among Jewish people in the U.S. and in Britain, very little is done in other so-called Christian countries such as France and Argentina. Pray the Lord of harvest to send forth more laborers into this part of His harvest, and their labor will bear much fruit to God's glory and the extension of His kingdom.

What do Jews believe? It is a mistake to identify Judaism with Old Testament religion and to overlook post-biblical teaching which forms a large part of present-day Jewish religion. It is also incorrect to assume that Judaism of the post-biblical period was the same kind of religion most commonly practiced among Jews today. Judaism is a conglomeration, the result of a long process of religious development. It has been influenced by ideas which cannot be traced back to the Old Testament, and has also incorporated some teachings which cannot be found in the Talmud which was compiled between the 3rd and 6th centuries of the Christian era, whose instructions are accepted as just as important as those of the Old Testament.

Strange as it may seem, it is difficult to summarize the fundamental teachings of Judaism. There is no formal summary of Jewish doctrine that would be acceptable to all Jews.

We hear of Orthodox, Conservative, and Progressive (or Reform) Judaism, but these are not always separated by rigid borderlines, and these terms do not always have the same meaning in every land.[3]

The majority of the Jews in this country came from the European ghettos and brought with them a strict, legalistic Orthodox Judaism. In a suburb of Detroit there's an Orthodox Jewish community where men may be seen wearing black Homberg hats, long overcoats, and full beards. There are 19 synagogues in the community, ten Jewish bakeries, an equal number of butcher shops, and two rabbinical colleges.

But most of the Jews discarded ghetto Judaism and the Yiddish language as they reformed their lifestyle and joined the Reform synagogue.

Many Jews have taken a middle-of-the-road position referred to as Conservative Judaism. In Conservativism there was a move to restore Jewishness without the legalism of the Orthodox. The three sects have about equal numbers of adherents, each with about 18% of the Jewish population.

The fourth and largest group of American Jews is the 2.7 million unaffiliated Jews. Many of these are business and professional people who have incomes about twice that of the national average. They have no inclination to lose their Jewishness, even though one-third of their youth marry Gentiles. They all declare "faith in the Torah" which is the entire body of written and oral Law, considered the "source of life" of the Jewish people.[4]

Centralization of power in the Jewish community has drifted away from the synagogue and the rabbi to the community federation and its president. When evangelizing the Jew, consideration of this power structure must be taken into account, together with the subsequent loss of power of the rabbi and synagogue. Surveys reveal that only about 9% of the Jews in America attend a synagogue with any degree of regularity.

Missionary work among Jews is primarily a one-on-one ministry. It may be a door-to-door ministry or a Bible correspondence course, or a telephone ministry. Whatever kind of ministry it is, it will require a good deal of patience and understanding.

Festive occasions are important to the Jews. Missionaries have discovered that Jews often accept invitations to banquets in which Jewish festivals are commemorated.

Education is given a high priority among the Jews, which means that quality Christian literature should be produced for them. It also suggests the need for a broad campus ministry.

Many believe that now is the day for Jewish evangelism. Jews are more responsive to the Gospel than ever before. But where will they go to church?

There are at least two options. First, of course, the Hebrew Christian may join a Gentile church. However, most churches are not prepared to receive Jewish believers. Another option would be to attend one of seventy messianic congregations. In this atmosphere the Jew can worship in a traditional manner centered around the Messiah who has brought new abundant life to Judaism. Moishe Rosen, founder of the Jews for Jesus Mission, popularized this approach in 1973.

But there are others who contend that messianic Judaism is neither messianic or Jewish, nor Biblical. Paul Feinberg of Trinity Evangelical Divinity School asks: "Does the Messianic Jewish approach make the Christian witness more credible in the Jewish community?"

In reply, Richard Quebedeaux, author of "Those Worldly Evangelicals," suggests that it does not when he says, "Because the established Jewish community feels that these Messianic Jews are really Christian evangelists masquerading as Jews to gain converts, it is extremely upset by their actions.[5]

If American Jews are to be won to Christ, Jewish home missions must enlarge their work force and expand geographicaly. They must reach into those cities where there are large numbers of Jews and little or no missionary presence. In addition, the church will have to recognize its privilege and responsibility to include the evangelization of the Jews in its own evangelistic outreach.

For many years the leaders of mission organizations have been offering training programs to local churches. All of the larger missions conduct seminars to train laymen to reach their Jewish neighbors, but the response has been meager. We need to pray that attitudes toward the Jews will be changed, that church members will have a genuine love and concern and passion for these precious souls for whom Christ died.

We praise God that there is a growing interest in Jewish evangelism. Bible schools, such as Moody Bible Institute, have developed a program of Jewish mission studies, and Jewish mission boards stand ready to assist any church that is interested in starting a Jewish evangelistic program.

NATIVE AMERICANS

When the white man arrived in North America back in the 15th century, there were about one million Indians living in what has since become the United States. But by 1887, because of wars, death marches, and the white man's diseases, the Indian population had dwindled to about one-fourth that number. But then their numbers began to increase again. Today there are about 1.4 million Indians in the United States.

Ninety-two percent of all the Indians in this country do not attend church. Tom Claus (American Indian Crusades), himself an Indian, estimates that only 3 to 5% are Christians. Most Indians are involved in native religious ceremonies including the Peyote Cult, incorporated as a National American church. Indians who live on reservations may live many miles from the nearest church. Those who live in the city do not live in groups as do other ethnics, but are scattered throughout the city. These Indians do not feel comfortable in other inner city churches, including black and Hispanic.

Why haven't more Indians become Christians? Many reasons could be given, but time and space will permit just a few. In the first place, the great majority of the early colonists were not interested in the evangelization of the Indians, but rather in their elimination. Secondly, even the ministers of the Gospel, until recent times, believed that the Indian could not be evangelized unless he was civilized first. That meant he must leave his culture, his clan, and his people. He had to dress and act like an Anglo-Saxon, and he must speak English. Thirdly, the U.S. government, a so-called "Christian" government, at times encouraged the wholesale slaughter of the Indians. Fourthly, the Indians were never fully accepted or trusted as bona fide citizens. And fifthly, the Indians have found it difficult to accept the Gospel message from the lips of the white man whose word was seldom trustworthy in other matters. Three hundred seventy treaties were signed between 1789 and 1871 (just 82 years), and every one of them was broken.[6]

Reservations were created by the U.S. government in 1786, supposedly to protect Indians' lands. But less than a half century later, in 1830, Congress passed the Indian Removal Act, and within ten years 100,000 Indians were rounded up from every state east of the Mississippi River and removed to Indian Country, which later became the state of Oklahoma.

In North Carolina the Cherokee nation resisted. Without provocation, 20,000 were put in stockades, where several thousand died. Then, during the winter, 16,000 were herded to Indian Country over the 1200-mile Trail of Tears that required nine months to travel. Twenty-five percent of the tribe died on that march, which had been ordered by President Andrew Jackson.

Another of the many negative experiences with the white man occurred in 1924 when the Indians were forced to reduce the size of their stocks of cattle by killing them. They lost their main source of income. Is it any wonder that the Indians have little love for the white man (so-called Christians) and are not inclined to believe anything the white man says? It is easy to understand their resistance to the message of salvation when brought to them by members of such a cruel and deceptive race.

Today about half of the 1.4 million Indians in the United States live on or around nearly a hundred reservations under the jurisdiction of the Bureau of Indian Affairs. The other half is scattered among major cities. Eighty percent of all Indians live west of the Mississippi River. The largest concentration is in California (201,300), about 50,000 of whom live in the Los Angeles area.

The second largest concentration of Indians is in Oklahoma where 170,000 of them are divided among 67 tribes. Arizona has 153,000 Indians, mostly Navajos in the northeastern part of the state. But the Navajo reservation spills over into New Mexico, Utah, and Colorado. The total number of Navajos is about 200,000. The reservation (25,000 square miles) is roughly the size of West Virginia.

Although there are about 100 reservations throughout the country, more than half of all reservation Indians live on one of twenty reservations. The Navajo reservation is by far the largest. Three others have 20,000 to 27,000 inhabitants. All others have less than 20,000. Most reservations have less than 6000 residents.

Before the coming of the white man, there were 460 tribes. Today there are fragments of 280 tribes speaking 158 languages. Only three have the entire Bible, six have only the New Testament, forty-six have only portions of God's Word. Fifty-seven languages are extremely bilingual, forty-nine are nearly extinct, and translation is in progress in twenty-three. There is need for work to begin in six others. Two languages need a new translation or revision.[7]

As we mentioned earlier, 92% of the American Indians do not go to church. Much remains to be done on the reservations as well as among the urban Indians.

One of the greatest needs on the reservation is the training of national pastors and evangelists. Another great need, especially on the Navajo reservation, is literacy work in their native tongue. They've had the New Testament for many years, and the translation of the Old Testament has just recently been completed. But half of the adult population is illiterate. What good will the Bible do them if they are unable to read it? If there is ever to be a strong national church on the Navajo reservation, these people must not only have the Word of God in their mother tongue, but they must be able to read it for themselves.

Another great need on the Navajo reservation and on many other reservations is the teaching of English as a second language. The Indians should be able to read God's Word in their own language, for that language is the one that really speaks to their heart. But they should also learn English since that is the national language of the country in which they live, and there is such a vast amount of Christian and other literature in English. Teaching English is a great door opener for the Gospel, for it gives the teacher opportunities day after day after day to share his faith with his students and their families.

One of the greatest problems facing Indian missions is the evangelization of urban Indians, because there are no native American communities in the city. Many Indians do not feel welcome in most urban churches, whether these be predominantly Anglo-Saxon, black, or Hispanic.

This is not the place to review Indian beliefs and practices nor the many problems and issues a missionary to these people must face. For more information about such subjects, we refer you to the brief bibliography at the end of this chapter. Meanwhile, pray for the 92% of the Indians who are unchurched, and pray the Lord of harvest to send forth workers—the right kind of workers—into His harvest.

Cross-References

Education & Schools, *13, 19, 21, 32, 36, 38, 50, 68, 83, 108, 110, 138, 192*

Teaching (English), *16, 21, 36, 151, 158*

BLACK AMERICANS

There are 28 million black Americans today, and 40% of them are unchurched. It is doubtful that even half of the 16.3 million church members are committed Evangelicals. This means that some 17 million blacks in this country are beyond the reach of normal evangelistic outreach of the established evangelical churches. Only four countries of black Africa have a greater population than black America.

One reason for the spiritual plight of black America is that there are so few evangelical black leaders. Until recently, most Bible colleges and seminaries would not accept black students. Even today only 4% of all seminary students are black, although blacks constitute 12% of the U.S. population.

Young blacks are not joining black churches, and others are leaving them because there are few programs designed specifically for them.

Because of the failure of black churches to meet the spiritual needs of their people, very few blacks are giving themselves to full-time Christian service at home or abroad. Many blacks are turning to cults. Two hundred thousand of them have turned to the Black Muslim movement, and 800,000 have become Catholic.

The black church has failed, but so has the white church. Blacks are not often made to feel very comfortable in white churches. And there has never been a consistant, concentrated effort on the part of whites to evangelize the black community.

It is ironic that Americans can see the needs of 320 million blacks in Africa and send 8,000 missionaries at a cost of $255 million annually but can't see the need of black Americans—or, if they can see the need, are not concerned about it.

As one missionary has pointed out, there is something *insincere* about the white church's concern for reaching blacks in Africa and neglecting blacks in our own country.

Blacks have been discriminated against ever since they began to arrive in this country as slaves in 1619. They have suffered the refusal of all so-called "inalienable rights," such as justice, education, and even the hearing of the Gospel.

Eighty-one percent of all black Americans live in an urban, central city setting. They live on about 59% of what whites make, and they are laid off from their employment twice as often as whites. That may be partly because 40% of blacks drop out of school, and only one in six goes to college. Blacks subsist in substandard housing often collecting welfare checks that further demoralize them.

Fifty-five percent of the black households have no father, 86% of the children born to teenagers are illegitimate, venereal diseases are 10 to 12 times higher than the national average. Alcoholism exists in nearly every household.

Blacks join gangs for survival in the streets and spend millions of dollars on drugs to escape a dead-ended existence. Then to support their habit, they turn to crime, mostly against their own people. The survival rate for gang life is only 3 out of 10 over a period of 5 years; for 4 die and 3 go to jail.

If black teenagers turn to the black church, as 60% of them do, they find an unresponsive organization. The black church is not offering the answers that blacks need to face the realities of life. Consequently, large numbers of them are commiting suicide.

What hope is there without education, job skills, good government, or a spiritual church? They cast about searching for answers. It is estimated that fifty black Americans turn to Islam every week, partly as a result of Muslim missionaries from Africa working in the black community.

Blacks believe that the virtual silence of the church in speaking out against the evils of slavery was tantamount to approval. Moreover, the involvement of Christians in the slavery movement, leading them to use Scripture and Christianity as tools for keeping blacks obedient, has prejudiced many against Christianity.

Cross-References
Slavery, *65, 127*

Due to many restrictions placed on the blacks in the 17th and 18th centuries, only a few of them joined organized churches. In the year 1800, only 4 or 5% of blacks were church members. That was approximately 50,000 out of a million people. By 1860 the number was 14%.

Today about 60% of all blacks belong to churches that are primarily black. There are 3 National Baptist Conventions with a combined membership of 8.6 million. The 3 Methodist Episcopal churches claim a membership of 2.4 million. There are probably 1.6 million blacks integrated into white churches. 3 million have joined the Pentecostal movement. 400,000 are Roman Catholics; 300,000 are Methodists; and 200,000 are Northern Baptists. Altogether there are about 16.3 million black Christians.

Sad to say, many black preachers are more concerned about how they sound than in how many people are being won to Christ. Howard Jones agrees that the ministry of evangelism is not given a high priority in the majority of black churches.

The black church has become highly institutionalized. It has so many auxiliary programs that people become too busy to have time for evangelism.

The sad spiritual condition of the black church is reflected in its attitude toward foreign missions. Joseph Washington states that blacks are difficult to recruit for anything that requires sustained sacrifice for others. There is largely an absence of missionary vision.

Another problem within the black church is its limited emphasis on the Sunday school. The need for black-oriented Sunday school literature is critical. What is available is geared too high for adequate understanding and is rarely related to black culture.

As for the pastors, they frequently have no formal education. This is often true of "store front churches" in the inner city which are often pastored by men who have retired from secular employment or who must work at a secular job to subsidize his salary. Obviously, he is not able to give the church the attention it needs.

To further complicate the picture, there are actually *three black groups* in America: the descendants of the "free persons of color" of pre Civil War America; the descendants of emancipated slaves (by far the largest group); and the West Indian immigrants. Each has his own ethnic identity to be considered for evangelization.

We need to pray daily for well-trained pastors, evangelists, and teachers for the black community, for a missionary vision for its leadership, and a real burden and passion for souls here in our own country and around the world.

HISPANICS

About ten percent of the world's Spanish speakers live in the United States. That is the estimate of mission organizations. Because of their high birth rate, they may soon become the largest minority in the U.S. At the moment, they are second only to the blacks (28 million).

By and large the Spanish speakers have been neglected by the Roman Catholic church as well as by the protestant churches.

The Spanish arrived in this part of the world as early as 1502. For three centuries they held all the southland from Florida to California. They also possessed the land from Texas to Mississippi and northward to Canada. In 1800, Spain gave this Mississippi Valley land to France, and three years later, the U.S. acquired it from France along with the rest of the Louisiana Purchase. The Gulf states and Florida were purchased from Spain in 1819. The Southwest from Texas to California was obtained through the Treaty of Quadalupe Hidalgo following the Mexican War in 1848.

Since 1800 millions of Mexicans have migrated to the U.S. to provide cheap unskilled labor in the mines, the cotton fields of Texas, the sugar beet industry, and the orchards, vineyards and truck farms of California and many other states. They also provided cheap labor for railroad construction and maintenance. Although legal channels allow Mexicans to enter the U.S., millions have entered the country illegally. Some estimate that as many as 12 million Hispanics now reside in this country illegally.

Mexicans constitute 60% of the Hispanics in the U.S. Puerto Ricans constitute the second largest Spanish speaking group. More than two million of them have taken up residence in this country, mostly in New York City.

Cubans began coming to this country in large numbers in 1959 to escape Communist rule. The Cuban refugees were quite different from other Spanish speakers who had come to the States. Among these refugees were doctors, lawyers, engineers, teachers, and successful businessmen, most of whom were affluent and were already fluent speakers of English as a second language. About 6% of the Hispanics in the U.S. are Cubans, and half of them live in Florida.

It is estimated that two million Central and South Americans have come to the U.S. In 1982 alone, some 100,000 El Salvadorians fled to Los Angeles. In New York City alone there are 25,000 Uruguayans and 50,000 Colombians. Another 100,000 Colombians live in Miami. The Central and South Americans total eight percent of all Hispanics in this country.

Sixty to eighty percent of all Hispanics live in a band fifty miles deep, running parallel to the border from Los Angeles to the Gulf of Mexico. California, Arizona, New Mexico, and Texas are home for more than 8 million Hispanics. The state of California is 25% Hispanic; Texas is 20% or more. One source says 49%.

South Florida is visited each year by 13 million foreigners, most of whom are Hispanics. By 1981, the Miami area was 40% Hispanic. Latins might well be in the majority in the very near future in that city.

Los Angeles, with 2 million Hispanics, is the second largest Mexican city in the world. Already 25% Hispanic, it is predicted to be 50% by the year 2000. San Antonio, Texas is 54% Hispanic. Dade County, Florida, is predicted to be 80% Hispanic by the turn of the century.

But not all Hispanics are city dwellers. Two to four million of them are migrant workers. Their jobs are unskilled and seasonal, so they must migrate with the ripening harvest along three major migrant streams—one on each coast and the other one—the major one— beginning in Texas, working its way northward to Colorado, then splitting. Some crews go into Wyoming, Utah, Idaho, Oregon, and

Washington, while the majority swing eastward to North Dakota, Minnesota, Wisconsin, Michigan, and Ohio.

Migrants may be white Appalachian, black, Indian, Oriental, Mexican, Mexican American, Puerto Rican, Canadian, Cuban, or Jamaican, but 40% of them are Mexican and are Roman Catholic in name. All members of the family work together in the fields. The 1.3 million children of these migrant workers usually have little education. They are the most forgotten and educationally deprived youth in the United States. 80% of them drop out of school.

Divorce, separation, commonlaw marriages, and unwed parenthood are common among these people.

These migrant workers need to be reached with the Gospel, but their mobility makes this difficult.

Most Hispanics never attend the Roman Catholic or any other church, because they don't feel welcome. They have been spiritually abused and neglected. Their former religious leaders have made promises and have not kept them. They are educationally deprived and economically exploited. Thus, they turn to radical forms of politics, cults, or distorted forms of Christianity. We must help the Hispanics find the truth, to establish churches among them, and train their own leaders with whom they can feel comfortable.

Missionary Activity

Missionary activity among the Hispanics is tragically small and scattered. Although most denominations have a token Hispanic ministry, it is primarily the Baptists and the Pentecostals who are ministering to these people. The Southern Baptists have 1400 Hispanic churches, most of which are served by Hispanic pastors. The American Baptists have 300 congregations. The Assembly of God reports 700 churches, and the Church of God (Cleveland, Tennessee) has a membership of 10,000. The Church of the Nazarene claims 89 churches, the Lutheran Church Missouri Synod has 39. Seventy-three congregations are affiliated with the Christian and Missionary Alliance. But the vast majority of Hispanics are not being touched by the Gospel. It is estimated that less than one percent of them are born again.[8]

Although numerous storefront churches have sprung up, most of them are so small that they cannot afford a full time pastor; therefore, lay pastors holding secular jobs are filling the void. There is a desperate need for a trained clergy among Hispanic congregations. A few seminaries and Bible Institutes have ethnic studies programs to prepare missionaries for Hispanic ministries, but the total number of theological students in Hispanic studies in 1978 was only 681.

Spanish language radio programs are effective and need to be multiplied across the country. Programs are produced by the Spanish World Gospel Mission, the Spanish "Back to the Bible," the "Radio Bible Class," the "Back to God Hour," the "Lutheran Hour," the "Mennonite Hour," the Southern Baptists, Plymouth Brethren, the Baptist General Conference, and Luis Palau.

Wherever there are many Hispanics, there are bound to be at least some of them who are deficient in English. Here is a great opportunity for average church members to get involved in a Hispanic ministry, teaching English and sharing their faith with their students. A one-month course in teaching English as a second langue will give the average layman the skills and the confidence that he needs for such a ministry.

Cross-References

Assemblies of God, *108*

Lutheran Church, *49, 115*

Radio Broadcasting, *15, 67, 72, 106, 111, 118, 123, 163, 191*

Teaching (English), *16, 21, 36, 147, 158*

OTHER ETHNIC GROUPS

According to the 1984 statistics there were 14 million ethnics in the United States in addition to the Indians, blacks, and Hispanics. More will continue to come since the U.S. government allows 700,000 immigrants to enter legally each year. In addition, up to a million enter illegally. Eighty-one percent of the immigrants come from Latin America and Asia, only about 16% from Europe. More than a third of them settle in California; 13% in Texas, and 12% in New York.

There are also six million temporary residents living here who are neither immigrants nor tourists. According to Don Bjork, former director of World Team's North American Ministries, these millions of newcomers are changing the face of America, compelling a new thrust for North American missions. The new thrust must include the cooperation of foreign missions because the number and the kind of newcomers is outpacing the timely and effective response from the existing churches and agencies. Most of the newcomers are from cultural groups previously unserved by home missions and churches of North America. Foreign missions have the intercultural expertise to effectively reach them.

CHINESE IN THE U.S.A.

Americans of Chinese descent numbered one million in 1984, and 94% of them were unchurched and could not be reached by existing churches, whether English or Chinese speaking. The Chinese church is not able to minister to the overseas-born Chinese who speak dialects that are not used in the church. Nor is she prepared to serve the American-born Chinese who speak English and have moved away from Chnatown to suburbia.

The Chinese first came to this country in great numbers as prospectors following the discovery of gold in 1848. Large numbers were also brought in as coolies or cheap labor to build the Central Pacific Railroad (1864-69) and to work on the huge farms in the West.

Widespread persecution of Chinese Americans developed during times of economic depression and unemployment. It culminated in the Oriental Exclusion Act of 1882, which excluded the entire race for more than sixty years. The law was finally repealed in 1943, but even then a strict quota of only one hundred immigrants per year was enforced. After 1965, the quota was relaxed so that now about 20,000 arrive annually.

California is home for 40% of the American Chinese. New York is home to 20%. Other large groups of them can be found in Hawaii (56,000), Illinois (29,000), Texas (26,000). Most of the Chinese live at least temporarily in ethnic communities known as Chinatowns. Because of hard work, long hours, frugal living and the pooling of family income, younger members have had opportunity to become educated and move up the social scale. Today the average Chinese American has reached a higher economic and educational level than the average white American.

More Chinese live outside Chinatown than within. Chinatowns have become places of transition for the suburb-bound newcomer. Immigrants are absorbed into the Chinatown economy without going on welfare.

Chinatowns are to be found in urban centers of all fifty states, but 18 states don't even have one Chinese church.

The first Chinese church was planted in San Francisco in 1853. The Chinese church grew slowly until Chinese pastors were trained and anti-Chinese sentiments diminished. After 1960, Chinese churches multiplied rapidly. By 1982, there were 468 Chinese churches serving 44,700 Chinese Christians. There are 136 Chinese churches in New York City; 126 in San Francisco; and 109 in Los Angeles.

There is a serious lack of churches for the more affluent population of the American-born Chinese who don't live in Chinatown. Although these American-born Chinese constitute more than half of all Chinese Americans, 90% of them are unchurched.

It may be that 25% of the 44,700 committed Chinese Christians are actively witnessing; so the Chinese church is not able to keep up with the growth of the North American Chinese population which is doubling every decade because of the large number of immigrants and a birth rate that is twice the national average.

In 1972, the North American Congress of Chinese Evangelicals (NACOCE) was formed to assist in the evangelization of Chinese Americans.

In 1979, the Fellowship of American Chinese Evangelicals (FACE) was founded to focus on evangelizing the American-born Chinese. Through its quarterly, "About Face," it endeavors to alert the Chinese church concerning the spiritual needs of American-born Chinese.

To promote evangelism among *all* Chinese in North America and to develop a missionary church among Chinese churches, the Evangelical China Office (ECO) was opened in 1980. It is sponsored by three groups engaged in Chinese evangelism—the North American Congress of Chinese Evangelicals, the Interdenominational Foreign Mission Association, and the Evangelical Foreign Missions Association.

By means of the ECO, most North American based evangelical foreign missions and Chinese congregations have banded together for the task of Chinese evangelism.

The Institute of Chinese Studies forms strategy profiles of unevangelized Chinese people groups worldwide and creates educational tools to graphically support these strategy profiles. ICS research supports "Watchman on the Great Wall," a periodical containing prayer profiles of Chinese people groups. ICS also published "Extended Family," containing more detailed profiles of unreached peoples. ICS is located at the U.S. Center for World Mission, 1605 E. Elizabeth Street, Pasadena, CA 91104.

America has long been referred to as a "melting pot" of the world's cultures and races. Many of the peoples who make up the seven other "worlds" are represented in America today. Each of these is a bloc of our world but should also be studied in its own context as well.

BUDDHISTS IN THE U.S.A.

Southeast Asians. Since 1975, millions of Indo Chinese have come to this country for asylum from the intolerable living conditions in their own part of the world. Half of them settled in California. Seventy percent of them are *Vietnamese.* They continue to arrive at the rate of 4,000 per month.

Altogether there are 2.7 million Vietnamese in the U.S. They are hardworking and honest people who desire to become self-supporting as soon as possible.

These Vietnamese refugees want to find the peace and acceptance they have never known. These people come from many different backgrounds, including Buddhism, Taoism, and Confucianism, but all are basically animistic. Some have been exposed to Roman Catholicism.

Southern Baptists have the largest ministry among these refugees. They had founded 35 Vietnamese congregations by 1981, using some of their foreign staff, who have learned the language, to work with the home staff.

Laotians. The Communists took over Laos in 1975, and thousands of Laotians fled to Thailand. By 1980, 120,000 had gathered in refugee camps to wait for opportunities to relocate in the free world. There are large numbers of Laotians in the San Francisco-Oakland Bay area, Los Angeles, as well as in Atlanta and Decatur, Georgia.

Thais. In 1984 there were 120,000 Thais in the United States. Sixty percent of them live in Los Angeles. 96% are Buddhist, but only one-fourth of them practice their religion. There's a large Thai Buddhist temple in northern Los Angeles.

About 60% of the Thais are students, many of whom will return to Thailand. What a tremendous opportunity to reach these people and win them to Christ, people who will someday become leaders in their own country where they can let their Gospel light shine in the darkness where fewer than one percent of their countrymen are followers of Jesus Christ.

Japanese. Seven hundred thousand citizens of Japanese descent live in the United States. One-third of them live in Hawaii where there are a hundred Buddhist temples in Honolulu. Here is a great mission field, almost untouched with the Gospel. Apparently the only mission work among the American Japanese Buddhists or any other Buddhists in the United States is being done in Hawaii on college campuses among international students.[9]

The Institute of Japanese Studies in Pasadena, California is engaged in research and the development of subsequent strategies for winning the Japanese people to Christ.

In cooperation with field leaders and mission agencies, IJS initiates grass-roots-level research to enable the Church to target and effectively evangelize groupings of Japanese people.

IJS staff also seek to mobilize the North American church for evangelism and church planting in Japan, beginning prayer groups and offering awareness seminars. In addition, the Institute of Japanese Studies plans to provide courses and teachers for orientation on evangelization of the Japanese, adding to courses already offered on the undergraduate and graduate levels. IJS presently offers credit-bearing courses through William Carey International University and the School of World Mission of Fuller Theological Seminary, both in Pasadena.

MUSLIMS IN THE U.S.A.

There are approximately 3 million Muslims in the United States today. They are found primarily in the larger cities, but they are found in nearly every town.

The largest Muslim concentration in the U.S. is in New York City and northern New Jersey where 128,000 from 25 ethnic backgrounds live. There are also large concentrations of Muslims in the Detroit and the Los Angeles areas.

Funded with petroleum dollars, Islam is on the march these days in a manner unmatched since its conquests of North Africa and Europe in the 7th and 8th centuries.

In America the number of Muslims increased sixfold in just 15 years. This growth, as reported by the Islamic Center in Washington, D.C., includes 300 Islamic centers in 41 states, including 84 mosques.

Students from Islamic countries form the largest group of international students in North American universities and colleges. Here is another tremendous opportunity to witness to Muslims who will someday be leaders in their own countries, many of which are closed to traditional mission work.

Numerous sects have developed within the Muslim fold. Leo Rosten suggests that there are 70 of them in the United States.[10]

One of these sects is Bahaism which began in Persia (Iran) in 1844. The largest Bahai temple in the world is in Evanston, Illinois. There are 900 groups totaling 100,000 members across the country. One of Bahais roots is Islam. The name Bahai means "brother" in Arabic and indicates its desire to be inclusive.

Another sect is the Black Muslim Movement. Although denounced in the 1950s as unorthodox because of illegal use of Islam to gain social and political ends, today its 100,000 to 200,000 members are generally accepted. In fact, the Muslims are making an all out effort to win the blacks. They've been especially successful in converting black ex-convicts. "Parole officers and the police say that the Black Muslims are the best rehabilitation agency at work among Negro criminals today. They arrange parole for their converts and then carefully watch over them" Some believe that Islam might eventually become the religion of the Negro in the U.S.A. if present trends continue. If so, Islam will win by default, since white and black Christians are doing very, very little to reach the unchurched or to meet the spiritual needs of black church members.

One large block of Muslims is from Iran. In 1984, there were 450,000 Iranians in the United States. Perhaps half of one percent are Christians, but the overwhelming majority of them are Muslims.

Fifty percent of all the Iranians in America live in California. Other concentrations are found in New York City, Boston, and Chicago.

One Christian fellowship, Iranian Christians International, Inc., includes missionaries from Iran and other individuals interested in church planting among Iranian believers and directing evangelicals toward winning Muslims to Christ. They have ten regional centers initiating national conferences for Iranian Christians, and preparing Bible study materials for printing in Persian.[11]

Palestinians. Another Muslim group is that of the Palestinians who have begun migrating to America since Israel occupied the land they considered their own by right of occupancy for nearly 13 centuries. By 1981, 110,000 Palestinians had become citizens of the United States.

Many Palestinian Americans are afraid to identify themselves because of the pro-Israel and anti-Palestinian bias that exists in the States. Even so, they are beginning to join national organizations that exist to promote Palestinian unity.

These Palestinian Americans are here to stay. Only 25% of them regularly support the Palestine Liberation Organization (PLO), although all Palestinians believe in creating a home for the homeless Palestinians.

American Palestinians are nominal Muslims, but secularism is far stronger among them than it seems to be among Palestinians elsewhere.

It is essential that protestant chrurches become aware of the presence of Palestinians in their community. At present there is no evidence of any organized effort to present the Gospel message to the Palestinians.

We have mentioned the Muslims from just two countries, but there are Muslims in this country from nearly every Muslim country from Indonesia to North Africa. Virtually every Muslim country is represented on the university and college campuses across the land. In Los Angeles alone there are an estimated 30,000 to 40,000 Syrians, Lebanese, Pakistanis, Indians, Yugoslavians, Turks, and Afghanis.

Several missions such as International Students, Inc., work among 4,000 Muslim students on college campuses.

International Missions established a summer ministry to train missionaries and laymen to witness to Muslim and Hindu people in Flushing, New York, where 200,000 aliens live, speaking fifty languages.

The Samuel Zwemer Institute in Pasadena, California offers training at every level for Muslim work, taught by a staff with 178 combined years of service in the Muslim world. Those preparing for ministry are offered a growing selection of courses to provide training for work in the Muslim world—within the broader framework of world mission studies. Practical fieldwork in the Los Angeles area is available to all students enrolled locally at the Institute.

The Zwemer Institute also offers Muslim Awareness Seminars. The Seminar is a stimulating and challenging nine-hour training program to prepare men and women to work cross-culturally with Muslim neighbors. Participants gain insights into Biblical models of cross-cultural ministry and how to apply them to Muslim outreach.

The SZI also directs field teams in outreach to Muslims. A fast-growing number of individuals are involved in outreach and discipleship ministries. In 1984 there were eighteen ethnic ministry teams, comprised of 80 laymen and missionary candidates, reaching out to Muslims in Southern California as part of preparation to work with Muslims overseas or in North America.

The Fellowship of Faith for Muslims prepares a monthly prayer bulletin and, among others, supplies materials necessary for Muslim evangelism. Materials are ready, training programs are available (through SZI and others), and missions are prepared to lead the way, but according to Raymond Joyce, long-time missionary to the Muslim world and executive director of the Fellowship of Faith for Muslims: ". . there is a tragic and almost total ignorance of what Islam really is. Where there is an attitude expressed, it is usually one of apathetic dismissal of the task of reaching the Muslim for Christ as being too hard and unproductive. So naturally there is little or no involvement."[12]

We agree with Mr. Joyce. How tragic the attitude of so many church members in this country toward the Muslim world, when Christ died for their sins and He wants all Muslims (and everytone else) to be saved and come to the knowledge of the truth (1 Tim. 2:4).

HINDUS IN THE U.S.

While the overwhelming majority of the world's 700 million Hindus live in India, there are an estimated 100,000 of them in the United States. There are concentrations of Hindus in Pittsburgh and New York City. There are Hindu temples in both of these cities.

Cross-References
Krishna, *43*
Nirvana. *30*

One of the main sects of Hinduism is the Hare Krishna movement. Thousands of disenchanted youth or college students give months of their lives to this cult as "an emphatic rejection of conventional affluent America.

The Hare Krishna cult, founded in 1944, maintains 30 centers and 7 self-sustaining farms in the U.S. The purposes of the movement are to explore the ideas presented in ancient India's Vedic literature, especially the Bhagavad Gita, and to teach Krishna consciousness throughout the English speaking world.

The devotees live in barn rooms built in a loft over the sacred cows that they venerate. They eat a vegetarian diet, wear rustic clothes, and repeat "Hare Krishna" 2,000 times a day. Many hours are spent chanting over sacred mantas 1728 times and then performing duties prescribed by the leader. In Moundsville, West Virginia, the work built a $500,000 palace for the founder, Swami A.C. Bhaktiredanta, whose life-sized statues adorn prominent places.

To many Americans, the act of meditating on a simple word or thought seems like a harmless way of obtaining peace in a hectic world. 300,000 such Americans are followers of Transcendental Meditation. They see no reason why tax dollars should not be spent in teaching TM in public schools. However, instant Nirvana, as it is called, is a sect of Hinduism. *Time* magazine reported in 1972 that TM may well be the fastest growing cult in the West.

The method of obtaining peace involves a daily 15 minute meditation on one's own personal Sanskrit mantra (saying) which is given by the guru (teacher) to fit one's personality. By means of this exercise, it is alleged that suffering can be eliminated. But, of course, there can be no real and lasting peace for people who do not know Jesus, the Prince of Peace.

The Institute of Hindu Studies in Pasadena, California has developed an introductory credit-bearing course on "Mission Among India's Peoples." IHS information services include maps, people group profiles, bibliographies, an audio library on Hinduism, evangelistic and church-planting strategy papers, and Indian language tracts and Scripture portions.

SIKHS IN THE U.S.A.

There are now (1985) some 150,000 Sikhs in the United States. They can be recognized by their well-kept beards and turbaned heads.

Sikhism is a syncretistic religion that drew its monotheism from Islam and the rest of its beliefs from Hinduism.

The earliest Sikhs came to this country from the Punjab in Northern India in the early 1900s. There are concentrations of them in Washington, D.C., New York City, Los Angeles, Espanola, New Mexico, and in Oregon where one can visit one of their temples.

The evangelical church must awaken and prepare literature and missionaries to reach these lost souls. Christians across America should be aware that some of the professionals in their community may be Hindus or Sikhs. They can be befriended and won to Christ.

The non-Christian religions of America are growing. The church is just beginning to recognize its responsibility to reach the foreign mission field right at our own doorstep. There is every opportunity to win Muslims,, Buddhists, Chinese,

Hindus, Sikhs, Jews, Mormons, Jehovah's Witnesses, Satanists and all kinds of people who are in spiritual darkness.

One excellent way to befriend these people and share your faith with them, especially the newcomers, is through teaching them English. If your church is surrounded by various immigrants and foreign students, why not start a TESOL (Teaching English to Speakers of Other Languages) program for them. There may be other TESOL programs available to them, but that shouldn't stop us from using this means to make new friends and lead them to Jesus.

Many universities offer certificates and advanced degrees in TESOL. But just a one-month methodology course can be very helpful. One of the better schools to acquire this kind of training is the William Carey International University in Pasadena, California. Most of us have been guilty of a great sin of omission by neglecting these foreigners whom God has been bringing to our door. We haven't even been praying for them. Let's repent of this prayerlessness and carelessness and sharelessness and darelessness and do all that we can to make disciples of these souls for whom Christ died.

Besides the ethnic groups referred to above, at least another 180 ethnic groups are represented here in the United States. But in addition to all of these opportunities for cross-cultural ministry, there are an almost unlimited number of opportunities and challenges for special ministry within our own culture. There are ministries to the blind, the deaf, and other handicapped people, to prisoners, students on various age levels, the military, to abandoned and abused children, to youth in trouble, to addicts and alcoholics, to senior citizens, to mobile Americans, etc. The list could go on and on.

Then, of course, there are special ministries to the Mormons, the Jehovah's Witnesses, the Satanists, the Spiritualists, and to all the other cults within our borders. An ABC-TV special in 1978 declared that six million Americans were involved in thousands of cults. Dave Hunt, author of "The Cult Explosion" reports "estimates of five thousand religious and pseudo-religious cults in the United States." Walter Martin, author of "The New Cults," says that cult membership in the U.S. may reach close to 20 million. A Gallup poll in 1979 indicated that the religious cult population of the United States is 54% of the total population. That would mean a total of 118,000,000 people in this country are cultists. That is a little hard to believe, but the twenty million suggested by Walter Martin seems to be a very conservative figure estimate. Earl Parvin, author of "Missions USA," compiled a list of less than 25 cults and found a total of 27 million persons involved.[13]

So there is much mission work to be done right here in America. There's no question about that. But that does not mean that we should stop sending missionaries overseas to the rest of the 3.5 billion unreached peoples. We must do all that we can on all fronts, especially where the people are responsive and the doors are open.

LATIN AMERICA

Throughout Latin America the Church is growing three times as fast as the population in general. In 1900, less than one percent were evangelicals (Protestants); today, nearly eight percent. There has been an average growth rate of 8% per year this century, and this has accelerated in recent years, due largely to the increasing confidence and aggressive witnessing of evangelical laymen. Ordinary church members have been better mobilized than in any other part of the world for personal witnessing and the starting of house churches.

Brazil, now the 6th largest nation in the world, is one of the most exciting areas for church growth. People are receptive and the national churches are vigorously multiplying through personal evangelism, forming satellite churches. One in every nine Brazilians is now an evangelical Christian.

For years the Wycliffe Bible Translators and other mission agencies have been seeking to evangelize the many small Amerindian tribes in the Amazon jungles. There are about 160 tribes with a total population of perhaps 100,000. But the government terminated this work in 1978. Pray that the government will allow the missionaries to return to Amazonia and complete the work among these isolated tribes. We'll have more to say about Brazil a little later.

In Chile the Protestant Church has grown dramatically over the last 60 years, and the troubles of the land since 1970 have caused this rate to accelerate. Seventeen percent of Chile is now Protestant. Yet there is great lack of unity among believers, and denominational rivalry based on strong leadership personalities. Some churches have great evangelistic zeal, but are often shallow spiritually and ill-taught. Pray that there may be more emphasis on solid Bible teaching.

In Bolivia there is a greater receptivity in all groups than ever before. The long resistant middle class and the growing student population are now open to the Gospel. The highland Quechuas and Aymaras, the lowland Indians, and the migrant populations are all turning to the Lord in large numbers.

In Equador there is a mighty moving of the Spirit among the long oppressed Quichua Indians, resulting in rapid church growth, moral uplift, and the development of the leadership gifts of these people. In 1967 there were only 120 believers among the 2.5 million Quichuas. Now there are more than 30,000, and the Lord is adding to His Church daily.

Colombia is a very troubled land. Nevertheless, the good testimony of believers during years of persecution, a new openness among Roman Catholics, and Evangelism-in-depth campaigns all help to bring people to Christ. Church membership increased sevenfold in just 17 years, and the growth continues. But there is much Communist guerrilla terrorist activity in Colombia as well as in many other Latin American countries. Missionaries and other Christians have been kidnapped and killed. Others have been persecuted in various ways. Pray daily for their safety and for the Lord's blessing upon their ministries.

Disasters, such as the earthquakes that devastated Nicaragua in 1972 and Guatemala in 1976, and the hurricanes that hit Honduras in 1975, and all the bloodshed in Central America in recent years have brought a new receptiveness to the Gospel. In just one year in Guatemala the church grew by 14%.

With all this church growth in Latin America there is a serious shortage of well-trained church leaders. More national Christian writers are also needed. Please take this to the Lord in prayer. Pray also that there will be more unity among the believers that they may work more closely together for the glory of God and for the extension of His Kingdom.

Central America

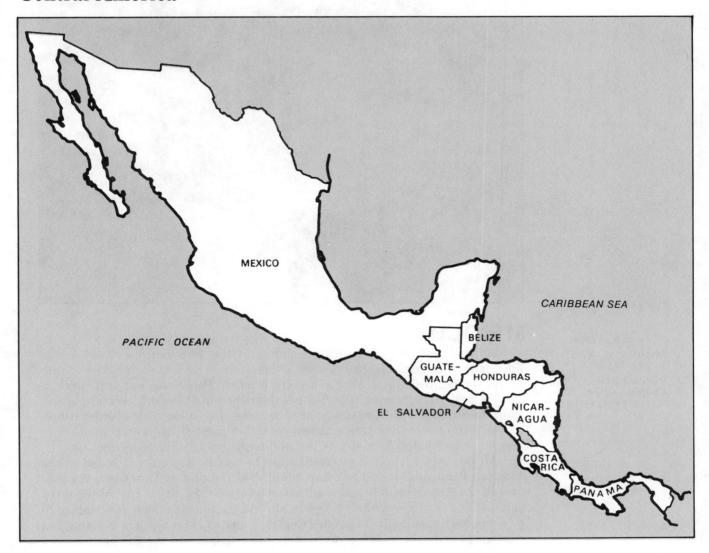

PACIFIC OCEAN

MEXICO

CARIBBEAN SEA

BELIZE

GUATE-
MALA

HONDURAS

EL SALVADOR

NICAR-
AGUA

COSTA
RICA

PANAMA

MEXICO

At the time of the Spanish conquest in the 16th century, Mexico was inhabited by Indians who had reached a high stage of developement. The culture of the Mayas, in southern Mexico and the Yucatan Peninsula, was at its peak in the 7th and 8th centuries. The Toltecs flourished in the south central plateau from the 9th to the 12th century, when they were driven south by stronger tribes. In the 15th century the Aztecs gained control of most of the central area. They may have numbered as many as ten million before the Spanish conquest.

Mexico was discovered by the Spanish in 1517 when Cordoba landed on the Yucatan Peninsula. In 1519 Cortez established the port of Vera Cruz. He conquered the Aztecs in 1521 and built Mexico City on the site of their devastated capital. The colony was named New Spain and, although much of it remained to be conquered, nominally it included Central America as far south as Panama and stretched northwest to Lower California and northeast to the Rio Grande.

The first missions were established in 1524. Together, Spanish troops and missionaries extended the boundaries of New Spain northward. The present states of New Mexico and Arizona were occupied in the early 17th century. By 1790 the land that is now Texas, California, Nevada, Utah, and part of Wyoming, Colorado, and Kansas fell within the teritory ruled from Mexico City.   The Catholic Church has been the principal influence in Mexico for all these centuries. Today 90% of Mexico's 78 million people are baptized Catholics. More than 80% have been confirmed and 77% married in the church. Only 15% however, could be classified as practicing Roman Catholics.

Mexican Catholicism has many syncretistic elements in it. The best known is the cult of the Virgin of Guadalupe. In December, 1531, an Indian named Juan Diego claimed visions of the Virgin Mary. Interest in these visions led to a movement which has grown into an intense and impassioned cult in which the Aztec worship of the earth goddess ("Madre Antigue" or "Ancient Mother"). has become fused with the worship of the Virgin Mary ("Madre Nueva", "New Mother"). Each year hundreds of thousands of pilgrims from across the world visit the shrine and basilica.

From 1520-1910 Mexico was under the domination of the Roman Catholic Church. The revolution of 1910 was directed largely against the church. As a result the church was stripped of all its property and much of its power. Though the church and state have made their peace, the church is still subject to restrictions. Mexico, however, remained, for all practical purposes, an overwhelmingly Roman Catholic country. Protestants have had to live with government restrictions and at the same time contend with Roman Catholic opposition.

There was never an evangelical church of any kind in Mexico until 1864. The first Protestant church was started in Monterey by a former Irish Roman Catholic. A few years later, in 1873, an American pioneer missionary organized a church in Guadalajara, but mob violence incited by the local Roman Catholic priests resulted in the death of this missionary and his Mexican evangelist. But in the face of continued persecution other missionaries followed and the number of believers grew steadily. Today there are several evangelical churches in Guadalajara.

Other missionaries from other denominations began work in Mexico City and in southern Mexico in the 1870s and 1880s. Today there are 125 mission agencies at work in Mexico and there are evangelical churches in every one of Mexico's 29 states. In fact, there is scarcely a town or village that does not have at least a small group of believers. The total number of evangelicals throughout the country is estimated at 600,000.

Only 20% of Mexico's 82 million people are of pure Spanish descent. 59% are Mestizos (part Spanish and part Indian). 1% are Negroes. 20% are Amerindians who speak more than 120 different languages and dialects.

Before 1935 there were no Scriptures in any of these Indian languages. Their languages had never even been written down. The Roman Catholics have never shown any interest in giving people the Word of God in their own language, and until recently, have never encouraged anyone to read the Bible in Spanish or Portuguese or any other language. Since 1935 some missions have been working exclusively among the Indian tribes in Mexico. The Wycliffe Bible Translators are working in more than a hundred languages. Thirty-seven tribes have the complete New Testament and another 48 have Scripture portions. There are believers in at least 76 of these Indian tribes. Thirty-seven languages await translators.

Until recently Christian radio in Mexico was impossible due to legal restrictions. During the administration of President Lopez Mateos (1958-1964) the law was revised. Religion is now permitted on the air provided it keeps out of politics and does not attack other religions. Today hundreds of programs are broadcast throughout the week.

Mexico City may soon be the largest city in the world. Some estimate that 15 million people are now crowded into this metropolis. Most of the newcomers have come to the city seeking employment but have been disappointed. There just aren't enough jobs to go around. Many are living in shacks thrown together with bits and pieces of scrap metal and sticks and cardboard—whatever they can find. They have no running water. Obviously this kind of living breeds all kinds of sickness and disease. But it also provides an excellent opportunity for the Gospel if those who bring the Message also are willing to show the love of Christ for these destitute people and help them with their physical needs. Pray that Mexican believers will be ready and willing to seize the opportunities, and that they will keep a balance between spiritual and social concern.

South America

BRAZIL

Brazil is one of the most exciting areas of church growth in the world today. This land of 138 million people is wide open to the Gospel, the people are receptive, and the national churches are vigorously multiplying through personal evangelism, forming satellite house churches. At the beginning of this century there were only a few thousand believers in Brazil. Today there are more than 14 million, and the church is growing three times faster than the general population growth rate.

Although the church is growing rapidly, the vast majority of Brazilians are still without Christ. Eighty-three percent of the people claim to be Roman Catholic, but only about ten percent show any interest in the Church. Spiritism is a major force throughout the land. Some have called it the "national religion of Brazil". Every stratum of society is influenced by the various forms of spiritism and witchcraft.

One of the greatest problems in the church is a direct result of its rapid growth. The present training of leadership for the churches cannot supply the needed manpower. Residential type Bible Schools and Seminaries cannot meet the demand for workers. Many thousands of church workers must be trained right where they are, through extension courses—without leaving their families or means of livelihood. More must be done to train lay leadership in the churches, for on these fall the main burden of the ministry. Pray for the missionaries and national pastors already engaged in training for ministry by extension, and pray for many more workers to join them in this crucial and urgent task.

Missionaries are still needed in Brazil to pioneer unreached areas and groups—especially in the vast Amazon Basin. The little settlements along the many jungle rivers are poor and needy physically and spiritually. The believers are few in number and very isolated. Most of them speak Portuguese but are unable to read God's Word. A few missionaries are doing good pioneer work in the upper reaches of the Amazon and its tributaries, but the churches they plant constantly suffer losses to the bigger towns where those most able to support the ministry are attracted by better job opportunities and better living conditions. We need to pray for more missionaries to reach the millions of settlers scattered throughout this vast area. Pray also for those already engaged in pioneer evangelism by means of river launches—a difficult and dangerous ministry.

In addition to the ever increasing number of Portuguese speaking settlers in the Amazon Basin, there are about 160 Indian tribes scattered throughout the jungle. Most of these tribes are very isolated and very small, usually numbering only 100 to 600 people. For many years Wycliffe Bible Translators and other missionaries were working in many of these tribes, but the government terminated the work in 1978. Pray that these pioneer missionaries and others will be allowed to return to the field and complete the task of giving these Indians the Word of God in their own language, teaching them to read it for themselves, and planting churches among them.

Pray for people in every part of this huge country and in every segment of society, from the humid green jungles of the north to the concrete jungles of the south (Sao Paulo, 9 million; Rio de Janeiro, 5 million). Pray that millions more will soon know Jesus as their personal Savior and their Lord.

Cross-References

Amazon River Basin, *159*

Brazil, *7, 91, 100, 159, 164, 172*

Poverty, *54, 79, 81, 150, 163*

Spiritism, *2, 39*

Europe

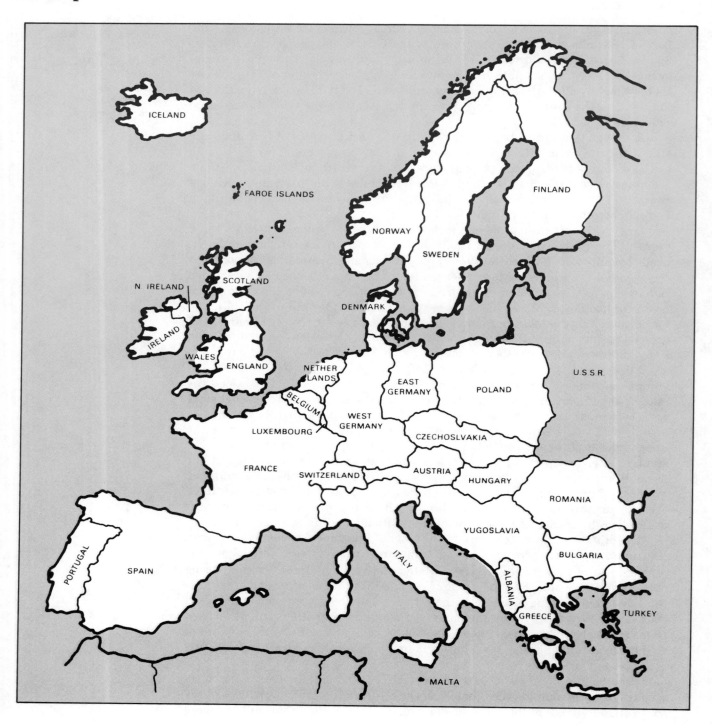

WESTERN EUROPE

God is at work in Western Europe today, in some countries more than ever before. Spain is one of the countries most open to the Gospel after centuries of ruthless persecution of evangelicals. Missionary efforts have had a marked effect in mobilizing and arousing young Spanish believers into aggressive evangelism through open air meetings, literature, and door-to-door evangelism. 180,000 university students are also more open to the Gospel than ever before.

The Gypsy people movement to Christ is noticeable in Spain as well as in Portugal, France, Germany, and Romania. Many thousands of these people are turning to the Lord and little Gypsy churches are springing up all over Spain. In France, over 1/3 of the Gypsies have come to the Lord in the last few years and there is now a community of about 60,000 believers. They have their own church and aggressively reach out to their fellow Gypsies in other lands.

Likewise in Portugal, since 1972 evangelicals may evangelize openly by any and all means. As a result, churches are growing rapidly and there are a number of good seminaries and Bible schools.

In Switzerland, the Netherlands, Austria, Belgium, France, Germany, Great Britain, Ireland, and Italy the evangelical voice, though small in some places, is growing and is more respected than it has been for centuries. Opportunities for evangelism have never been greater, especially among the university students.

In Finland, the mission vision has grown considerably in recent years. There are now 522 missionaries from Finland serving in 51 countries.

All over Germany house groups are springing up for Bible study and prayer. The quantity of good evangelical literature and books has enormously increased in recent years. Many young people are turning away from immorality, drug use, and leftist radicalism—turning to Christ—and aggressively evangelizing other young people. Bible schools are full and a stream of keen young people are moving out into full time service at home and abroad. Several German and international groups are working among the Turks (Muslims). There are now more Turkish believers in Germany than in Turkey itself.

In Great Britain, the Evangelical movement is now stronger and more respected than for many years, especially among young people. The proportion of

Christian students in the universities is far higher than the national average. The house-church movement has become a significant factor in the spiritual life of the country.

Also in the Netherlands many prayer and Bible study groups are springing up. These house meetings are where most of the real Bible teaching and conversions occur.

In Norway, many voluntary organizations have sprung up within the State Church with a burden for home and overseas evangelism. Many fine missionaries have gone forth from these groups. This little land (four million) has probably more missionaries than any other nation on earth for the size of its population.

Sweden, too, has had exceptional missionary outreach. This country has about 1,700 missionaries serving all over the world.

Praise God for all He is doing in Europe. Pray that much more will be done in the years ahead, for the vast majority of the people in Western Europe are indifferent to the Gospel. In most countries, less than five percent attend church regularly. In France, 36,000 towns and villages are without a resident evangelical witness. Pray the Lord of the harvest to send forth laborers into His harvest.

THE PHILIPPINES

The Republic of the Philippines with its 156 million inhabitants is nominally a Christian country—83% Roman Catholic and 5% Protestant. Another 5% are members of the Filipino Independent Church (Aglipayan) which broke away from the Roman Catholic Church in 1902 in protest against the foreign dominated Catholic clergy.

Less than one month after Magellan had discovered the Philippines for Spain (1521), the first Roman Catholic baptisms took place. In the years that followed, Spanish explorers together with Roman Catholic missionaries continued the conquest of the Philippines with the cross and the sword. By 1876 there were 1962 Roman Catholic missionaries on these islands.

During the Spanish occupation the church and state were joined. It was a treasonable offense to advocate any other religion, and the church members were taught that it was evil to read the Bible without proper authorization and instruction. Then, as now, Roman Catholic religion revolves around images, rituals, processions, festivals, and fiestas rather than God's Word.

The revolution against Spain was mainly caused by the religious system of the friars. The 1896-98 revolution put an end to Spanish rule, giving rise to the first Philippine Republic. At the same time (1898), the treaty which ended the Spanish American war ceded the Philippines to the U.S.

With American rule in the Philippines came religious freedom, and evangelical missionaries were quick to enter. Several denominations and interdenominational groups entered the field almost immediately. By 1922, twenty-two independent non-Roman Catholic churches had registered with the government. Many more mission agencies have begun work since 1922, especially since 1945. But Protestant Church growth was very slow until the 1970s.

Today the Republic of the Philippines is *one of the most open and responsive countries in Asia.* Roman Catholics and others are more eager to read and study the Bible and are more responsive to the Gospel than ever before.

There are far more opportunities for Christian service than there are laborers to use them—opportunities in evangelism and church planting as well as

Cross-References
Philippines, *7, 23, 69, 91, 101, 173*
Roman Catholic Church, *118, 143, 148, 150, 162, 199*

The Philippines

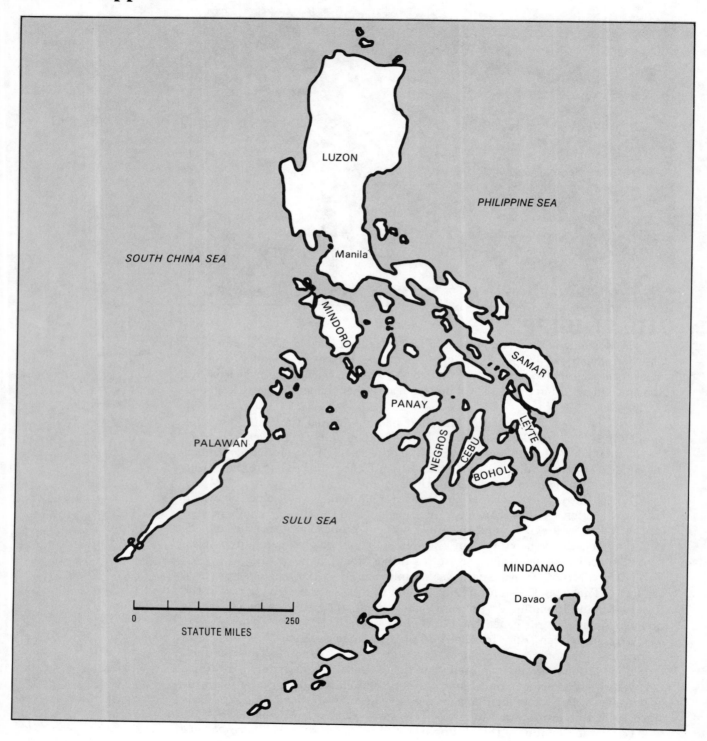

LUZON

PHILIPPINE SEA

SOUTH CHINA SEA

Manila

MINDORO

SAMAR

PANAY

LEYTE

PALAWAN

NEGROS

CEBU

BOHOL

SULU SEA

MINDANAO

Davao

0   250

STATUTE MILES

teaching and helping in established churches. Several agencies need additional workers such as Bible translators for the remaining 34 Bibleless tribes and literacy workers for the millions of adults who are still unable to read God's Word for themselves. Others are needed to train national writers, and to help evangelize the 1,500,000 university students. Technicians must also be found for radio and TV ministries.

About six percent of the inhabitants of the Philippines (over 3 million) are Muslims who have been very resistant to the Gospel, though some have been converted in recent years. They live mainly in Mindanao, the Sulu Islands, and Palawan. Work among these people has been greatly hindered by the continual war (armed and financed by Libya) in which the Muslims seek to secede.

Another half a million inhabitants of these islands are Chinese. Only about 3% of them are Christians. Buddhism and Confucianism are still the religions of 97% of the Chinese people. There are, however, 40 Chinese Christian churches in the Manila area alone.

Praise God for the advances that have been made in recent years among the Chinese, the Muslims, and the animistic tribal peoples as well as among the nominal Christians.

Pray that more workers may soon be trained and sent to those who are still without any clear Gospel witness in their own language or area.

Praise God that the missionary vision of the Filipino Church is growing and 13 agencies have sent out 170 or more missionaries to other lands. Pray that this missionary vision may grow, that hundreds or even thousands of Filipino missionaries may be trained and sent to Indonesia and Malaysia and other Asian countries where the need is so very, very great.

THE ROMAN CATHOLIC WORLD

Since the reformation Christian thought has been divided between the extremes of rigid episcopalianism under papal control and independent evangelical protestantism. Between them, many shades of belief have developed. The free expression of differing views under protestant influence has been a catalyst to church growth, missions, and evangelical fervor in areas where it has not been repressed. The dominance of the Roman Catholic church in many other areas of the world has discouraged free thought and the enthusiasm that should accompany one's faith.

The impact of catholicism is, therefore, not universally the same. In some countries, especially those which have not repressed protestantism, catholic missions have been active and prosperous. This irony results in strange contrasts as one views the so-called Christian World. Generally speaking, where a very strong central Roman catholic body exists, there will be found an enormous thirst for God's Word and a needy mission field.

Cross-References

Buddhism, *2, 18, 29, 32, 35, 39, 122, 199*

Chinese People, *83, 152*

Confucianism, *29, 35, 39, 122, 154*

Indonesia, *6, 23, 59, 65, 69, 83, 85, 91, 100, 177*

Libya, *6, 68, 69, 92, 100, 103, 104*

Malaysia, *6, 23, 33, 34, 59, 69, 91, 100*

Muslims, *2, 32, 46, 48, 65, 72, 75, 83, 107, 110, 155, 167, 191, 199*

The Roman Catholic World

Countries that are professedly 5% or more Roman Catholic and of more than a hundred thousand.

REGION OR COUNTRY	1986* TOTAL POPULATION (IN MILLIONS)	PERCENT ROMAN CATHOLIC**	REGION OR COUNTRY	1986* TOTAL POPULATION (IN MILLIONS)	PERCENT ROMAN CATHOLIC**
WORLD	**4,943.0**		Czechoslovakia	15.5	50%
LATIN AMERICA	**419.0**		France	55.4	76%
Argentina	31.2	92%	Germany, E.	16.7	6%
Bahamas	.2	25%	Germany, W.	60.7	43%
Barbados	.3	8%	Hungary	10.6	54%
Belize	.2	67%	Ireland	3.6	95%
Bolivia	6.0	92%	Italy	57.0	83%
Brazil	134.4	88%	Netherlands	14.5	42%
Chile	11.9	82%	Poland	37.5	81%
Colombia	28.2	96%	Portugal	10.1	94%
Costa Rica	2.7	90%	Spain	38.8	97%
Cuba	10.2	32%	Switzerland	6.5	53%
Dominica	.1	90%	United Kingdom	56.6	13%
Dominican Republic	6.4	96%	Yugoslavia	23.2	26%
Ecuador	9.1	96%			
El Salvador	5.1	96%			
French Guiana	.05	87%	**AFRICA**	**583.0**	
Granada	.1	64%	Angola	8.2	69%
Guadeloupe	.3	95%	Benin	4.1	18%
Guatemala	8.6	94%	Botswana	1.1	9%
Guyana	.8	18%	Burundi	4.9	78%
Haiti	5.9	83%	Cameroon	10.0	35%
Honduras	4.6	96%	Cape Verde Is.	.3	96%
Jamaica	2.3	10%	Central Africa Rep.	2.7	33%
Martinique	.3	95%	Chad	5.2	21%
Mexico	81.7	95%	Equatorial Guinea	.4	71%
Nicaragua	3.3	95%	Ghana	13.6	18%
Panama	2.2	85%	Guinea Bissau	.9	9%
Paraguay	4.1	96%	Ivory Coast	10.5	18%
Peru	20.2	95%	Kenya	21.0	26%
Puerto Rico	3.3	91%	Madagascar	10.3	26%
St. Lucia	.1	88%	Malawi	7.3	27%
St. Vincent	.1	19%	Mozambique	14.0	13%
Surinam	.4	36%	Namibia	1.1	19%
Trinidad & Tobago	1.2	36%	Nigeria	105.4	12%
Uruguay	3.0	59%	Reunion	.5	96%
Venezuela	17.8	94%	Rwanda	6.5	55%
			Senegal	6.9	6%
			Seychelles	.1	89%
NORTH AMERICA	**267.0**		South Africa	33.2	10%
Canada	25.6	47%	Swaziland	.7	11%
United States	241.0	30%	Tanzania	22.4	28%
			Togo	3.0	29%
			Uganda	15.2	50%
EUROPE	**493.0**		Upper Volta (Burkina Faso)	7.1	10%
			Zaire	31.3	48%
Austria	7.6	89%	Zambia	7.1	26%
Belgium	9.9	90%	Zimbabwe	9.0	14%

The Roman Catholic World (Continued)

REGION OR COUNTRY	1986* TOTAL POPULATION (IN MILLIONS)	PERCENT ROMAN CATHOLIC**	REGION OR COUNTRY	1986* TOTAL POPULATION (IN MILLIONS)	PERCENT ROMAN CATHOLIC**
ASIA	**2,782.0**		**OCEANIA**	**25.0**	
Hong Kong	5.7	8%	Australia	15.8	30%
Lebanon	2.7	36%	Fiji	.7	9%
Philippines	58.1	84%	French Polynesia	.2	39%
Sri Lanka	16.6	6%	New Zealand	3.3	19%
Timor	.7	29%	Papua New Guinea	3.4	33%
			Samoa, W.	.2	21%
			Solomon Islands	.3	19%
			Vanuatu (New Hebrides)	.1	17%

* Population Statistics are from the 1986 World Population Data Sheet of the Population Reference Bureau, Inc., Washington, D.C.

** These figures are from the World Christian Encyclopedia (David Barret, ed.), Oxford University Press, 1982.

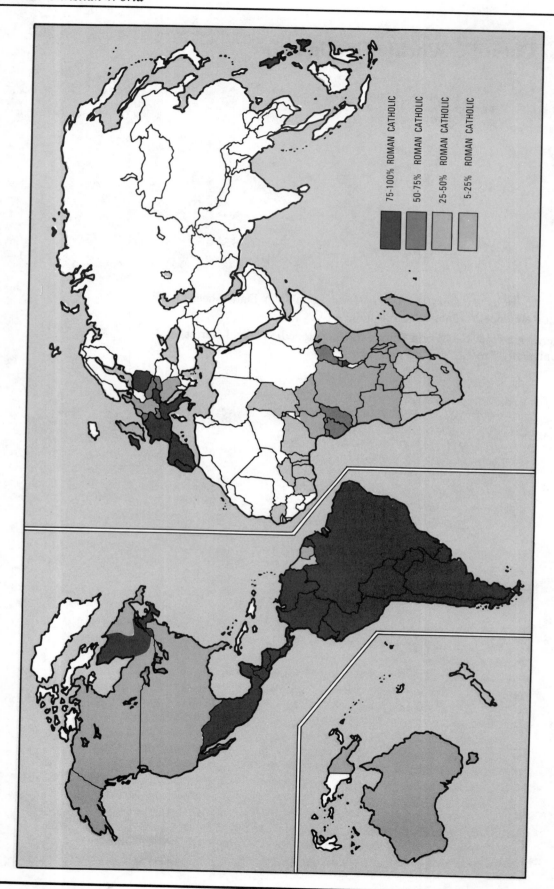

75-100% ROMAN CATHOLIC
50-75% ROMAN CATHOLIC
25-50% ROMAN CATHOLIC
5-25% ROMAN CATHOLIC

The Roman Catholic World

The Protestant World

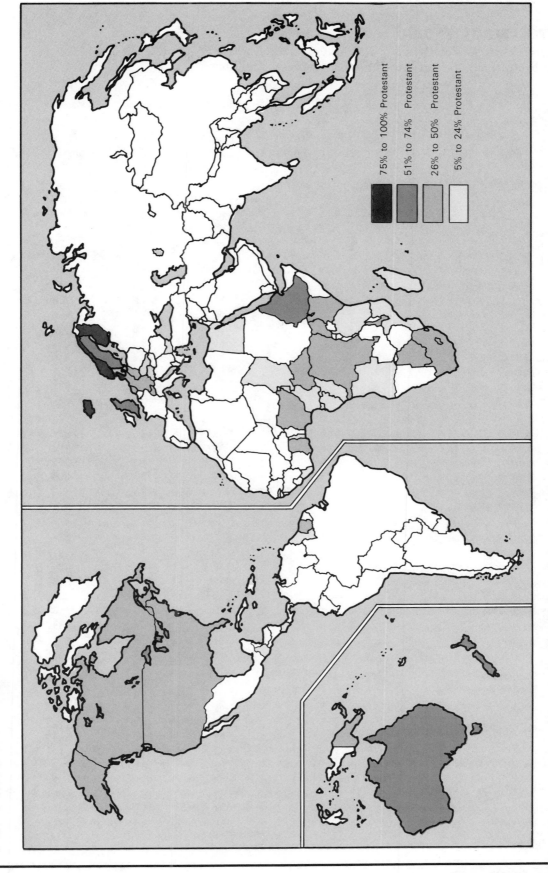

Note: Ethiopia is 52% Orthodox. Markings for all other countries are for the total percentage of all Protestants and Anglicans.

Legend:
- 75% to 100% Protestant
- 51% to 74% Protestant
- 26% to 50% Protestant
- 5% to 24% Protestant

The Protestant World

Countries having a population of 100,000 or more and where 5% or more are professing Protestants or Anglicans. Numbers represent millions.

	Profess. Anglican	Percent	Professing Protestant	Percent	Evangelicals	Percent
North America						
Canada	2.58	10.5	6.85	28.0	1.5	6.3
U.S.A.	5.38	2.4	89.5	40.0	59.487	26.5
Europe						
Channel Islands	.984	63.3	.018	13.8	.024	17.9
Czechoslovakia			1.078	7.1	.221	1.5
Denmark			4.85	95.0	.367	7.2
Finland			4.33	92.5	1.45	31.0
Germany, East			7.4	43.0	2.6	15.0
Germany, West			28.9	46.7	6.45	10.4
Hungary			2.31	21.6	1.16	10.5
Iceland			.22	96.4	.018	8.0
Netherlands			5.9	41.8	1.8	13.0
Norway			4.02	97.6	1.05	25.5
Romania			1.28	5.8	—	—
Sweden			5.795	69.9	1.010	11.8
Switzerland			2.89	42.9	.518	7.7
United Kingdom (Great Britain & N. Ireland)	32.671	56.8	8.63	15.0	11.55	20.0
Oceania						
Australia	4.208	27.8	7.6	50.0	1.557	14.1
Fiji	.009	1.4	.246	38.8	.129	20.5
French Polynesia			.07	46.0	.016	10.6
New Caledonia			.026	18.1	.004	2.9
New Zealand	1.067	32.7	1.157	35.5	.740	22.7
Papua New Guinea	.160	5.4	1.74	58.4	1.14	38.2
Samoa			.131	67.6	.028	14.8
Solomon Island	.072	33.5	.081	37.8	.053	24.6
Africa						
Angola			1.42	19.8	64	8.9
Botswana	.017	2.2	.211	26.6	.032	4.1
Cameroon			1.25	17.6	1.05	14.8
Cen. African Republic			.99	49.0	.6	29.9
Chad			.52	11.6	.39	8.8
Congo			.37	24.4	.186	12.2
Egypt			2.6	6.2	.143	.3
Gabon			.10	18.0		
Ghana	.24	2.1	2.86	25.0	.95	8.3
Kenya	1.129	7.2	3.02	19.3	3.367	21.5
Lesotho	.147	11.4	.382	29.8	.087	6.8
Liberia			.360	18.6	.112	5.8
Madagascar			2.05	22.0	.485	5.2
Malawi	.122	2.2	1.75	31.5	.78	14.0
Mozambique	.072	.7	.705	6.8	.47	4.5
Namibia	.028	3.6	.508	63.9	.24	30.2
Nigeria	7.622	10.5	11.03	15.2	8.40	11.9
Rwanda	.282	5.8	.564	11.6	.733	15.1
Sierra Leone	.040	1.2	.159	4.7	.114	3.3

The Protestant World (Continued)

	Profess. Anglican	Percent	Professing Protestant	Percent	Evangelicals	Percent
South Africa	1.968	6.9	11.013	38.6	5.705	20.0
Swaziland	.018	3.4	.180	33.2	.087	16.0
Tanzania	.722	4.0	2.027	11.2	1.966	10.9
Togo			.150	5.8	.054	2.1
Transkei	.235	9.4	.834	.334	.420	16.8
Uganda	3.463	26.2	.251	1.9	2.329	17.7
Zaire			8.106	29.0	4.540	16.2
Zambia	.135	2.3	.804	13.7	.362	6.2
Zimbabwe	.367	4.9	1.547	20.6	.778	10.4
Latin America and the Caribbean						
Bahamas	.047	20.7	.11	46.6	.026	11.3
Barbados	.125	49.7	.08	32.2	.022	7.0
Costa Rica			.123	5.4	.68	3.0
Grenada	.020	21.0	.012	12.6	.006	6.1
Guatemala			.348	4.9	.425	6.0
Guyana	.141	16.0	.159	18.0	.054	6.1
Haiti			.634	12.8	.520	10.5
Jamaica	.347	16.0	1.187	54.7	.412	19.0
Panama	.020	1.0	.090	4.7	.8	4.6
Suriname			.179	36.6	.037	7.6
Trinidad/Tobago			.132	12.5	.109	10.3
Asia						
Hong Kong			.329	7.3	.230	5.1
Indonesia			7.43	4.8	6.81	4.4
Korea, South			4.45	11.9	2.39	6.4

SUGGESTED READING

WHAT ARE WE MISSING: *By C. Peter Wagner. Ventura, CA: Regal Books*
The exciting story of the advance of the Gospel in Latin America where the church is growing three times faster than the exploding population. ($4.95)

THE BATTLE FOR THE MIND: *By Tim LaHaye. Power Books*
Old Tappen, NJ: Fleming H. Revell Co., 1980
"Have you ever wondered why America has become one of the most immoral nations on earth, yet has more Christians than any other? This book reveals the real enemy—secular humanism—in simple terms that laymen can understand. The Battle for the Mind is a shocking and detailed exposé of the humanist onslaught, as well as a practical handbook for waging war against this subtle but deadly infiltration. This is "must reading" for every Christian. (237 pp.)

IF MY PEOPLE: A HANDBOOK FOR NATIONAL INTERCESSION: *By Jimmy and Carol Owens. Waco, TX: Word Books, Publ.,1974*
The Bible says, "If my people which are called by My name, shall humble themselves, and pray, and seek My face, and turn from their wicked ways; then will I hear from heaven, and will forgive their sin, and will heal their land" 2 Chron. 7:14. This book is a call to repentence and intercession for this increasingly immoral nation. Excellent! (153 pp.)

AMERICA IS TOO YOUNG TO DIE: A CALL TO REVIVAL: *By Leonard Ravenhill. Minneapolis: Bethany Fellowship, 1979*
This straight forward message is meant to avert the untimely death of a "child" among nations. In a time when nations all over the world point at America, calling her everything but Christian, the voice of a "minor" prophet once again speaks a major truth: "It is time to quit playing church."

THE CULT EXPLOSION: *By Dave Hunt. Eugene, OR: Harvest House Publishers, 1978*
The cult explosion is an exposé of today's cults and why they prosper. Hunt shows the real danger and the strategy employed by the old and new cults—and how we can win over these sinister forces using the power of truth. Facts and personal experiences are related by people who escaped to tell about it. (270 pp.)

PEACE, PROSPERITY AND THE COMING HOLOCAUST: *By Dave Hunt. Eugene, OR: Harvest House Publishers, 1983*
Dave Hunt lays claim to an accurate look into the future, taking into account considerations that most Christian and non-Christian prognosticators have overlooked. He sees the one-world government and worship of the Anti-Christ close at hand. (282 pp. $6.95)

NONE DARE CALL IT CONSPIRACY: *By Gary Allen. Seal Beach, CA: Concord Press, 1971*
This book does an admirable job of amassing information to prove that Communism is socialism, and socialism (a plot to enslave the world) is not a movement of the downtrodden but a scheme supported by the wealthiest people. Over 5 million copies sold. (138 pp.)

YOU CAN TRUST THE COMMUNISTS (TO BE COMMUNISTS): *By Dr. Fred Schwarz. Long Beach, CA: Christian Anti-Communist Crusade, 1972*
The fascinating, forceful history that gives you the inside facts on how Communism affects you... and tells you what you can do about it. (182 pp.)

ON THE CREST OF THE WAVE Becoming a World Christian: *By C. Peter Wagner. Ventura, CA: Regal Books, 1983*

In all of history there has never been a more exciting time to be a Christian. A wave of world Christians is carrying the Gospel to those who are still un- reached. Members of the Church are wanting to get involved personally and be fully informed, but we must face this challenge realistically. Not many are called to be missionaries, yet we can be involved right where we are. Peter Wagner gives us the facts in this popular up-to-date missions books. ($8.95)

NEA: TROJAN HORSE IN AMERICAN EDUCATION
By Samuel L. Blumenfeld
Boise, Idaho: The Paradigm Co., 1984

An educational Mafia captured the high ground of American public education in the late 1800s. By their own words and deeds, Sam Blumenfeld shows how their carefully orchestrated, partially hidden agenda has deliberately steered the public schools, its teachers and children down a disaster road to socialism, secular humanism, radicalism, planned failure in reading and writing, suffocation of Christianity, the trashing of basic values and the establishment of one of the most powerful and dangerous unions, the National Education Association (NEA). The country owes Mr. Blumenfeld a great debt of gratitude for his outstanding and courageous work.

THE STEALING OF AMERICA
By John Whitehead
Westchester, IL: Crossway Books, 1983

Like millions of Americans, the author is alarmed by the growing encroachment of the state into areas where it has no business. Whitehead shows how the state has increasingly gained control over education, family life, and the church—areas that were previously under the control of individuals or local governments. The result has been the erosion of our God-given and constitutionally guaranteed freedoms and the rise of atheistic secularism.

CHILD ABUSE IN THE CLASSROOM
By Phyllis Schlafly (ed.)
Alton, IL: Pere Marquette Press, 1985

This book consists of selected excerpts from the Official Transcripts of Proceedings before the U.S. Department of Education in the matter of Proposed Regulations to Implement the Protection of Pupil Rights Amendment, also known as the Hatch Amendment. Highlights of the testimonies of hundreds of parents, teachers, and concerned citizens regarding the violations of the Pupil Rights Amendment. The testimonies at these Hearings were given by men and women who were, for the most part, total strangers to each other. Yet their message was the same from every part of the country. It came through loud and clear that child abuse in the classroom is a national disease carried to every state by the Typhoid Marys of federal spending. Many actual examples of how children have been abused in the classroom are included.

MISSIONS USA
By Earl Parvin
Chicago: Moody Press, 1985

This invaluable handbook, replete with tables, lists, maps, and appendixes, describes 45 unchurched groups, countless mission agencies geared toward serving them, and resources the church can use in training and sending missionaries to neglected peoples right here in America, is a MUST. It should be in the hands of every Christian leader, and all Christians, for that matter.

THE HOME INVADERS
By Donald E. Wildmon
Wheaton, IL: Victor Books, 1985

A shocking analysis of TV and the media, and how you can help stem the mind-polluting tide seeking to submerge us all. The startling facts of the media's attempted overthrow of our faith and our families, and a challenge to believers to fight back. Another MUST for all who are concerned about the future of this country.

PIONEERS IN MISSIONS
by R. Pierce Beaver. Grand Rapids: Eerdmans, 1966

THE AMERICAN HERITAGE BOOK OF INDIANS
by William Brandon, New York: Dell, 1961

THE NAVAJOS ARE COMING TO JESUS
by Thomas Dologhan and David Scates. Pasadena: Wm. Carey Library, 1978

THE NATIVE AMERICAN CHRISTIAN
by Gordon Frazier. Flagstaff, AZ: Southwestern School of Missions, 1977

THE INDIAN TRIBES OF THE UNITED STATES
by D'Arcy McNickle. New York: Oxford University Press

INDIANS OF THE SOUTHERN PLAINS
by William Powers. New York: Capricorn Books, 1972

INDIAN MISSIONS
by James Ronda and James Axtell. Bloomington, IN: University of Indiana Press, 1978

THE STORY OF RELIGION IN AMERICA
by William Sweet. New York: Harper & Row, 1950

THE AMERICAN INDIAN IN URBAN SOCIETY
by Jack Waddell & Michael Watson. Boston: Little, Brown & Co., 1971

THE WORLD OF THE AMERICAN INDIAN
Washington, D.C.: National Geographic Society

THE FIELDS AT HOME
by Peter Gunther, (ed.). Chicago: Moody Press, 1963

Black Americans

THE BLACK CHURCH IN THE U.S.
by William Banks. Chicago: Moody Press, 1972

A CHRONOLOGICAL HISTORY OF THE NEGRO IN AMERICA
by Peter M. Bergman and Mort N. Bergman. New York: New American Library, 1969

THE BLACK CHURCH IN AMERICA
from Good News Broadcaster, March, 1973
by Howard Jones.

THE BLACK EXPERIENCE IN RELIGION
by Eric C. Lincoln. New York: Doubleday, 1974

A QUIET REVOLUTION
by John Perkins. Waco, TX: Word, 1976

THE WORLDLY EVANGELICAL
by Richard Quebedeaux. New York: Harper & Row, 1980

RELIGIONS OF AMERICA
by Leo Rosten (ed.). New York: Simon & Schuster, 1975

AMERICAN ETHNIC GROUPS
by Thomas Sowell. Chicago: The Urban Institute, 1978

BLACK SECTS AND CULTS
by Joseph Washington. New York: Doubleday, 1973

MISSION HANDBOOK: North American Protestant Missions. 13th edition
by Sam Wilson (ed.). Monrovia, CA: MARC, 1986

Latin Americans

THE PROUD PEOPLES
by Harold Alford. New York: New American Library, n.d.

PROPHETS DENIED HONOR
by Antonio Arroyo. New York: Orbis, 1980

THE EXPLODING HISPANIC MINORITY: A Field in Our Back Yard
from Christianity Today, August 1980
by John Maust.

NORTH FROM MEXICO
by Carey McWilliams. New York: Greenwood, 1968

THE MEXICAN PEOPLE ON THE MOVE
by Griffith Smith, Jr.
from National Geographic, June, 1980

NO GRAVEN IMAGE
By Elisabeth Elliott
Westchester, IL: Crossway Books. (Paper, $5.95)

A sensitive, skillfully crafted novel about a young missionary to Ecuador who finds her faith tested to the limit.

AN URBAN STRAGEGY FOR LATIN AMERICA
By Roger Greenway
Grand Rapids: Baker Book House, 1973

ADVENTURES WITH THE BIBLE IN BRAZIL
By Frederick C. Glass
New York: Loizeaux Bros., 1943

LATIN AMERICAN CHURCH GROWTH
By William Read, V.M. Monterroso, and H. A. Johnson
Grand Rapids: Zondervan, 1969

MIRACLES IN MEXICO
By Hugh Steven and James Hefley
Chicago: Moody Press, 1972

MANUEL
By Hugh Steven
Old Tappan, NJ: Fleming H. Revell, 1970

Philippines

THE PHILIPPINE CHURCH
By Arthur Tuggy
Pasadena, CA: William Carey Library, 1978

BROKEN SNARE
By Caroline Stickley
Robesonia, PA: OMF Books, 1984

This is the sometimes luridly frank story of the initial outreach to a "hidden people" on Mindoro Island in the Philippines. It carries its reader right into jungle life and tells how a "good" spirit prepared the Tadyawan tribe to receive the gospel.

CAPTAIN MAHJONG
By Philip Holder
Robesonia, PA: OMF Books, 1984

Philippine parables based upon some of the parables of Jesus. The fictitious stories reflect realistically life in a Filipino barrio (village). In some cases they refer to the Japanese occupation during World War II.

ASSIGNMENT IN THE PHILIPPINES
By Marti Hefley
Chicago: Moody Press, $6.95

Jared and Marilee Barker traveled to the Philippines with great expectations. But they found their field completely hostile to Christianity. What progress could they possibly make? But God slowly began to heal the land. Poignant, touching, even humorous, those little, almost insignificant touches of the hand of God formed the miracle that is occurring there today.

STREET BOY
By Fletch Brown
Chicago: Moody Press, $2.95

The story of Jaime as he grows up in the streets of Manila in the Philippines, where he steals food and money to support his family.

STREET BOY RETURNS
By Fletch Brown
Chicago: Moody Press, $2.95

Jaime faces mockery and threats when he witnesses in his Manila neighborhood. A true story.

So-Called Christian World References

1. Parvin, Earl. *MISSIONS U.S.A.* Chicago: Moody Press, 1985:240.
2. Parvin, Earl. *MISSIONS U.S.A.* Chicago: Moody Press, 1985:159.
3. Anderson, Lorna. *YOU AND YOUR REFUGEE NEIGHBOR.* Pasadena: William Carey Library, 1980:78
4. Anderson, Lorna. *YOU AND YOUR REFUGEE NEIGHBOR.* Pasadena: William Carey Library, 1980:55-56
5. Quebedeaux, Richard. *THOSE WORLDLY EVANGELICALS.* San Francisco: Harper & Row, 1980:161
6. Parvin, Earl. *MISSIONS U.S.A.* Chicago: Moody Press, 1985:51.
7. Grimes, Barbara. *ETHNOLOGUE.* Huntington Beach: Wycliffe Bible Translators, 1984:52.
8. Parvin, Earl. *MISSIONS U.S.A.* Chicago: Moody Press, 1985:127.
9. Parvin, Earl. *MISSIONS U.S.A.* Chicago: Moody Press, 1985:171-175.
10. Rosten, Leo (Ed.). *RELIGIONS IN AMERICA.* New York: Simon & Schuster, 1975:382.
11. Parvin, Earl. *MISSIONS U.S.A.* Chicago: Moody Press, 1985:110.
12. Joyce, Raymond H. "Islam is Here in North America." *INTERLIT* Magazine, Dec. 1977:7.
13. Parvin, Earl. *MISSIONS U.S.A.* Chicago: Moody Press, 1985:183.

THE LORD'S PRAYER FOR MISSIONS

OUR FATHER WHO ART IN HEAVEN, HALLOWED BE THY NAME. Grant that the Gospel of Jesus Christ may be proclaimed among us and throughout the world in all its truth and purity, and that all believers may live holy and consecrated lives to the glory of Thy Holy Name.

THY KINGDOM COME. Grant that the proclamation of the Gospel may bear much fruit, that large numbers of men, women, and children from every nation, tribe, and language may be brought into Thy Kingdom of Grace in this life and Thy Kingdom of Glory in the life to come.

THY WILL BE DONE ON EARTH AS IT IS IN HEAVEN. Grant that we may never forget that it is Thy Will that ALL men be saved and come to the knowledge of the truth. Grant that we may always remember that WE are to be witnesses unto Christ unto the uttermost part of the earth. And help us to remember that it is also Thy Will that we live a holy life, that men may be led to their Savior, not only by our words, but by everything we do.

GIVE US THIS DAY OUR DAILY BREAD. Grant that we may always remember that every good gift is from above, that the earth is Yours and the fulness thereof, that we may always trust Thee to give us our daily bread, that we may therefore share our blessings with others and return unto Thee a large measure of the gifts You have entrusted unto us, that Thy Kingdom may be spread from pole to pole around the globe to every mountain hamlet and every jungle village.

AND FORGIVE US OUR TRESPASSES AS WE FORGIVE THOSE WHO TRESPASS AGAINST US. Forgive us for all the times we have given offense and thus kept others from coming to Thee. Forgive us for not witnessing unto Christ in our own community and throughout the world. Forgive us for so often forgetting that Christ died for us, that we who live might not henceforth live unto ourselves, but unto Him who died for us and rose again. Grant that we may also forgive those who trespass against us, That we may love our enemies, bless them that curse us, do good to them that hate us, and pray for them who despitefully use us and persecute us, that we might by all means lead some to Christ.

AND LEAD US NOT INTO TEMPTATION. Grant that Satan, the world and our own flesh may not tempt us to neglect the supreme task of the church. Grant that we may not be tempted to fiddle away our time while the world rushes toward eternal flames, that we may never be tempted to squander our money on luxuries and the pleasures of this world and deny to others the Bread of Life. Grant that we may never be tempted to use our God-given talent to our own glory and selfish interests, but that we may always use these talents to show forth the praises of Him who called us out of darkness into His marvelous light.

BUT DELIVER US FROM EVIL. Protect us from all harm and danger, but grant that we may boldly confess our faith in Jesus no matter what the circumstances, no matter what may be the result. Grant that we may be willing and happy to deny ourselves and take up the cross of self sacrifice that others might live.

FOR THINE IS THE KINGDOM AND THE POWER AND THE GLORY FOREVER AND EVER. AMEN!

Available in tract form from All Nations Missions, P.O. Box 5491, Ft. Wayne, IN 46895.

HOW TO PRAY FOR MISSIONARIES

Every missionary has his own particular problems with which to cope, depending on the country he's in and the nature of his ministry and several other factors. But all missionaries have a lot of common problems and pressures—some that you might expect them to have and others that you might not expect.

Some of these problems are personal and some concern his work. Understanding them will help you pray more effectively for him.

SPIRITUAL PRESSURES

Missionaries are usually under a lot of pressure to get things done, and because of this they sometimes neglect their own quiet time with the Lord. Their devotional life begins to deteriorate. So pray that your missionary will maintain his daily communion with God.

If he doesn't walk closely with the Lord, he may become irritable toward his fellow missionaries and national coworkers. This is very serious, especially with regard to his national colleagues who attribute such bahavior to racial predjudice.

Neglect of one's own quiet time with the Lord may also result in pride—that attitude which regards his own opinions or actions as the only right ones, or at least the best ones. Pride may show itself in high-handed treatment of others, impatience with other people's shortcomings, or seeking personal popularity.

Losing daily communion with God also exposes your missionary to temptations. It's possible for a missionary, like any other Christian to fall morally. The devil would like nothing better than to destroy the missionary personally and ruin his work. Complete honesty in the handling of money and goods, truthfulness in word and deed, purity of mind and body—all of these may be attacked. The Enemy may use loneliness or the influence of low moral standards around him to aggravate temptation.

PHYSICAL PRESSURES

Ill health can cause spiritual depression and inefficiency and can be used by Satan to hinder the Lord's work and put a strain on those who have to carry the extra load.

Fatigue is a common condition on the mission field, especially in the tropics, where humidity and temperatures are high and where physical exertion can make one drip with perspiration.

Car accidents are increasingly prevalent with the growing number of vehicles crowding the highways and city streets. Pray for your missionary's protection. Pray, too, that your missionary may drive with skill and caution, that he may not harm other people. How tragic, blameless or not, to maim or kill another person.

EMOTIONAL PRESSURES

One of the chief causes of emotional difficulties is loneliness. This affects single workers particularly, especially if there are no other single people for companionship. Even couples in isolated places can become despondent due to lack of friends of their own race.

Anxiety is another source of emotional pressure. This may be anxiety over the work, or a problem in the local church, or trouble back home in the States. In other countries where there is political upheaval, there can be anxiety over friends and fellow workers.

In the case of missionary parents there can be anxiety about the children—and not just over their physical health or safety, but with regard to their education. "Should we send them home for schooling? Should we stay at home with them?" These are heart-rending questions for parents. And those who have left sons or daughters at home for higher education are subject to severe concern for their moral and spiritual welfare.

Other problems should be mentioned, such as incompatibility with fellow workers or other conditions, discouragement at apparent lack of results, and the subtle strain of just being an alien 24 hours a day.

FINANCIAL PRESSURES

Most of us face financial pressures to one extent or another. But the missionary is in a situation where he can't do much about the lack of money except pray. He can't increase his income by changing jobs, or by moonlighting, or by starting his own business.

The cost of living can be a source of pressure. Travel for children going to school, clothing, hospitality to travelers, repairs and replacements for equipment, the high price of imported foods—all of these mount up.

The missionary expects these inconveniences, but his skill at managing financial affairs may not always equal them. He may fall into debt, if only with the Mission, but that also is a cause for worry.

Properly committed to God, of course, all the missionary's pressures can become a source of blessing, as he discovers that his heavenly Father can supply all his needs.

AN OUTPOURING OF THE HOLY SPIRIT

Within the past decade, many missionaries have been murdered. Others have been shot at, stoned, beaten and imprisoned. Many have had their property confiscated or homes destroyed simply for preaching the Gospel or due to some misunderstanding. Still others have seen little fruit of their labors because the people have been resistant, often out of fear of being ostracized or even killed by their own relatives for becoming Christian.

In situations like these, it is easy to lose one's courage or enthusiasm. But no missionary, no matter how enthusiastic or courageous, no matter how intelligent, no matter how well-trained, can do anything in his own strength. "Not by might nor by power but by my Spirit", says the Lord (Zech. 4:6). Jesus told His disciples, "You will receive power after the Holy Spirit comes on you; and you will be my witness...to the ends of the earth" (Acts 1:8). Earlier He had said, "When He (the Holy Spirit) comes, He will convict the world of guilt in regard to sin and righteousness and judgment" (John 16:7,8). "He will guide you into all truth. He will tell you what is yet to come" (v.13). "He will bring glory to Me!..." (v.14). Of course, no one can even say, "Jesus is Lord," except by the Holy Spirit (I Cor. 12:3). So pray for a tremendous outpouring of the Holy Spirit on your missionary and on the people to whom he has been sent, that multitudes may be won to Christ and incorporated into the Church, and that they may be strong in the faith, reaching out to others locally and beyond, glorifying the Lord in all they do. Or, as St. Paul, that great missionary to the Gentiles put it, "Pray...that whenever I open my mouth, words may be given me so that I will fearlessly make known the mystery of the Gospel, for which I am an ambassador in chains. Pray that I may declare it fearlessly as I should" (Eph.6:19-20). "Pray for us, that the message of the Lord may spread rapidly and be honored" (II Thess. 3:1).

These are just a few suggestions that will help you pray for your missionaries. But every missionary has many specific people and projects and problems and pressures that need your prayer support. And every missionary experiences many blessings that he would like to share with you—that you may rejoice in what God is doing in and through his ministry and otherwise in that part of the world.

If you haven't already adopted a missionary, we urge you to do so—that you may hear from him regularly and be able to pray for his specific needs and praise the Lord when those prayers are answered.

Available in tract form from All Nations Missions, P.O. Box 5491, Ft. Wayne, IN 46895.

HOW TO PRAY FOR THE LOST

In a little Muslim village in Niger (in the Sahara) a young man named Ahmed became a Christian. His father and his brothers beat him unmercifully and left him for dead. But Ahmed recovered and fled southward to Nigeria. When his brothers learned that Ahmed was not dead, they pursued him to Nigeria, then westward to Benin where they finally caught up with him and stoned him to death.

Is it any wonder that so few Muslims ever turn to Christ for life and salvation? New Christians in Muslim lands certainly need our prayers, as do the missionaries who work among such resistant people. But the need to pray for the lost—the fanatically lost—is even greater. Ahmed is with his Savior. But his brothers and hundreds of millions of others like them are without Christ and thus without God and hope. They will be punished with everlasting destruction and shut out from the presence of the Lord and from the majesty of His power on the day He comes to be glorified in His holy people and to be marvelled at among all those who believe (II Thess. 1:9-10).

No wonder St. Paul urged Christians everywhere to strive together with him in prayers (Rom. 15:30), praying always with all prayer and supplication for all saints, and for himself, that utterance may be given unto him, that he might open his mouth boldly to make known the mystery of the gospel (Eph.6:18,19), that the word of the Lord may have free course and be glorified, and that he and his coworkers may be delivered from unreasonable and wicked men. (II Thess. 3:2).

The need for intercessory prayer has never been greater than it is today. Twenty-five hundred million people are living in places beyond the reach of national churches or existing missionary efforts. More than 100,000 of them die every day without ever hearing a clear presentation of the Gospel of Jesus Christ. Many of them, like Ahmed, live in countries that are 99.9% Muslim or Buddhist, or Communist, walled off from the Gospel by linguistic, cultural, social and political barriers, unable to break the chains that bind them. And the Evil One is determined to keep these people in his clutches for all eternity.

But even in the United States and in other nominally Christian countries, Satan is hard at work. As a roaring lion he stalks the earth, seeking whom he may devour.

No missionary, no matter how intelligent, no matter how well-trained or how well-acculturated or how determined, can win the battle for souls without long and regular hours in intensive prayer. He may learn the language well and speak with all the eloquence of men and of angels, but unless he can pray with a faith that draws all heaven to his aid, his speaking will be "as sounding brass or a tinkling cymbal." It is the one who goes forth weeping (not preaching great sermons, but agonizing for souls), bearing precious seed, who shall come again rejoicing, bringing his sheaves with him (Ps.126:5,6).

But it is not enough for the *missionaries* to be men and women of prayer. All Christians must be intercessors. *All* Christians must storm the gates of heaven continously in behalf of those still held by the Enemy and in behalf of the new Christians (and older ones too) and those soldiers of the cross who are fighting the battle in areas held by the powers of darkness. If we do, we can be certain of victory, for greater is He that is in us than he that is in the world. But if we fail to pray, we can expect little advance against the forces of evil. The Gospel moves with slow and timid pace when the saints are not on their knees—early, and late, and long.

How can we pray effectively for the Lost?

Volumes have been written on this subject. But we pray that the few suggestions here will help you in your own personal walk with the Lord and in your effectiveness as a prayer-warrior.

First of all, we must come before the throne of grace with a pure heart, we must repent of all selfishness and pride, worldliness and greed, deceitfulness and lust. We must put away all bitterness and wrath and thoughts of revenge, and forgive one another, even as God for Christ's sake has forgiven us. For if we cherish sin in our hearts, the Lord will not hear us (Ps. 66:18 and 24:3-5). But the eyes of the Lord are on the righteous, and his ears are attentive to their cry (Ps. 34:15).

Second, we should approach the throne of grace seriously and humbly but cheerfully, serving the Lord with gladness in our prayer life as in everything we do. While it is true that we are to be fervent in prayer, wrestling with God, striving in the Spirit, earnestly contending for the souls of men, we are to count it a great privilege and honor to so so. As David wrote so many years ago, "Delight yourself in the Lord, and He will give you the desires of your heart" (Ps. 37:4).

Third, we must pray in the Name of Jesus. We often feel that we cannot come into the presence of God because we are so unworthy. We feel that we don't have enough faith, or we don't have enough love and concern for the lost, or that we aren't spiritual enough. That, of course, is true, and there would be no hope for us if we were to pray in our own name. But we are to pray in the Name of Jesus. It is for Jesus' sake that our requests are granted.

Fourth, we do need a little faith. We do need faith enough to come to Jesus with our requests. Jesus assures us that whatever we ask for in prayer, believing, we shall receive (Matt. 21:21) and that even if our faith is as small as a mustard seed, we can move mountains, and nothing will be impossible for us (Matt. 17:20).

God doesn't want anyone to perish in his sins; he wants all people everywhere to be saved (I Tim. 2:4). He wants this so much that He sent His only Son into the world to be mocked, slapped, spit upon, scourged, crowned with thorns, and crucified that He might pay for the sins of all mankind, that whoever believes in Him should not perish but have everlasting life. God is much more concerned about the lost than we are. With this in mind, it shouldn't take much faith to come to Him in behalf of those still held by the powers of darkness, heading down that broad road which leads to everlasting destruction.

Fifth, we should keep in mind that even the worst of sinners can be saved. Some of the most proud and arrogant, selfish, vicious, and degraded people that ever lived have become lovable and loving children of God, zealous to spread the Good News about Jesus to their friends and to the ends of the earth. Jesus is able to save to the uttermost all that call upon Him in repentance and true faith, and He really does want all people everywhere to be saved.

Sixth, we must be persistent in our prayers—not to persuade God, but *because of the Enemy*—the awful powers and rulers of darkness. It is our duty to *fight* for souls for whom Christ died. Just as some must preach to them the Good News about Jesus—over and over again—others must fight the powers of darkness on their knees, interceding for the lost, day in and day out. Satan gives up only what he must, and he renews his attacks in subtle ways. Thus, prayer must be definite and persistent, even after definite results are seen. Remember that one soul is worth all the gold and silver and precious stones and everything else this world contains. If we were as concerned for souls as we ought to be, we would be willing to crawl through a thousand miles of broken glass or swim the widest ocean if possible to bring people the Message of God's redeeming love. Certainly we will be willing to spend an hour a day making intercession for them, especially for those who have never had an opportunity to hear the Good News of Jesus before.

Seventh, we must be early with our prayers. We ought to pray before we see anyone. The men who have done the most for God in this world have been early on their knees. David's heart was ardent after God. He hungered and thirsted after God, and so he sought God early, before daylight (Ps. 63:1). Jesus longed for communion with His heavenly Father; and so rising a great while before day, He would go out into a solitary place to pray (Mark 1:35). We need to put first things first, and nothing is more important than getting close to God and storming the gates of heaven in behalf of precious souls. Intercession is no petty duty, no piecemeal performance made out of the fragments of time snatched from business and other earthly pursuits; it demands the *best* of our time and energy and strength.

Eighth, we should pray for specific individuals and groups. We cannot overemphasize this point. Probably the best way to learn of specific needs in other lands is to "adopt a missionary". He and his family desperately need your prayer support, as do the people with whom he works—Christians and non-Christians alike. Your missionary will be grateful for your prayers and will be happy to send you specific prayer requests and keep you informed as to how God is answering your prayers and blessing the work.

Available in tract form from All Nations Missions, P.O. Box 5491, Ft. Wayne, IN 46895.

ON PRAYING FOR THE MUSLIM WORLD

Here are a few suggestions for those concerned to pray for Muslims.

1. Pray against the spiritual forces that blind Muslims. Islam holds a wrong view of Christ. They consider Him as a good prophet but no more. They do not see Him as God the Son, cannot understand His death, nor appreciate His place in the Godhead. The Scriptural explanation is considered to be a distortion produced by later Christians.

2. Pray against the social forces that hold Muslims back from faith. For a Muslim to confess Christ usually means rejection by his family. Such pressures are hard to bear. Commitment to Christ is costly, and there are few Christians to strengthen the new believer.

3. Pray for those who do confess Christ openly:
For a close walk with Jesus involving a deep study of the Bible—their only hope if they are to root Islam out of their thinking.
For a warm fellowship with other believers. There is often little chance of fellowship and Bible teaching as we have in the West.
For strength and boldness to overcome depression, fears and doubt, and to manifest the fruit of the Spirit, along with a strong witness.
For a love among Christians, and a love for Muslims which will break down the barriers that so often exist between Christian converts and Muslims. Many times converts from Islam are not trusted and are rejected by the Christian community.

4. Pray for foreign workers.
For determination . . .
In their own personal spiritual lives.
In language study. This is no easy task
In cultural adaptation. This takes time.
In pressing through the problems and disappointments that do come, to the Lord's victories.
To persevere to see God's church established.
To apply Biblical truth to their situation.
To perceive the needs of the people among whom they work, whether Christian or Muslim, and the answers to them.

5. Pray for the more established forms of Christian witness—schools, hospitals, clinics, bookshops. They need Christian doctors, teachers, nurses and evangelists.
Normally in hospitals and schools there is some time during the day, a short meeting for all patients or children when the Gospel is presented. Literature is distributed in the hospital to outpatients who take it back to their homes—often in villages and tribes. Patients in bed are visited by the hospital evangelist, if there is one. In many hospitals nurses are being trained. This is a large opportunity and responsibility. In the schools Christian teachers need strength both physically and spiritually to be persevering witnesses for Christ. Almost everywhere more workers are needed to fill key gaps.

6. Pray for more modern methods of witness.
Radio: There are many broadcasts for Muslims. The least reached area, as far as radio is concerned, is the Middle East from Pakistan through North Africa.
Often only prayer will make people tune to the right wavelength at the right time. Often only radio will reach into the villages and tribes. But nationals from the countries concerned are needed to write and often produce the radio

programs. For example, where are the Afghans to write and produce the programs?

Literature: The rapid spread of literacy has opened wide doors for books. Pray for the work of literature committees, the Bible Societies, the Scripture Gift Mission, the Arabic Literature Mission and Operation Mobilization who among others, seek to seize the opportunity. Pray for more literacy workers and for literacy organizations such as the All Nations Literacy Movement. Most Muslim countries are still 50% or more illiterate; many are 85% to 90% blind to the printed page. Often literature exists, but it is not distributed. Often literature exists, but it is translated from books intended for the West. Pray for national authors who can write relevant and interesting Christian literature for new literates as well as for more advanced readers.

Gospel Recordings: Records exist in hundreds of languages spoken by Muslims, but distribution is a critical problem. Again, the records in so many dialects need to be distributed.

Newspaper Advertising: Leads many to seek Jesus.

Bible Correspondence Courses: Thousands are applying for such courses throughout the Muslim World. Probably more are reading the Bible in this way than ever before. Think what this means in practice. A person in a small town, having never seen a Christian, finds a tract and writes for the course. His friends get to know about it (through the Post Office which checks letters). He gets interested. They begin to mock. He has questions. A foreigner comes to visit. His friends put pressure on him and he is scared off, or if strong enough, he makes a secret profession of faith. Only prayer can overcome the spiritual barriers and support such interested inquirers. In many countries such courses need to be developed. National workers are needed to help answer questions, to produce courses for students, for those who have little education, and for women and children.

7. Pray for areas of need where advance must be made: the less open countries such as Afghanistan, Turkey, Libya, Morocco, Saudi Arabia, the Sudan, Muslims in the Communist World, and Bangladesh. Women in some countries are far freer than previously, yet their lot is still unhappy. Pray for tribespeople, villages, the rising middle class, refugees, foreign workers, the student world with universities in Tehran, Bagdad, Istanbul, Amman, and Cairo. Some Final Thoughts: Be informed and ask for regular prayer information from Missions to Muslims. Join the Fellowship of Faith for Muslims: FFM 205 Yonge Street . .25, Toronto, Ont. M5B 1N2. Literature may be obtained from them. Correspond with a missionary family or national Christian worker and make them your personal prayer target. Get to know some Muslims in your own area and share your faith with them. Let them tell you what they believe. Don't give up. Remember, the effectual fervent prayer of a righteous person availeth much (James 5:16). So be stead-fast, unmovable, always abounding in the work of the Lord, forasmuch as you know that your labor is not in vain in the Lord. (1 Cor. 15:58).

Available in tract form from All Nations Literacy Movement, P.O. Box 5491, Ft. Wayne, IN 46895.

NO CHRISTIAN IS GREATER THAN HIS PRAYER LIFE

The church has many organizers, but few agonizers; many who pay, but few who pray; many resters, but few wrestlers; many who are not praying are playing.

The prerequisites of dynamic Christian living are vision and passion, and both of these are generated in the prayer closet. The ministry of preaching is open to a few. The ministry of praying is open to every child of God.

Dont mistake action for unction, commotion for creation, and rattles for revivals.

The secret of praying is praying in secret. A worldly Christian will stop praying, and a praying Christian will stop worldliness.

When we pray, God listens to our heartbeat. Hannahs lips moved, but her voice was not heard (II Sam. 1:12,13). When we pray in the Spirit, there are groanings which cannot be uttered (Rom.8:26).

Tithes may build a church, but tears will give it life. That is the difference between the modern church and the early church. Our emphasis is on paying, theirs was on praying. When we have paid, the place is taken. When they prayed, the place was shaken (Acts 4:31).

In the matter of effective praying, never have so many left so much to so few. Brethren, let us pray.

Leonard Ravenhill
from Why Revival Tarries

Used by permission.

SUGGESTED READING

ALL THINGS ARE POSSIBLE THROUGH PRAYER, *By Charles L. Allen*

DESTINED FOR THE THRONE, *Paul Billheimer*

POWER THROUGH PRAYER, E.M. Bounds

WHAT HAPPENS WHEN WOMEN PRAY, Evelyn Christenson

NO EASY ROAD, Dick Eastman

HOW DO I KNOW GOD ANSWERS PRAYER, Rosalind Goforth

WHAT WILL IT TAKE TO CHANGE THE WORLD S.D. Gordon

REES HOWELLS: INTERCESSOR, Norman Grubb

PRAYER, O. Hallesby

OPERATION WORLD: A HANDBOOK FOR INTERCESSORS Patrick Johnstone

WHY REVIVAL TARRIES, Leonard Ravenhill

HUDSON TAYLOR'S SPIRITUAL SECRET Mr. and Mrs. Howard Taylor

GOD'S CHOSEN FAST Arthur Wallis

DIVIDING THE MISSIONARY DOLLAR

By Ted W. Engstrom

Let me admit from the start that I have an axe to grind, After more than 35 years in full-time Christian work, I am still amazed at the number of people who do not realize that churches and charitable organizations both have operating costs. Often I'm asked, "Why can't you operate World Vision the way my church is run, without any overhead?" That probably is the most exasperating question anyone could ask. And I can picture my many friends in other Christian organizations cringing inwardly every time the question is directed to them.

The fact is, you see, that most churches use practically all their income on overhead-type expenditures—staff salaries and benefits, office supplies, printing, maintenance, utilities, Christian education materials, etc. Few churches devote more than 20% of their annual budgets to overseas missions or to local community outreach programs.

Of course, a church is a unique institution essentially serving its own membership who help establish the budget and set priorities. Any other Christian charity that devoted 80% of its income to overhead and only 20% to outside ministries would be severely criticized—and rightly so.

But charity—be it World Vision, the Salvation Army, YMCA, or the mission arm of any denomination—must manage its "business" so that most of the gifts it receives actually go to an ongoing ministry; to whatever ministry for which the funds were solicited.

The agency that is maintaining a low 15% overhead rate is doing a remarkable job, but anywhere between 15 and 25% is respectable. This holds true for secular charities as well. Early last year, a U.S. Senator investigating a number of charities labeled the 24% overhead of a national society that solicits funds for crippled children as "one of the best." Unfortunately, the American public all too often supports, without question, organizations whose overheads run as high as 60 to 80%.

After wrestling with overhead expenses at Youth for Christ International (1951 to 1963) and at World Vision (since 1963), I know there's no way a responsible organization can be run with 5 or 10% overhead, administration and fund-raising costs. And I know no responsible agency that makes such a claim.

The word "responsible" is most important. Many organizations report their salaries, administration and fund-raising costs as one overhead figure. Others slyly include only salaries and administration in that total; fund-raising costs are disguised as "literature","public information" or "educational programs". Still others would rather take you off their mailing lists than divulge overhead costs.

Now, the most important overhead-related variable within any charitable organization—and, incidentally, within any secular corporation—is management. Some Christian organizations thrive and grow and maintain a low overhead cost because they are blessed with good leadership and good management. Some organizations enjoy a dynamic leadership but have mediocre management; they, too, thrive and grow, but overhead costs are high. Still other Christian organizations have poor management; the commitment of their managers to our Lord Jesus Christ may be every bit as sincere as mine, yours or Billy Graham's, but their knowledge of business management leaves much to be desired.

It is the decisions of management that determine how efficiently an organization operates and how well its overhead is controlled. For instance, is it good stewardship to continue spending $10,000 in eight magazines every month to run an advertisement that produces $20,000? How about $30,000? At what level is it good stewardship? Or at what point do you stop hiring people to manually perform a job that a machine could do more efficiently?

Unfortunately, a few organizations—a very few, I think—are not run efficiently and the adverse publicity they eventually receive throws a cloud of suspicion on all. I'd like to point out that most of the "exposés" I've heard about during the past two years have concerned secular rather than Christian charities. I think that's one good reason for supporting Christian organizations.

Most concerned Christians want to contribute funds to an agency that will use their money responsibly. But it's not easy to know who these groups are.

Perhaps someday Christian organizations will adopt standard accounting procedures for reporting their financial data. We could issue our own "Christian Seal of Approval". But until someone does come up with such a standard procedure it will remain up to the discerning Christian to research and judge the evidence before contributing. That's difficult, especially when one is confronted with an urgent emotional appeal, but I still recommend it.

When you research a charity, you should be able to inquire—and receive without any difficulty—information about: a charity's ministries and its areas of involvement; the names of its board of directors and whether they are paid or serve voluntarily; information about key management personnel; the number of people it employs; whether it employs an independent certified public accounting firm, and how often its books are audited; and a copy of its most recent financial report which should contain information concerning its sources of income and overhead, i.e., salaries, administration and fund-raising costs and ministry expenses.

An efficient charity organization carrying out an effective ministry requires operating funds. However, it is the percentage of overhead that an agency requires—not the fact that overhead exists—that should determine whether we contribute or not. Overhead is not a dirty word, but a natural part of the work we do.

Used by permission.

SOME THINGS YOUR CHURCH CAN DO
To Help Win The Seven Worlds to Christ

1. Appoint a Missions Chairman.

2. Try to have a Missions Committee.

3. Adopt a missionary (or several missionaries). Support him (them) in full or in part (a certain amount each month) and pray for him (them) daily at home as well as in the church services each week, in the Sunday School, Day School, Vacation Bible School, etc. It is best to adopt someone from the local congregation if possible. Otherwise, adopt someone known to the members. Write to your missionary (ies) regularly and read his (their) letters to various church groups.

4. Have a Missions Library which includes periodicals as well as books. Also a filing cabinet full of information on various countries and mission endeavors. Wall maps, atlases, a globe, etc.

5. Have a mission program each month, with a missionary speaker if possible. Otherwise, many good mission films and filmstrips exist. Have a missionary speak or show a mission film Sunday morning occasionally.

6. Have an entire week of mission promotion once each year beginning on a Sunday and ending the following Sunday evening. Emphasize one continent one night, another the next. Or emphasize one kind of ministry one night, (e.g., radio) and another the next (e.g., literacy).

7. Witness to immigrants, refugees, foreign students, seamen, etc, Invite them to dinner frequently. Teach English to those who need help several times each week, and use the opportunity to witness.

8. Use church bulletins or bulletin inserts that emphasize what God is doing in various lands and what remains to be done.

9. Have projects to raise money for missions. For example, the young people could wash cars for a dollar or two and use the money to buy cars for the mission field. Others could collect paper and aluminum for recycling and use the money for publication of Christian literature. It could be called the Litter for Literature project.

10. Visit one or more mission fields as a group. If the group can't visit a distant field in Asia perhaps a visit to a field in Mexico or an Indian reservation in the States could be arranged.

11. Study missions in the Sunday School and adult Bible Class and/or Vacation Bible School. Many good books exist which would be suitable for this purpose. Some are excellent.

12. Encourage students to take basic mission courses. They are offered on several college campuses and seminaries. In such, students sit at the feet of missionaries and professors of missions and mission directors who have worked for many years in many parts of the world.
    for fourteen weeks. Students sit at the feet of missionaries and professors of missions and missions directors who have worked for many years in many parts of the world.

13. Add the Great Commission Study Guide to the instruction given to the confirmation class. This could be called The Biblical Basis for Missions or The Unfinished Task or Our Lords Last Commandment. This can be ordered through R.C. Law & Co., 579 S. State College Blvd., Fullerton, CA 92631.

GET THE MOST FOR YOUR DOLLAR

All agree that the needs on the various mission fields throughout the world are staggering, to say the least. For example, just to reach every non-Christian with a one-cent tract would require $35 million, for printing alone. Think what it would cost to effectively reach the 2.5 billion people who have no church within reach where their language is spoken! Unfortunately the numbers of concerned Christians are very few. For this reason those of us who are committed to the fulfillment of the Great Commission—"to make disciples of all nations"—must not only give sacrificially, but we must make every penny count.

How to Use Mission Funds to the Greatest Advantage

1. Support only those missionaries who know and love the Lord Jesus, are doctrinally sound, and saturated with His Word, tenaciously clinging to it and boldly proclaiming it.

2. Support servants of Christ who are living holy, loving and joyful lives, lives that attract others to our Lord and Savior.

3. Support missionaries who have been well-trained in cross-cultural communications and missionary strategy, and who are able to communicate effectively.

4. Give top priority to supporting missionaries whose primary objective is winning people to Christ and helping them become responsible members of His Church.

5. Support agencies that are good stewards of funds they receive. (Some do the right things on the mission field but spend too much on administration at home. Other agencies have been able to cut expenses at home and still meet the above requirements.)

6. Support Christian radio broadcasts, and the production and distribution of Christian literature (including Bible correspondence courses and courses in theological education by extension), and tape recordings especially prepared for those who have no viable church in their midst. Under certain circumstances these may be more economical ways to spread the Gospel, and in some cases the *only* way.

7. Support ministries among international students. (There are 400,000 of them in North America.) This is strategic for several reasons: (a) Muslim, Buddhists and others are easier to win to Christ in this country than in their homelands. (b) Many of these students will become leaders in their own countries. For example, forty presidents and prime ministers in third-world countries today received their training in the U.S.A. What a pity they were not converted as well while in the States! (c) Witnessing to international students in our country is of course more economical than sending missionaries overseas, but even if money were not a problem, (d) many Muslim and Buddhist countries are closed to traditional mission work.

8. Support efforts to win refugees, immigrants, seamen and other visitors to this country. Teaching English as a second language (TESL) offers an excellent way to spend time with them, which will give opportunity to share your faith with them. The cost in dollars for this kind of witnessing is minimal.

9. Support adjunct training institutes near large universities in major cities of Asia, Africa, and Latin America, where tomorrow's leaders can receive instruction and inspiration from God's Word while training to be doctors, professors, business men, etc. A much higher percentage of the educated people in these countries can be reached in this way than in any other, and again, the cost in dollars is relatively little.

10. Support efforts to promote missions in Christian Day Schools, high schools, and colleges and in local congregations. Sadly, this has been neglected. But it is something that *must be done* if we are to reach the 2.5 billion who thus far have not been touched by the existing missionary efforts.

THE WORLD AT A GLANCE

The World at a Glance
Facts and Figures Concerning the World and Its Need

World Population: 5,026,000,000 (1987)

If all the people living today continued to live long enough to be counted, and if no more people were born during that time, and if you counted one person per second, 24 hours every day, it would take 153 years to count them all.

Population of Continents and Regions
(Population Reference Bureau, 1987)

Africa	601 million	ªEurope	779 million
Americas	691 million	ᶜOceania	25 million
ᵇAsia	2,930 million		

ªIncludes U.S.S.R.
ᵇIncludes Indonesia & the Philippines.
ᶜIncludes Australia, NZ, Papua New Guinea & islands to the north & east.
ᵈ1987 statistics are from the 1987 World Population Data Sheet of the Population Reference Bureau, Inc.
All other statistics are from McEvedy & Jones, Atlas of World Population History, Penguin Books, 1978.

Population Explosion

In the days of Christ there were about 200 million people in the world. In 1500 there were about 400 million people. In 1830 the population reached one billion. By 1930 there were two billion, and by 1984 there were 4.7 billion inhabitants on this planet. Although some 130,000 people die every day, about 330,000 babies are born every day. So there is an increase in the population of about 200,000 every day, or 73 million per year. At the present annual growth rate of 2%, there will be 6.2 billion people in the world by the year 2000. (Pop Ref. Bureau)

World Religions

The following figures are at best approximations but they do show the relative numerical balance of the major religions of the world. (Estimated figures for mid-1985—World Christian Encyclopedia, p. 6)

Total Christian	1,548,592,000	Buddhist	295,570,780
Roman Catholic	884,221,982	Chinese folk-religionist	187,994,026
Protestant	292,733,699	Atheist	210,643,540
Orthodox	130,837,380	Tribal religionists (animists)	91,130,380
Anglican	68,048,221	New Religionists	106,317,600
Others	172,750,718	Jewish	17,838,060
Muslim*	817,065,000	Sikhs	16,149,890
Hindu	647,567,465	Other	842,255,234

Islamic Center, Washington, D.C. claims one billion Muslims worldwide.

The Protestant Church is growing rapidly in Africa and Latin America, in South Korea and in Indonesia and other places. But Buddhism is also on the upsurge, and Islam is spreading very fast, especially in Africa, but also in Europe and North America.

An Extreme Imbalance

- 90% of the world's ordained ministers work among the 9% who speak English.
- More people attend Sunday School in the U.S. than in all the rest of the world.
- There are more young people in Bible Institutes and Bible Colleges in the U.S. than in all the rest of the world.
- There is more evangelical literature printed in English than in all the other languages of the world combined.
- We have many times more Christian radio broadcasts than any other nation.
- The U.S., with 6% of the world's population, has 50% of the world's wealth

World Missions and Needs

- In Latin America, the Church is growing three times faster than the population growth rate, but thousands of church groups are without trained leadership.
- In Africa, 1000 new church groups spring up every week, but trained leadership is not keeping pace. Thousands of pastors, teachers, evangelists and Christian writers must be trained as soon as possible.
- In Asia, where 57% of the world's population dwell and where only 5-7% are professed Christian, there's only one full-time church worker (national or missionary) for every 50,000 people. If we train a million more workers, there will still be only one worker for every 2400 people.
- Some 900 million Chinese, 800 million Muslims, 500 million Hindus, and 400 million others have never heard a clear presentation of the Gospel. There's no Christian church in their midst that speaks their language.
- 83% of the Western missionary force is serving the area of 402 million non-Christians while only 17% work among the other 2.6 billion non-Christians, most of whom are in Asia.
- Only 2% of the world's missionaries work among the 817 million Muslims.
- 4000 languages are still without a single word of Scripture. These languages are spoken by about 160 million people.
- More than a billion adults and teenagers are unable to read the Scriptures that exist in their languages.

The Selfishness and Indifference of Americans.

God wants all people to be saved and come to the knowledge of the truth. Jesus gave Himself a ransom for all, and He gave His followers the Great Commission to make disciples of all nations (every ethnic group). And yet, many church members, as well as the unchurched in America, continue to spend hundreds of times more money on fun and games and even on sinful pursuits than on spreading the Gospel. Here, for example, is...

How Americans Spent Some of Their Money in 1981.
(From Information Please Almanac-'83)

Food $329,100,000,000
Housing 295,300,000,000
Household operation 256,500,000,000
Transportation 260,800,000,000

Clothing, etc. 136,400,000,000
Medical care 194,600,000,000
Recreation 117,200,000,000
*Legal Gambling 45,500,000,000
Alcoholic drinks 46,200,000,000
Personal care 24,600,000,000
Tobacco 23,100,000,000
Religion & Welfare 25,400,000,000
Radio, TV, records, etc. 20,300,000,000
*Pets 10,150,000,000
*Missions (foreign) 1,000,000,000

Jesus said, "Much is required from those to whom much is given, for their responsibility is greater." And yet, even though so abundantly blessed, American Christians give less than 1% of their income for foreign missions. American Communists, on the other hand, spend 38% of their income for their cause. No wonder Communism now dominates some 1.6 billion people (more than a third of the world's inhabitants).

American Christians must repent of their selfishness and disobedience to the Lord's command to preach the Gospel to every creature...and begin to live sacrificially unto Him who died for them and rose again (II Cor. 5:15; Rom.12:1,2; Luke 9:23 and 14:33). Those who do will be richly blessed. There's no greater joy than serving Christ and leading others to Him. No one has ever given up anything for the love of Jesus and the spreading of the Gospel, who will not receive a hundred times more in this present life. Mark 10:29,30.

Information from previous year from other sources.

Available in tract form from All Nations Missions, P.O. Box 5491, Ft. Wayne, IN 46895.

Languages of the World Spoken by More Than a Million People

Source of Information: The World Almanac and Book of Facts, 1987

LANGUAGE COUNTRY	MILLIONS	LANGUAGE COUNTRY	MILLIONS
1. Mandarin (China)	788	49. Sinhalese (Sri Lanka)	12
*2. English	420	50. Sindhi (India, Pakistan	12
3. Hindi (India)	300	51. Nepali (Nepal, India)	11
4. Spanish	296	52. Amharic (Ethiopia)	11
5. Russian	285	53. Fula (West Africa)	11
6. Arabic	177	54. Greek	11
7. Bengali (India & Bangladesh)	171	55. Uzbek (U.S.S.R.)	11
8. Portuguese	164	56. Swedish	9
9. Malay Indonesian	128	57. Cebuano (Philippines)	10
10. Japanese	122	58. Malagasy (Madagascar)	10
11. German	118	59. Bulgarian	9
12. French	114	60. Byelorussian	9
13. Urdu (Pakistan & India)	82	61. Madurese (Indonesia)	9
14. Punjabi (Pakistan & India)	72	62. Afrikaans (South Africa)	9
15. Korean	66	63. Azerbaijani (U.S.S.R., Iran)	9
16. Italian	63	64. Oromo (Ethiopia)	9
17. Telegu (India)	62	65. Bihari (India)	8
18. Tamil (India)	61	66. Kurdish (SW of Caspian Sea)	8
19. Marathi (India)	60	67. Malinke-Bambara-Dyula (Africa)	8
20. Cantonese (China)	59	68. Quechua (South America)	7
21. Wu (China)	58	69. Rajasthani (India)	7
22. Javanese	51	70. Ruanda (So. Central Africa)	7
23. Turkish	51	71. Tatar (or Kazan-Turkic/USSR)	7
24. Vietnamese	51	72. Catalan (Spain, France, Andorra)	7
25. Min (China)	45	73. Kazakh (U.S.S.R.)	7
26. Thai	44	74. Khmer (Kampuchea)	7
27. Ukranian (mainly USSR)	43	75. Zulu	7
28. Polish	41	76. Somali (East Africa)	6
29. Kannada (India)	38	77. Twi-Fante (or Akan) (W. Africa)	6
30. Swahili (E. Africa)	38	78. Uighur (Sinkiang, China)	6
31. Gujarati (India)	36	79. Xhosa (South Africa)	6
32. Malayalam (India)	32	80. Yi (China)	6
33. Tagalog (Philippines)	31	81. Tibetan	5
34. Persian (Iran, Afghanistan)	30	82. Danish	5
35. Hausa (West & Central Africa)	29	83. Finnish	5
36. Oriya (India)	28	84. Norwegian	5
37. Burmese	28	85. Shona (Southeast Africa)	5
38. Hakka (China)	25	86. Slovak	5
39. Romanian	24	87. Armenian	5
40. Netherlandish (Dutch & Flemish)	20	88. Ilocano (Philippines)	5
41. Serbo Croatian (Yugoslavia)	20	89. Minankabau (Indonesia)	5
42. Pushtu (mainly Afghan)	20	90. Panay-Hiligaynon (Philippines)	5
43. Sundanese (Indonesia)	18	91. Rundi (So. Central Africa)	5
44. Assamese (India)	16	92. Miao (and Meo) (S.E. Africa)	5
45. Yoruba (Nigeria)	16	93. Provencal (South France)	4
46. Hungarian (or Magyar)	14	94. Albanian	4
47. Ibo or Igbo (Nigeria)	14	95. Bhili (India)	4
48. Czech	12	96. Georgian (U.S.S.R.)	4

Languages of the World Spoken by More Than a Million People (Continued)

LANGUAGE	COUNTRY	MILLIONS	LANGUAGE	COUNTRY	MILLIONS
97. Santali (India)		4	131. Turkoman (U.S.S.R.)		3
98. Tigrinya (Ethiopia)		4	132. Achinese (Indonesia)		2
99. Efik (Nigeria)		4	133. Bemba (S. Central Africa)		2
100. Hebrew		4	134. Chuvash (U.S.S.R.)		2
101. Kanuri (W. of Central Africa		4	135. Fang-Bulu (W. Africa)		2
102. Mossi (or More) (W. Africa)		4	136. Gilaki (Iran)		2
103. Ngala (or Lingala) (Africa)		4	137. Gondi (India)		2
104. Nyanja (S.E. Africa)		4	138. Kirghiz (U.S.S.R.)		2
105. Sotho, Southern (S. Africa)		4	139. Kongo (Congo River)		2
106. Tajiki (U.S.S.R.)		4	140. Latvian (or Lettish)		2
107. Wolof (W. Africa)		4	141. Luo (Kenya)		2
108. Balinese (Indonesia)		3	142. Macedonian (Yugoslavia)		2
109. Baluchi (Pakistan, Iran)		3	143. Mazandarani (Iran)		2
110. Ewe (West Africa)		3	144. Mbundu (Kimbundu gp.) (Angola)		2
111. Galician (Spain)		3	145. Nyamwezi-Sukuma (S.E. Africa)		2
112. Ganda (or Luganda) (E. Africa)		3	146. Samar-Leyte (Philippines)		2
113. Guarani (Mainly Paraguay)		3	147. Sango (Central Africa)		2
114. Kashmiri		3	148. Shan (Burma)		2
115. Kikuyu (Kenya)		3	149. Slovene (Yugoslavia)		2
116. Kituba (Congo River)		3	150. Sotho, Northern (S. Africa)		2
117. Lao (Laos)		3	151. Tiv (Nigeria)		2
118. Lithuanian		3	152. Aymara (Bolivia, Peru)		2
119. Luba-Lulua (Zaire)			153. Kamba (E. Africa)		2
120. Makua (Southeast Africa)		3	154. Kurukh (India)		2
121. Mbundu (S. Angola) (Umbundu Gp.)		3	155. Luhya (Kenya)		2
122. Tswana (S. Africa)		3	156. Thonga (S.E. Africa)		2
123. Yiddish		3	157. Dayak (Borneo)		1
124. Batak (Indonesia)		3	158. Edo (W. Africa)		1
125. Bikol (Philippines)		3	159. Esperanto		1
126. Bugi (Indonesia)		3	160. Estonian		1
127. Ijaw (Nigeria)		3	161. Mende (Sierre Leone)		1
128. Khalkha (Mongolia)		3	162. Mordvin (U.S.S.R.)		1
129. Konkani (India)		3	163. Tulu (India)		1
130. Luri (Iran)		3			

TOTAL: 4,509,000,000 speakers . . . 95.6% of the world's total population in 1986.

* English is also spoken by at least 300 million additional people as a second language, and the demand for English is great in almost every land, and the demand is steadily growing.

Note: In addition to the above 163 languages, there are some 5,200 other languages with fewer than a million speakers each. While some are spoken by many hundreds of thousands of people, others are spoken by fewer than a hundred people. The total number of people speaking these 5,200 languages is probably not more than 200 million, so the average language would be spoken by about 38,000. About 3,000 of these languages, including many that are spoken by 100,000 or more people, have never been written down. Most of these people are unable to read the national language or trade language, so they are completely blind to the world of print.

AREA AND POPULATION OF STATES (U.S.)

(Information Please Almanac, 1983).

RANK	STATE	AREA IN SQ. MI.	STATE	POPULATION, 1980
1.	Alaska	566,432	California	23,667,565
2.	Texas	262,234	New York	17,558,072
3.	California	156,361	Texas	14,229,288
4.	Montana	145,587	Pennsylvania	11,863,895
5.	New Mexico	121,412	Illinois	11,426,518
6.	Arizona	113,417	Ohio	10,797,624
7.	Nevada	109,889	Florida	9,746,324
8.	Colorado	103,766	Michigan	9,262,078
9.	Wyoming	97,203	New Jersey	7,364,823
10.	Oregon	96,184	North Carolina	5,881,813
11.	Idaho	82,677	Massachusetts	5,737,037
12.	Utah	82,096	Indiana	5,490,260
13.	Kansas	81,787	Georgia	5,463,105
14.	Minnesota	79,289	Virginia	5,346,818
15.	Nebraska	76,483	Missouri	4,916,759
16.	South Dakota	75,955	Wisconsin	4,705,521
17.	North Dakota	69,273	Tennessee	4,591,120
18.	Missouri	68,995	Maryland	4,216,975
19.	Oklahoma	68,782	Louisiana	4,206,312
20.	Washington	66,570	Washington	4,132,180
21.	Georgia	58,073	Minnesota	4,075,970
22.	Michigan	56,817	Alabama	3,893,888
23.	Iowa	55,941	Kentucky	3,660,257
24.	Illinois	55,748	South Carolina	3,121,833
25.	Wisconsin	54,464	Connecticut	3,107,576
26.	Florida	54,090	Oklahoma	3,025,290
27.	Arkansas	51,945	Iowa	2,913,808
28.	Alabama	50,708	Colorado	2,889,735
29.	North Carolina	48,798	Arizona	2,718,425
30.	New York	47,831	Oregon	2,633,149
31.	Mississippi	47,296	Mississippi	2,520,638
32.	Pennsylvania	44,966	Kansas	2,364,326
33.	Louisiana	44,930	Arkansas	2,286,435
34.	Tennessee	41,328	West Virginia	1,950,279
35.	Ohio	40,975	Nebraska	1,569,825
36.	Virginia	39,780	Utah	1,461,037
37.	Kentucky	39,650	New Mexico	1,302,981
38.	Indiana	36,097	Maine	1,125,027
39.	Maine	30,920	Hawaii	964,691
40.	South Carolina	30,225	Rhode Island	947,154
41.	West Virginia	24,070	Idaho	944,038
42.	Maryland	9,891	New Hampshire	920,610
43.	Vermont	9,267	Nevada	800,493
44.	New Hampshire	9,027	Montana	786,690
45.	Massachusetts	7,826	South Dakota	690,768
46.	New Jersey	7,521	North Dakota	652,717
47.	Hawaii	6,425	District of Columbia	638,432
48.	Connecticut	4,862	Delaware	594,317
49.	Delaware	1,982	Vermont	511,456
50.	Rhode Island	1,049	Wyoming	469,557
			Alaska	401,851

AREAS OF INDEPENDENT COUNTRIES OF THE WORLD

1. USSR 8,649,489
2. CANADA 3,851,787
3. CHINA 3,705,387
4. USA 3,540,939
5. BRAZIL 3,286,487
6. AUSTRALIA 2,967,892
7. INDIA 1,269,338
8. ARGENTINA 1,068,296
9. SUDAN 967,494
10. ALGERIA 919,595
11. ZAIRE 905,562
12. SAUDI ARABIA 829,995
13. MEXICO 761,600
14. LIBYA 679,362
15. IRAN 636,296
16. MONGOLIA 604,250
17. INDONESIA 581,655
18. PERU 496,222
19. CHAD 495,752
20. NIGER 489,191
21. ANGOLA 481,350
22. MALI 478,766
23. ETHIOPIA 471,778
24. SOUTH AFRICA 471,445
25. COLOMBIA 439,735
26. BOLIVIA 424,162
27. MAURITANIA 397,955
28. EGYPT 386,661
29. TANZANIA 364,900
30. NIGERIA 356,669
31. VENEZUELA 352,143
32. NAMIBIA 318,261
33. PAKISTAN 310,404
34. MOZAMBIQUE 302,328
35. TURKEY 301,380
36. CHILE 292,257
37. ZAMBIA 290,586
38. BURMA 261,217
39. AFGHANISTAN 249,999
40. SOMALIA 246,201
41. CENTRAL AFRICAN EMPIRE 240,535

42. BOTSWANA 231,804
43. MADAGASCAR 226,658
44. KENYA 224,960
45. FRANCE 211,208
46. THAILAND 198,455
47. SPAIN 194,897
48. CAMEROUN 183,569
49. PAPUA NEW GUINEA 178,259
50. SWEDEN 173,732
51. MOROCCO 172,414
52. IRAQ 167,925
53. PARAGUAY 157,047
54. ZIMBABWE 150,803
55. JAPAN 143,750
56. CONGO 132,046
57. FINLAND 130,119
58. VIETNAM 128,302
59. MALAYSIA 127,316
60. NORWAY 125,182
61. POLAND 120,725
62. PHILIPPINES 115,831
63. YEMEN, DEM. 111,074
64. ECUADOR 109,483
65. UPPER VOLTA 105,870
66. NEW ZEALAND 103,736
67. GABON 103,346
68. YUGOSLAVIA 98,766
69. GERMANY, W. 95,791
70. GUINEA 94,925
71. UNITED KINGDOM 94,529
72. GHANA 92,100
73. ROMANIA 91,700
74. LAOS 91,429
75. UGANDA 91,134
76. GUYANA 83,000
77. OMAN 82,030
78. SENEGAL 75,750
79. YEMEN 75,290
80. SYRIA 71,498
81. KAMPUCHEA 69,898
82. URUGUAY 68,536,

83. TUNISIA 63,170
84. SURINAM 63,037
85. BANGLADESH 55,598
86. NEPAL 54,362
87. GREECE 50,944
88. NICARAGUA 50,193
89. CZECHOSLOVAKIA 49,373
90. KOREA, N. 46,540
91. MALAWI 45,747
92. CUBA 44,218
93. BENIN 43,483
94. HONDURAS 43,277
95. LIBERIA 43,000
96. BULGARIA 42,823
97. GUATEMALA 42,042
98. GERMANY, E. 41,923
99. ICELAND 39,768
100. KOREA, W. 38,022
101. JORDAN 37,738
102. HUNGARY 35,919
103. PORTUGAL 35,553
104. AUSTRIA 32,375
105. UNITED ARAB EMIRATES 32,278
106. PANAMA 29,208
107. SIERRA LEONE 27,699
108. IRELAND 27,136
109. SRI LANKA 25,332
110. IVORY COAST 24,504
111. TOGO 21,622
112. COSTA RICA 19,575
113. DOMINICAN REP. 18,816
114. BHUTAN 18,147
115. TRANSKEI 17,000
116. DENMARK 16,629
117. ITALY 16,304
118. SWITZERLAND 15,941
119. NETHERLANDS 15,750
120. GUINEA-BISSAU 13,948
121. TAIWAN 13,893
122. BELGIUM 11,781
123. LESOTHO 11,720

124. ALBANIA 11,100
125. EQ. AFRICA 10,830
126. BURUNDI 10,741
127. HAITI 10,714
128. RWANDA 10,169
129. DJIBOUTI 8,494
130. EL SALVADOR 8,260
131. ISRAEL 7,992
132. FIJI 7,055
133. KUWAIT 6,880
134. SWAZILAND 6,704
135. BAHAMAS 5,382
136. GAMBIA 4,361
137. QATAR 4,247
138. JAMAICA 4,232
139. LEBANON 4,015
140. CYPRUS 3,572
141. TRINIDAD & TOBAGO 1,980
142. CAPE VERDE IS. 1,557
143. W. SAMOA 1,097
144. LUXEMBOURG 999
145. COMORO IS. 838
146. MAURITIUS 790
147. SAO TOME & PRINCIPE 372
148. TONGA 270
149. BAHRAIN 240
150. SINGAPORE 226
151. ANDORRA 175
152. BARBADOS 166
153. SEYCHELLES 145
154. GRENADA 133
155. MALTA 122
156. MALDIVES 115
157. LIECHTENSTEIN 61
158. SAN MARINO 23
159. NAURU 8
160. MONACO .73
161. VATICAN .17

AREAS OF DEPENDENCIES
AND INTEGRAL PARTS OF OTHER COUNTRIES

1. GREENLAND (DEN) 839,999
2. TIBET (CHINA) 471,660
3. FR. GUIANA (FR) 35,135
4. SOLOMON IS. (UK) 10,983
5. SICILY (ITALY) 9,927
6. SARDINIA (ITALY) 9,301
7. BELIZE (UK) 8,867
8. NEW CALEDONIA (FR) 7,201
9. NEW HEBRIDES (ANGLO-FR) 5,700
10. FALKLAND IS. (UK) 4,618
11. PUERTO RICO (USA) 3,421
12. CORSICA (FR) 3,367
13. CRETE (GR) 3,207

14. GALAPAGOS IS. (EC) 3,029
15. CANARY IS, (SP) 2,808
16. BRUNEI (UK) 2,226
17. FR POLYNESIA 1,544
18. REUNION (FR) 970
19. AZORES (PORT) 924
20. RYUKYU (JAPANESE) 848
21. FERNANDO PO (EQ. G.) 785
22. GUADALOUPE (FR) 688
23. MICRONESIA (USA) 687
24. FAEROE IS. (DEN) 540
25. MARTINIQUE (FR) 425
26. HONG KONG (UK) 391

27. NETH. ANTILLES 383
28. CANAL ZONE (USA) 362
29. DOMINICA (UK) 290
30. ST. LUCIA (UK) 238
31. GUAM (USA) 212
32. ANTIGUA (UK) 171
33. TURKS & CAICOS (UK) 166
34. ST VINCENT (UK) 150
35. VIRGIN IS. (USA) 132
36. ST KITTS (UK) 118
37. CAYMAN IS. (UK) 104
38. GILBERT IS. (UK) 102
39. COOK IS (NZ) 99

40. ST PIERRE (FR) 93
41. AMERICAN SAMOA 76
42. BRIT. VIRGIN IS. 59
43. CHRISTMAS IS. (AUST.) 52
44. ST. HELENA (UK) 47
45. MONTSERRAT (UK) 40
46. ASCENSCION IS. (UK) 34
48. BERMUDA (UK) 21
48. MACAO (PORT) 6
49. GILBRALTER (UK) 2

RATIO OF CHURCH MEMBERS PER MISSIONARY
How does your church measure up?

Church membership statistics were obtained from the Yearbook of American and Canadian Churches, 1986. The number of missionaries for each church was obtained from the 13th edition of the Mission Handbook, 1987.

CHURCH BODY (U.S.A.)	1984 INCLUSIVE MEMBERSHIP	1985 MISSIONARIES	MEMBERS/ MISSIONARY RATIO
Brethren Assemblies (Plym. Br.)	98,000	554	176
Church of the Lutheran Brethren	11,006	57	193
The Missionary Church	26,124	125	208
Mennonite General Conference	37,000	162	228
Christian & Missionary Alliance	158,218	874	255
Grace Brethren	42,118	119	353
Conservative Baptists	225,000	525	428
Evangelical Free Church	90,000	209	430
North American Baptist Conf.	43,215	81	533
Free Methodists	72,072	119	605
Seventh Day Adventists	638,929	1,052	607
Wesleyan Church	106,250	176	620
Presbyterian Church in America	168,239	263	639
Orthodox Presbyterian	17,660	22	802
Christian Reformed Church	224,764	266	845
Church of the Nazarene	516,020	595	867
Evangelical Covenant Church	84,185	92	915
Mennonite	90,347	90	1,003
Pentecostal Free Will Baptists	10,674	10	1,067
Pentecostal Holiness Church	113,000	105	1,076
Baptist General Conference	130,193	101	1,289
Christian Churches/Chs of Christ	1,043,642	709	1,471
Assoc. of Free Lutheran Congregations	17,665	12	1,472
Church of Christ (Dallas)	1,600,500	982	1,629
Assemblies of God	2,036,453	1,237	1,646
Open Bible Standard	46,351	28	1,655
Church of God, General Conf.	34,424	20	1,721
Int'l Church of 4 Square Gospel	171,928	83	2,071
Moravian Church in America	53,925	25	2,157
Free Will Baptists	212,527	105	2,205
United Pentecostal Church	475,000	212	2,240
Baptist Bible Fellowship Int'l	1,400,900	620	2,259
Church of God (Anderson, IN)	185,404	76	2,439
Liberty Baptist	130,000	50	2,600
Church of God of Prophecy	74,430	28	2,658
Pentecostal Church of God	93,338	26	3,589
Friends United Meeting	57,432	16	3,589
Church of the Brethren	161,824	43	3,763
Reformed Church in America	341,866	86	3,975
Southern Baptists	14,341,821	3,346	4,286
Church of God (Cleveland TN)	505,775	109	4,640
Baptist Missionary Assn.	228,868	39	5,868
United Church of Christ	1,696,107	229	7,406
American Lutheran Church	2,339,946	310	7,548
Lutheran Church-Missouri Synod	2,631,374	310	8,477
American Baptist Churches	1,620,153	186	8,710
Cumberland Presbyterian Church	98,829	11	8,984
Wisconsin Evangelical Lutheran Synod	415,630	44	9,446
Christian Churches (Disciples)	1,132,510	106	10,684
Presbyterian Church, USA	3,092,151	266	11,624
Lutheran Church in America	2,910,281	246	11,830
United Methodist Church	9,291,936	516	18,007
Episcopal Church	2,775,424	118	23,520

Note: Several church bodies with less than 10,000 members have more than one missionary for every 500 members.

Note 2: Most, if not all, of the above denominations have many missionaries serving under interdenominational boards.

YOUR GUIDE FOR WORLD INTERCESSION
Estimated Population of the World's Nations, 1987

Please pray for seven independent countries or dependencies each day. In this way you can pray for each of them once each month. The number after the name of the country is the population in millions.
Source: Population Reference Bureau, Inc.

AFGHANISTAN 14.2	EQ. GUINEA 0.3	LUXEMBOURG 0.4	SOMALIA 7.7
ALBANIA 3.1	ETHIOPIA 46.0	MADAGASCAR 10.6	SOVIET UNION 284.0
ALGERIA 23.5	FIJI 0.7	MALAWI 7.4	SOUTH AFRICA 34.3
ANDORRA . . . . <.1	FINLAND 4.9	MALAYSIA 16.1	SPAIN 39.0
ANGOLA 8.0	FRANCE 55.6	MALDIVES 0.2	SRI LANKA 16.3
ARGENTINA 31.5	GABON 1.2	MALI 8.4	SUDAN 23.5
AUSTRALIA 16.2	GAMBIA 0.8	MALTA 0.4	SURINAM 0.4
AUSTRIA 7.6	GAZA 0.6	MAURITANIA 2.0	SWAZILAND 0.7
BAHAMAS 0.2	GERMANY, E. 16.7	MAURITIUS 1.1	SWEDEN 8.4
BAHRAIN 0.4	GERMANY, W. 61.0	MEXICO 81.9	SWITZERLAND 6.6
BANGLADESH 107.1	GHANA 13.9	MONACO . . . . <.1	SYRIA 11.3
BARBADOS 0.3	GREECE 10.0	MONGOLIA 2.0	TAIWAN 19.6
BELGIUM 9.9	GRENADA 0.1	MOROCCO 24.4	TANZANIA 23.5
BENIN 4.3	GUATEMALA 8.4	MOZAMBIQUE 14.7	THAILAND 53,6
BHUTAN 1.5	GUINEA 6.4	NAMIBIA 1.3	TOGO 3.2
BOLIVIA 6.5	GUINEA-BISSAU 0.9	NAURU . . . . <.1	TONGA . . . . <.1
BOTSWANA 1.2	GUYANA 0.8	NEPAL 17.8	TRANSKEI . . . . <.1
BRAZIL 141.5	HAITI 6.2	NETHERLANDS 14.6	TRINIDAD & TOBAGO 1.3
BULGARIA 9.0	HONDURAS 4.7	NEW ZEALAND 3.3	TUNISIA 7.6
BURKINA FASO 7.3	HUNGARY 10.6	NICARAGUA 3.5	TURKEY 51.4
BURMA 38.8	ICELAND 0.2	NIGER 7.0	UGANDA 15.9
BURUNDI 5.0	INDIA 800.3	NIGERIA 108.6	UNITED ARAB EMIR. 1.4
CAMEROON 10.3	INDONESIA 174.9	NORWAY 4.2	UNITED KINGDOM 56.8
CANADA 25.9	IRAN 50.4	OMAN 1.3	ENGLAND
CAPE VERDE 0.3	IRAQ 17.0	PAKISTAN 104.6	WALES
CENTRAL AFR. REPUB. 2.7	IRELAND 3.5	PANAMA 2.3	SCOTLAND
CHAD 4.6	ISRAEL 4.4	PAPUA NEW GUINEA 3.6	N. IRELAND
CHILE 12.4	ITALY 57.4	PARAGUAY 4.3	CHANNEL IS.
CHINA 1062.0	IVORY COAST 10.8	PERU 20.7	ISLE OF MAN
COLOMBIA 29.9	JAMAICA 2.5	PHILIPPINES 61.5	UNITED STATES 243.8
COMOROS 0.4	JAPAN 122.2	POLAND 37.8	UPPER VOLTA (SEE BURKINA FASO)
CONGO 2.1	JORDAN 3.7	PORTUGAL 10.3	URUGUAY 3.1
COSTA RICA 2.8	KAMPUCHEA 6.5	QATAR 0.3	VANATU 0.2
CUBA 10.3	KENYA 22.4	ROMANIA 22.9	VATICAN . . . . <.1
CYPRUS 0.7	KOREA, N. 21.4	RWANDA 6.8	VENEZUELA 18.3
CZECHOSLOVAKIA 15.6	KOREA, S. 42.1	SAN MARINO . . . . <.1	VIETNAM 62.2
DENMARK 5.1	KUWAIT 1.9	SAO TOME & PRINCIPE 0.1	W. SAMOA 0.2
DJIBOUTI 0.3	LAOS 3.8	SAUDI ARABIA 14.8	YEMEN, NORTH. 6.5
DOMINICAN REP. 6.5	LEBANON 3.3	SENEGAL 7.1	YEMEN, SOUTH. 2.4
E. TIMOR 0.7	LESOTHO 1.6	SEYCHELLES 0.1	YUGOSLAVIA 23.4
ECUADOR 10.0	LIBERIA 2.4	SIERRA LEONE 3.9	ZAIRE 31.8
EGYPT 51.9	LIBYA 3.8	SINGAPORE 2.6	ZAMBIA 7.1
EL SALVADOR 5.3	LIECHTENSTEIN . . . . <.1	SOLOMON ISLANDS 0.3	ZIMBABWE 9.4

DEPENDENCIES AND INTEGRAL PARTS OF OTHER COUNTRIES

AMERICAN SAMOA . . . . <.1	EASTER IS. (CHILE) . . . . <.1	GREENLAND . . . . <.1	PUERTO RICO (USA) 3.3
ANTIGUA & BARBUDA 0.1	FAEROE IS. (DEN) . . . . <.1	GUADALOUPE (FR) 0.3	REUNION (FR) 0.6
BELIZE 0.2	FALKLAND IS. (UK) . . . . <.1	GUAM . . . . <.1	ST. HELENA . . . . <.1
BRIT. VIRGIN IS. . . . . <.1	FERNANDO PO (EQ. G.) . . . . . . <.1	HONG KONG 5.6	ST. KITTS (UK) . . . . <.1
BRUNEI (UK) 0.2	FRENCH GUIANA . . . . <.1	MACAO 0.4	ST. LUCIA 0.1
CANAL ZONE (USA) . . . . <.1	FRENCH POLYNESIA 0.2	MARTINIQUE (FR) 0.3	ST. PIERRE (FR) . . . . <.1
CANARY IS. (SP) . . . . <.1	FR. GUIANA (FR) . . . . <.1	MICRONESIA (USA) . . . . <.1	ST. VINCENT (UK) 0.1
CAYMAN IS. (UK) . . . . <.1	GALAPAGOS IS.	MONTSERRAT (UK) . . . . <.1	TIBET (CHINA) 2.0
CHRISTMAS IS. (NZ) . . . . <.1	(ECUADOR) . . . . <.1	NETH. ANTILLES 0.2	TURKS & CAICOS (UK) . . . . . . <.1
COOK IS. . . . . <.1	GIBRALTAR (UK) . . . . <.1	NEW CALEDONIA (FR) 0.2	VIRGIN IS. (USA) . . . . <.1
DOMINICA (UK) 0.1	GILBERT IS. (UK) . . . . <.1	OKINAWA (JAPAN) . . . . <.1	

PER CAPITA INCOME

AFGHANISTAN ('78) ....$ 168	GHANA ('80) 420	NORWAY ('80)...............12,432
ALBANIA ('79)..................830	GREECE ('84) 3,260	OMAN ('76)...................2,400
ALGERIA ('84)................2,085	GUATEMALA ('84) 1,085	PAKISTAN ('80) 280
ANGOLA ('76)..................500	GUINEA ('84)...................305	PANAMA ('78).................1,116
ARGENTINA ('78)..............2,331	GUINEA BISSAU ('83)...........165	PAPUA NEW GUINEA ('78)......480
AUSTRALIA ('83)...............9,960	HAITI ('83) 300	PARAGUAY ('83)...............1,614
AUSTRIA ('80) 8,280	HONDURAS ('82) 590	PERU ('79) 655
BANGLADESH ('83) 119	HUNGARY ('82) 4,180	PHILIPPINES ('82) 772
BELGIUM ('84) 7,803	ICELAND ('79) 9,000	POLAND ('84) 2,750
BELIZE ('84)...................1,000	INDIA ('77) 150	PORTUGAL ('84)...............1,930
BENIN ('83) 290	INDONESIA ('82) 560	ROMANIA ('80) 5,250
BHUTAN ('83) 120	IRAN ('77) 2,160	RWANDA ('84) 270
BOLIVIA ('82)...................570	IRAQ ('81) 2,410	SAUDI ARABIA ('79)........11,500
BOTSWANA ('78)................544	IRELAND ('84) 4,750	SENEGAL ('82).................342
BRAZIL ('78)..................1,523	ISRAEL ('83) 5,609	SIERRA LEONE ('80)...........176
BULGARIA ('80) 2,625	ITALY ('80) 6,914	SINGAPORE ('85) 6,526
BURMA ('81)....................174	IVORY COAST ('84) 1,100	SOMALIA ('83)........ less than 500
BURUNDI ('84).................273	JAMAICA ('81) 1,340	SOUTH AFRICA ('85) 1,296
CAMBODIA (See Kampuchea)	JAPAN ('84) 10,266	SPAIN ('79) 5,500
CAMEROON ('84) 802	JORDAN ('76)..................552	SRI LANKA ('84)...............340
CANADA ('84) 13,000	KAMPUCHEA ('84) 100	SUDAN ('82) 361
CENT'L AFRICAN REP. ('82).....310	KENYA ('83)....................309	SWEDEN ('85).................14,821
CHAD ('84) 88	NORTH KOREA ('78)...........570	SWITZERLAND ('85)..........14,408
CHILE ('79) 1,950	SOUTH KOREA ('78)..........1,187	SYRIA ('75) 702
CHINA ('80) 566	KUWAIT ('75) 11,431	TANZANIA ('82) 240
TAIWAN ('84) 3,000	LAOS ('76).......................85	THAILAND ('85)................828
COLOMBIA ('81)...............1,112	LEBANON ('83)...............1,150	TOGO ('82) 348
CONGO ('78)...................500	LESOTHO ('79) 355	TRINIDAD & TOBAGO ('82)....6,800
COSTA RICA ('81)............2,238	LIBERIA ('82)...................400	TUNISIA ('83) 844
CUBA ('83) 1,590	LIBYA ('84) 7,000	TURKEY ('84) 1,000
CZECHOSLOVAKIA ('80)......5,800	LUXEMBOURG ('81)..........10,444	UGANDA ('76)..................240
DENMARK ('80)..............12,956	MADAGASCAR ('82)...........279	USSR ('76).....................2,600
DJIBOUTI ('82)................400	MALAYSIA ('75) 714	UNITED ARAB EMIR. ('83) ...23,000
DOMINICAN REP. ('80)........1,221	MALI ('81) 140	UNITED KINGDOM ('79) 7,216
ECUADOR ('83).................1,428	MAURITANIA ('84) 466	UNITED STATES ('85) 13,451
EGYPT ('83) 686	MAURITIUS ('82) 1,240	UPPER VOLTA
EL SALVADOR ('84) 854	MEXICO ('80) 1,800	(Burkina Faso) ('81) 180
EQUAT. AFRICA ('83)...........250	MONGOLIA ('76) 750	URUGUAY ('85)...............1,665
ETHIOPIA ('84).................141	MOROCCO ('81).................800	VENEZUELA ('84) 4,716
FIJI ('84).......................1,086	MOZAMBIQUE ('83)............220	VIETNAM ('82) 189
FINLAND ('80) 10,477	NEPAL ('82)....................140	NORTH YEMEN ('78)...........475
FRANCE ('83) 7,179	NETHERLANDS ('83) 9,175	SOUTH YEMEN ('83)............310
GABON ('83) 2,613	NEW ZEALAND ('82) 7,916	YUGOSLAVIA ('85).............3,109
GAMBIA ('81)...................330	NICARAGUA ('80)...............804	ZAIRE ('75)....................127
GERMANY, E. ('84) 8,000	NIGER ('81) 475	ZAMBIA ('82)...................570
GERMANY, W. ('85)...........9,450	NIGERIA ('80) 750	ZIMBABWE ('83)...............640

Source of information: The World Almanac and Book of Facts, 1987, pages 545-633.

Note: Statistics vary from 1975 for some countries to 1985 for others.

POPULATION DENSITY
(per square mile)

AFGHANISTAN 60	GUINEA BISSAU 62	PANAMA 75
ALBANIA 274	HAITI......................538	PAPUA NEW GUINEA..........19
ALGERIA 24	HONDURAS...................104	PARAGUAY 25
ANGOLA......................18	HONG KONG............13,568	PERU.........................40
ARGENTINA 29	HUNGARY....................296	PHILIPPINES................490
AUSTRALIA....................5.2	INDIA 606	POLAND......................308
AUSTRIA 230	INDONESIA..................235	PORTUGAL...................283
BANGLADESH............1,824	IRAN 71	QATAR........................68
BELGIUM 837	IRAQ.........................92	ROMANIA 248
BENIN.......................92	IRELAND 132	RWANDA 601
BHUTAN......................78	ISRAEL.....................526	SAUDI ARABIA 13
BOLIVIA 15	ITALY......................491	SENEGAL.....................89
BOTSWANA....................5	IVORY COAST................81	SIERRA LEONE 140
BRAZIL......................37	JAMAICA....................535	SINGAPORE.............11,411
BULGARIA...................210	JAPAN 840	SOMALIA.....................31
BURKINA FASO 65	JORDAN......................71	SOUTH AFRICA.............69
BURMA 141	KAMPUCHEA 89	SPAIN......................199
BURUNDI 435	KENYA.......................90	SRI LANKA 645
CAMBODIA (See Kampuchea)	KOREA, NORTH 431	SUDAN 24
CAMEROON...................53	KOREA, SOUTH 1,121	SWEDEN 68
CANADA 7	KUWAIT 249	SWITZERLAND 405
CENTRAL AFRICAN REP.......11	LAOS 39	SYRIA 147
CHAD........................10	LEBANON....................652	TAIWAN 1,393
CHILE 41	LESOTHO 129	TANZANIA....................59
CHINA (PRC) 280	LIBERIA 58	THAILAND...................260
COLOMBIA...................67	LIBYA 6	TOGO.......................140
CONGO.......................14	MADAGASCAR 44	TRINIDAD & TOBAGO 599
COSTA RICA.................135	MALAWI 154	TUNISIA 115
CUBA 229	MALAYSIA...................121	TURKEY 168
CZECHOSLOVAKIA...........314	MALI 16	UGANDA 161
DENMARK 307	MAURITANIA 4	USSR 32
DOMINICAN REPUB.........352	MAURITIUS...............1,280	UNITED ARAB EMIRATES 40
ECUADOR 86	MEXICO.....................105	UNITED KINGDOM...........599
EGYPT.......................127	MONGOLIA....................3	*UNITED STATES..............66*
EL SALVADOR...............603	MOROCCO...................134	UPPER VOLTA (See Burkina Faso)
ETHIOPIA....................90	MOZAMBIQUE 44	URUGUAY 43
FINLAND 38	NEPAL 313	VENEZUELA..................49
FRANCE......................261	NETHERLANDS 918	VIETNAM 417
GERMANY, East............399	NEW ZEALAND...............32	YEMEN, NORTH 122
GERMANY, West 635	NICARAGUA..................64	YEMEN, SOUTH 17
GHANA......................141	NIGER......................13	YUGOSLAVIA 234
GREECE.....................195	NIGERIA 288	ZAIRE 34
GUATEMALA 199	NORWAY 33	ZAMBIA 24
GUINEA 59	PAKISTAN...................320	ZIMBABWE...................58

This is the population per square mile for the 48 contiguous states.

Source:This information comes from the 1987 World Almanac, pp. 545-633.

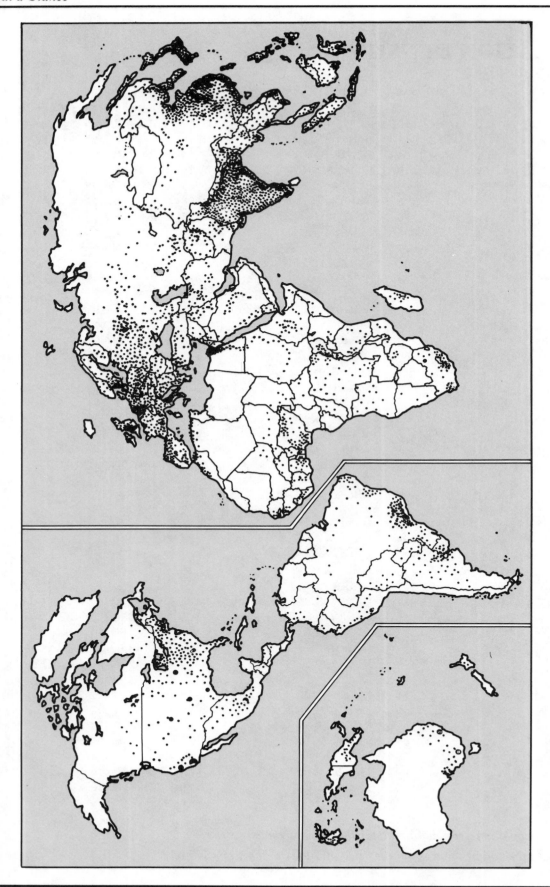

World Population Distribution

World Population Increase as Projected 1970-1985

PROJECTED POPULATION INCREASE

1 MILLION   10 MILLION   100 MILLION   250 MILLION

MILES

1500
1000
500
0

WORLD POPULATION, 400 BC to 1984 AD
(Population in Millions)

1984 statistics are from the 1984 World Population Data Sheet of the Population Reference Bureau, Inc. All other statistics are from McEvedy & Jones, Atlas of World Population History, Penguin Books, 1978.

YEAR	aEUROPE	bASIA	AFRICA	AMERICAS	cOCEANIA	WORLD
400 BC	20	70	7	3.0	.8	100.8
200 BC	26	105	10	4.0	.9	145.9
AD 1	31	115	16	4.5	1.0	167.5
200	36	130	18	5.0	1.1	190.1
400	31	130	19	6.0	1.2	187.2
600	26	140	20	7.0	1.3	194.3
800	29	155	25	8.0	1.4	218.4
1000	36	185	33	9.0	1.5	264.5
1100	44	230	35	10.0	1.6	320.6
1200	58	250	38	11.0	1.7	358.7
1300	79	230	40	12.0	1.8	362.8
1400	60	235	45	13.0	1.9	354.9
1500	81	280	46	14.0	2.0	423.0
1600	100	375	55	11.5	2.1	543.6
2650	105	370	58	12.0	2.2	547.2
1700	120	415	61	13.0	2.3	611.3
1750	140	495	65	16.0	2.4	718.4
1800	180	625	70	24.0	2.5	901.5
1850	265	795	81	59.0	2.2	1202.2
1900	390	970	110	145.0	6.7	1621.7
1950	515	1450	205	325.0	14.0	2509.0
1975	635	2300	385	545.0	23.0	3888.0
1984	765	2782	531	659.0	24.0	4761.0

a. Includes U.S.S.R.
b. Includes Indonesia & the Philippines.
c. Includes Australia, NZ, Papua New Guinea & islands to the north & east.

WORLD CHRISTIANS, AD 100 to 2000

YEAR	% CHRISTIAN	YEAR	% CHRISTIAN	YEAR	% CHRISTIAN
100	.6	1000	18.7	1800	23.1
200	3.4	1200	19.4	1850	27.2
300	10.4	1350	24.1	1900	34.4
330	12.0	1500	19.0	1950	34.1
400	17.1	1550	19.5	1970	33.7
500	22.4	1600	20.7	1975	33.2
630	22.5	1650	21.2	1980	32.8
800	22.5	1700	21.7	1985	32.4
950	19.0	1750	22.2	est. 2000	32.3

From World Christian Encyclopedia, 1982, pp. 23-32.

SELECTED INFORMATION SOURCES

GENERAL INFORMATION

Background Notes on the countries of the world. Superintendent of Documents, U.S. Government Printing Office, Washington, D.C. 20402. (1) complete set of all looseleaf Background Notes currently in stock (at least 125). (2) One—year subscription service for approximately 75 updated or new Background Notes. (5) Subscriptions. Write for prices.

UNESCO Publications: 152 W. 42 St.; New York, NY 10036.
U.S. Populations Bureau, P.O. Box 35012; Washington D.C. 20013
World Almanac & Book of Facts 1983. Write: Newspaper Enterprise Association, Inc.; 200 Park Avenue; New York NY 10166.
Information Please Almanac. Theodore B. Dolmatch, ed.;New York: Simon & Schuster.

GENERAL MISSIONS INFORMATION

Mission Handbook, 13th edition, 1986, MRL/MARC. Listing of over 600 North American Protestant mission agencies working overseas, with analysis of last decade in missions and trends in next decade. Includes statistics on number of personnel, fields in which active, finances, and brief organizational descriptions. Listings are alphabetical by agency, by country, and by function. Includes list of institutions with professors of mission. Bibliography.
MARC. 919 W. Huntington Dr., Monrovia, CA 91016.

Association of Church Mission Committees. An excellent source of information on promoting missions in the local congregation. P.O. Box ACMC; Wheaton IL 60189.

Missions Directory. Goddard, Horton, eds. The Encyclopedia of Modern Christian Missions. Camden: Thomas Nelson & Sons, 1967. Alphabetical listing of over 1400 mission agencies.

Missionary News Service. Published on the 1st and 15th of each month by Evangelical Missions Information Service, P.O. Box 794, Wheaton, IL 60187. It can be secured on a single subscription basis or as part of a package plan from EMIS associates. The package plan includes area editions of PULSE (Asia, Africa, Chinese World, Muslim World, Europe, and Latin America) published regularly. Also included in the package plan is a subscription to Evangelical Missions Quarterly. EMQ may be ordered separately.

International Bulletin of Mission Research. Quarterly update on mission issues on all six continents, reports from significant mission conferences, profiles of mission leaders, book reviews, current book notes, and checklist of mission periodicals and films. Circulation Department, P.O. Box 1308—E, Ft. Lee NJ 07024.

MARC Newsletter. See address under Mission Handbook, above. Standing order subscription rates for all MARC publications are available.

Mission Frontiers, deals with reaching the unreached peoples of the world. A publication of the U.S. Center for World Mission; 1605 E, Elizabeth St.; Pasadena, CA 91104. Also available is the **Frontier Fellowship Daily Prayer Guide.**

World Christian. A excellent and colorful magazine regarding the unreached peoples of the world. Write for subscription rates: World Christian, P.O. Box 5199, Chatsworth, CA 91313.

World Christian Encyclopedia, David Barrett, ed. New York: Oxford University Press, 1982. A comprehensive study of churches and religions in the modern world (AD 1900—2000). Information about the status of Christianity in every land. 997 pages.

Global Church Growth. A worldwide missiological magazine dedicated exclusively to the Great Commission. They believe the main thrust of Scripture is that the evangelization of the world is the most important task of the Church and therefore is the prime responsibility of mission—now and until Christ comes. Church Growth; P.O. Box 66, Santa Clara, CA 95052.

William Carey Library. Over 280 books, tapes, and magazines covering many topics such as general missions, strategy, linguistics, history, anthropology, Islamic ministries, TEE, and theology. Substantial discounts are given to members of the Church Growth Book Club (by subscribing to Global Church Growth, above). 1705 N. Sierra Bonita, Pasadena, CA 91104.

BIBLE TRANSLATION, PUBLICATION & DISTRIBUTION

Wycliffe Bible Translators. Huntington Beach CA 92648 (Administrative offices). Wycliffe has six regional offices around the U.S. They publish a magazine entitled In Other Words, as well as offering translation and literacy courses for prospective missionaries.

Ethnologue. Published by Wycliffe Bible Translators, above. A directory of the languages of the world with notes on the Bible translation needs.

American Bible Society Record. The Official periodical of the American Bible Society; 1865 Broadway; New York NY 10023. A report of their activities. Sent to anyone contributing $3 or more a year to ABS, Free to members of the Bible-a-month Club, wherein you regularly donate money to be used to print and distribute Bibles in a needy country. ABS sends you a description of the country and a sample of the language.

LITERACY

All Nations Literacy Movement. P.O. Box 5491, Ft. Wayne, IN 46895. An organization dedicated to producing literacy materials, teaching people to read, training national literacy teachers, training and encouraging national Christian writers, training the laity and the ministry through Bible extension courses, and helping the nationals carry the Gospel to others in their own and other lands.

Wycliffe Bible Translators. See above under: BIBLE TRANSLATION, PUBLICATION & DISTRIBUTION.

Center for Applied Linguistics. 3520 Prospect St. NW; Washington D.C. 20007.

The Committee of World Literacy and Christian Literature. 475 Riverside Dr., New York NY 10027.

HINDU WORLD

Institute of Hindu Studies. 1605 E. Elizabeth St., Pasadena CA 91104.

Asia Pulse. (See EV. Missionary Information Service)

Church Growth Research Quarterly. Roger Hedlund; Post Bag 768; Kilpauk, Madras 600-010 INDIA

Mission Outreach. The official monthly magazine of the India Evangelical Mission; 38 Langford Road; Bangalore 560-025 INDIA.

AIM. A monthly magazine published by the Evangelical Fellowship of India; 804/92 Deepali; Nehru Place, New Delhi 110—019 INDIA.

TRIBAL WORLD

In Other Words. See: Wycliffe Bible Translators, above.

Africa Pulse. See: Missionary News Service, above.

MUSLIM WORLD

Samuel Zwemer Institute, located at 1539 E. Howard St., Pasadena CA 91104. Mailing Address: P.O. Box 365, Altadena CA 91101. Publishes the Samuel Zwemer Institute Newsletter. Content of articles does not necessarily reflect the position of the Zwemer Institute. The purpose is to enable Muslims everywhere to have a valid opportunity to accept Jesus as Lord and Savior and to see that the Church is planted among each Muslim unreached people group. They also have Muslim Awareness Seminars, training programs, handbooks, and a film entitled, Islam; Unlocking the Door.

Fellowship of Faith for Muslims. The main objectives of this service are to mobilize prayer, provide information and supply literature on Islam in the interest of work among Muslims worldwide. It also operates a manuscript resource pool of tracts and Muslim Prayer Watch (see: SIM Now, below). Write: 205 Yonge St. Room 25, Toronto M5B 1N2 CANADA.

Middle East Media. Publishes a magazine, Magallati, aimed at Muslims living in Europe and North America. P. O. Box 3324, Tulsa OK 74101.Muslim World. A magazine published by the Samuel Zwemer Institute. See above.

Muslim World Pulse. See: Missionary News Service, above.

COMMUNIST WORLD

Sparks. Published every other month by the Slavic Gospel Association. Provides news and mission information about Eastern Europe and the Soviet Union. Special attention is given to the subject of the persecution of believers. Write P.O. Box 1122, Wheaton, IL 60189.

Diane Books. Publishes many books written by Richard Wurmbrand. P.O. Box 2948, Torrance, CA 90509.

Dr. McBirnies Newsletter. United Community Churches of America, P.O. Box 90, Glendale, CA 91209. Dr. W. S. McBirnie, News Analyst

Christian Anti Communist Crusade. P.O. Box 890, Long Beach, CA 90801. Dr. Fred C. Schwarz.

CHINA

China Prayer Letter. Published by Chinese Church Research Center; 7 Kent Road; Kowloon; HONG KONG. The Chinese Church Research Center studies Christian life in China, makes analyses, and reports to the worldwide Christian community. It is non-denominational, evangelical, and supported by free will offerings. Distributed free. The China Prayer Letter is distributed in North America by Christian Nationals Evangelism Commission, 1470 N. Fourth St., San Jose, CA 95112.

Chinese Around the World. Published by the Chinese Coordination Center of World Evangelism as a monthly news service to promote prayer and support for the evangelization of the Chinese people worldwide. Sent free of charge upon request; donations accepted. Write: Chinese Coordination Center of World Evangelism, 19, Mong Kok Road, 2nd floor, Kowloon, Hong Kong.

China and the Church Today. Published six times a year by the Chinese Church Research Center. See: China Prayer Letter above.

Institute of Chinese Studies. 1605 E. Elizabeth St., Pasadena, CA 91104

Watchman on the Great Wall. Published by the Institute of Chinese Studies. A small prayer guide sent free of charge upon request. Write: ICS, 1605 E. Elizabeth St., Pasadena, CA 91104.

Chinese World Pulse. See: Missionary News Service, above.

ASIA

East Asia Millions. A magazine published by Overseas Missionary Fellowship; 404 S. Church St., Robesonia, PA 19551.

Asian Report. A publication of Asian Outreach; 1 Sugar St., 15th Floor; Causeway Bay Commercial Bldg., HONG KONG. Focuses primarily on the Chinese world, SE Asia and Indonesia.

Asia Pulse. See: Missionary News Service, above.

Muslim Pulse & Chinese Pulse. See Missionary News Service, above.

AFRICA

AIM Now. A magazine published by Africa Inland Mission; Cedar Grove, NJ 07009

Inland Africa. Published by the Sudan Interior Mission; P.O. Box 178; Pearl River, NY 10965.

Africa Pulse. See: Missionary News Service, above.

EUROPE

Europe Pulse. See: Missionary News Service, above.

LATIN AMERICA

Latin America Pulse. See: Missionary News Service, above.

IMPORTANT NOTE:

Resources listed in this book are not intended to be complete. Major denominations generally sustain their own mission boards and sending agencies. Consult the offices of your denomination for further information on these.

SUGGESTED READING

GOD'S PLAN, MAN'S NEED, OUR MISSION: *By G. Christian Weiss. Lincoln, NE: Back to the Bible Broadcast Publication, 1971.*

G. Christian Weiss sets forth a scriptural view of world missions. He shows the imperative of knowing what God's program is, the urgency of having a new consciousness, and a new conviction of man's need and the importance of realizing that Christ has sent us into the world even as the Father sent Him into the world. (172 pp.)

A HISTORY OF CHRISTIAN MISSIONS: *By Stephen Neill. Middlesex. England, 1964*

This volume of the Pelican History of the Church gathers the most important material from many sources in different languages. Bishop Neill gives a clear outline of the greatest and sustained campaign in the propagation of a faith that the world has ever experienced.

THE 25 UNBELIEVABLE YEARS 1945-1969: *By Ralph Winter. Pasadena, CA: William Carey Library, 1970*

The period under consideration marked by the end of the colonial era, recorded a growing cynicism among youth and yet an unexpected expansion of the Kingdom of God in places and ways no man was expecting. (126 pp.)

FORWARD THROUGH THE AGES: *By Basil Mathews. New York: Friendship press, 1951*

Simple, easy to read history of the expansion of Christianity from Pentecost to 1950. (254 pp.)

OPERATION WORLD: A HANDBOOK FOR WORLD INTERCESSION: *By P.J. Johnstone. Bromley, Kent, England: STL Publications, 1986*

A unique and comprehensive "global prayer atlas". A survey of the basic prayer needs of each country of the world backed by information on population, ethnic groups, economy, religious and political situations.

SEVEN IMPERATIVES FOR WORLD EVANGELIZATION: *By Morris Watkins, 1984*

A thought provoking handbook on how the Christian should walk. Chapter titles included are Penitence; Prayer; Publicity, Promotion, and Personal Involvement; Proper Priorities; Proper Preparation of Missionaries; Partnership in Missions; Power from on High.

All Nations Mission Education Materials, P.O. Box 5491, Ft. Wayne, IN 46895

GREAT COMMISSION STUDY GUIDE: *By Morris Watkins. Fullerton, CA: R.C. Law & Co.*

Questions and answers regarding the supreme task of the church throughout the world. Includes biblical basis for missions, needs and opportunities.

LITERACY, BIBLE READING AND CHURCH GROWTH THROUGH THE AGES: *By Morris Watkins. Pasadena, CA: William Carey Library 1978*

Americans and Europeans take for granted the printed page, as it is so readily available. Only through reading the Bible does a Church firmly stand with the principles taught therein. The author builds a case for literacy as a foundation for strong churches.

IN THE GAP What It Means to be a World Christian: *By David Bryant. Madison, WI: Inter-Varsity Missions, 1979*

A book that clearly calls us to see the whole world as the object of God's missionary concern and our identification with Him in this as life's high purpose. Filled with exciting facts that can become fuel for prayer and action, this call to dynamic discipleship with a global dimension amply documents the fact that we are walking into the sunrise of mission. (272 pp.)

FROM JERUSALEM TO IRIAN JAYA: A BIOGRAPHICAL HISTORY OF CHRISTIAN MISSIONS: *By Ruth Tucker. Grand Rapids: Academic Books, 1983*

This is history at its best. It is readable, informative, gripping, and honest. The author never covers up the weakness of criticisms of the subjects. We see these men and women as fallible and human in their failures as well as their successes. It's the most moving book ever written, touching the whole scope of the least understood...effort in the annals of human achievement.

HAVE WE NO RIGHT?: *By Mabel Williamson. Chicago: Moody Press*

While serving the Lord in China for many years, Miss Williamson learned that she was not her own—she was bought with price. She could not stand up for her rights. She had no rights. Her sincere and frank remarks about her problems of adjusting on the mission field provide fascinating, instructive, and extremely valuable material for missions, students, churches and all Christians.

ON THE CREST OF THE WAVE: *By C. Peter Wagner. Ventura, CA: Regal Books.*

Invaluable and truly unsurpassed for all those in the local churches, Bible studies, student groups—even for pastors—who want the sober, astounding truth about the missionary movement in highly edible form.

MISSIONS RESOURCE HANDBOOK: *By Morris Watkins. Fullerton, CA: R.C. Law & Col, Inc, 1987*

A resource book for missions and, in particular, for the promotion of missions in the local church. This text is an aid in locating those resources which may be most helpful to the missions emphasis of your church, a library of missions books, films, and references. You will find a wealth of help available if you seek it through the sources named in this book.

SHORT TERM OPPORTUNITIES

Many short-term ministries are oriented to technically skilled workers and professionals while others are intended for lay evangelism and volunteer work projects. The following composite list includes non-denominational agencies known to place a degree of emphasis upon short-term assignments. This list is not complete and does not include denominational agencies. You may wish to consult your own denominational office for further information. Also refer to *Missions Resource Handbook,* Fullerton, CA: R.C. Law & Co., 1987.

Agape Force	P.O. Box 386 Lindale, TX 75771
Agape Movement	Arrowhead Springs San Bernardino, CA 92414
Bethany Fellowship	6820 Auto Club Rd. Minneapolis, MN 55438
CAM International	8625 La Prada Dr. Dallas, TX 75228
Gospel Missionary Union	10000 N. Oak Kansas City, MO 64155
Greater Europe Mission	P.O. Box 668 Wheaton, IL 60189
InterVarsity Christian Fellowship	233 Langdon St. Madison, WI 53703
International Teams	P.O. Box 203 Prospect Heights, IL 60070
English Lang. Institute/China	P.O. Box 265 San Dimas, CA 91773
Missions Outreach	P.O. Box 73 Bethany, MO 64424
OMS International	P.O. Box A Greenwood, IN 46142
Operation Mobilization	P.O. Box 148 Midland Park, NJ 07432
Teen Missions	P.O. Box 1056 Merritt Island, FL 32952
Wycliffe Associates	P.O. Box 2000 Orange, CA 92669
Wycliffe Bible Translators	7500 W. Camp Wisdom Rd. Dallas, TX 75236
Youth With A Mission	P.O. Box 4600 Tyler, TX 75712

MISSIONARY PLACEMENT SERVICES

The following agencies specialize in recruiting and placement of missionaries and prospective missionaries.

Global Opportunities	1600 E. Elizabeth St., Pasadena, CA 91104 (818) 797-3233
Intercristo Christian Placement Network	P.O. Box 33487 Seattle, WA 98133 (800) 426-1342
Overseas Counseling Service	P.O. Box 33836 Seattle, WA 98133 (800) 251-7739

Global Opportunities and Overseas Counseling Service offer information on serving overseas in various "tent-making" ministries such as Teaching English as a Second Language.

Intercristo puts prospective missionaries in touch with mission agencies which specialize in the kind of missionary service the prospect is considering.

INDEX

INDEX (Continued)

INDEX (Continued)

INDEX (Continued)

INDEX (Continued)

INDEX (Continued)

INDEX (Continued)

INDEX (Continued)